Give Me 10,000 Men!

The Incredible True Story of Pvt. Alfred Petty at San Juan Hill

William M. Holden

Copyright © 2011 by William M. Holden

No part of this book may be reproduced or utilized in any form or by any means: electronic, mechanical or otherwise, including photocopying, recording or by any informational storage and retrieval system without permission in writing from the author.

Although the author has researched all sources to ensure the accuracy and completeness of the information contained within this book, no responsibility is assumed for errors, inaccuracies, omissions, or inconsistency herein. Any slights of people, places or organizations are completely unintentional.

Many of the photographs and illustrations contained herein are reproduced in the fair use of public domain material. All photographs and illustrations produced prior to January 1, 1923 are in the public domain, pursuant to the Copyright Law of the United States of America and Related Laws Contained in Title 17 of the United States Code.

ISBN
0-9824777-1-6 (10 digit)
978-0-9824777-1-7 (13 digit)

Library of Congress Control Number: 2011927474

First Edition

Published by
23 House Publishing
405 Moseley St.
Jefferson, TX 75657
SAN 299-8084
www.23house.com

Printed in the United States of America

Front cover photographs (clockwise):
Soldiers entrenched on San Juan Hill; Pvt. Alfred Petty; the USS Maine.

Contents

Rendezvous With Destiny 1
Foreword 3
Chapter 1: Calamity at Havana 7
Chapter 2: Hue and Cry 24
Chapter 3: Chaos at Tampa 39
Chapter 4: Expedition Against Cuba 57
Chapter 5: Rust-Bucket Armada 66
Chapter 6: Invasion 81
Chapter 7: Confusion Compounded 98
Chapter 8: Spoiling for Action 110
Chapter 9: Ordeal: The Road to Santiago 115
Chapter 10: Moving Up 126
Chapter 11: Bullets for Breakfast 134
Chapter 12: The Balloon Fiasco 143
Chapter 13: Hell in Panorama 147
Chapter 14: "Sound the Charge!" 156
Chapter 15: Agony on the Ridge 167
Chapter 16: Shafter Ponders Retreat 178
Chapter 17: Desperation and Disaster 189
Chapter 18: Surrender Talks 199
Chapter 19: Last Days of an Empire 212
Chapter 20: Comic-Opera Invasion of Puerto Rico 226
Chapter 21: Home From the Hill 231
Chapter 22: Forty Years After 246
Chapter 23: Petty's Final Days 257
Epilogue 263

Rendezvous With Destiny

After bottling up Spain's Atlantic Fleet in the harbor of Santiago de Cuba, Admiral William T. Sampson, commander of the U.S. Atlantic Fleet, cabled Washington on June 6, 1898:

```
IF 10,000 MEN WERE HERE CITY AND FLEET WOULD
BE OURS . . . EVERY CONSIDERATION DEMANDS
IMMEDIATE ARMY MOVEMENT. IF DELAYED, CITY
WILL BE DEFENDED MORE STRONGLY BY GUNS TAKEN
FROM FLEET
```

Give Me 10,000 Men!

Foreword

In terms of numbers engaged, the American assault on San Juan Hill in the Santiago campaign was not one of history's greatest battles.

But it was the battle that won the campaign.

The campaign that won the war.

The war that dismantled the empire that had flown the blood-and-gold colors of Spain since Columbus.

This book is based on the true story of Pvt. Alfred C. Petty's role in the adventure that changed the world.

In all the annals of war, there may be no more reckless adventure than this: the frantic embarkation of an expedition of 17,000 Americans, the voyage to Cuba in a rust-bucket armada, the headlong incursion into the pestilential jungles of the big island dominated by nearly 200,000 Spanish soldiers, and the storming of the gates of Santiago: El Caney, Kettle Hill and San Juan Hill.

Some 1,500 Americans were killed or wounded on that torrid July 1, 1898, at Santiago.

Contrary to legend, it was not the Rough Riders but the infantry who captured San Juan Hill. The infantry took it while Teddy Roosevelt and his Rough Riders were capturing Kettle Hill, half a mile away, in a rip-roaring charge. The Rough Riders fought as bravely as soldiers anywhere, but truth must be told: the infantry did the job at San Juan.

But not before the army teetered on the brink of disaster.

Someone had blundered – and not just once. The ailing, 315-pound commanding general, age 63, and top brass committed four egregious blunders.

And how could this proud corps of elite career officers admit that a cheeky Southern bumpkin had done the incredible in the near-debacle at San Juan? An ex-cottonpicker with no formal schooling? A buck private who had been in the army only forty-three days? A soldier who had disobeyed orders to retreat? An inelegant rustic still wearing chiefly his shabby civilian hand-me-downs?

Unthinkable.

Forget him.

So they euchred him out of the honors he deserved as one of our military immortals.

This is his story…

Foreword

Alfred C. Petty, who charged up San Juan Hill in his civilian hand-me-downs, was later outfitted in a proper uniform. (author's collection)

Give Me 10,000 Men!

Chapter 1:
Calamity at Havana

The date was one of the most momentous in world history: the evening darkness of February 15, 1898.

In a gas-lit office of the New York *Journal*, an editor stared under his green eyeshade at the clattering ticker of *The Associated Press*, scowling at the latest bulletin from Havana. Plunking a cigar butt into a brass cuspidor, he shoved back his eyeshade and reached for the telephone to call his young employer, William Randolph Hearst.

"Hate to bother you this time o' night, sir, but thought you oughta know. AP bulletins from Havana say the *Maine* just blew up – killing hundreds of American sailors."

"Good heavens!" Hearst gasped. "What have you done with the story?"

"Plastered it big on the front page, sir."

"Have you put anything else on the front page?"

The editor coughed, realizing his error. "Only the other big news," he said.

"*Other* big news? There *is* no other big news! Spread the story all over the page – this means *war*!"

Next evening, at the cold and drizzly hamlet of Pacific, Missouri, twenty-five miles west of St. Louis, the Missouri Pacific mail train belched smoke and cinders as it chuffed into the depot. As it grumbled past the loading platform without stopping, two porters began to fling heavy canvas "US MAIL" bags and hemp-tied bundles of newspapers.

Out of the baggage room door bounded a strapping six-footer, the twenty-one-year-old railroad telegrapher, Alfred C. Petty, whose duties encompassed receipt of mail and newspapers. Dancing about the platform, he kicked and punched the bouncing and flying bags and bundles, imparting – usually – just the right impetus and direction to deflect the missiles into the baggage room. Most skidded or rolled through the doorway, while some boomed against the wall to be fetched later. As fast as the porters hurled bags and bundles onto the platform, Petty shagged them into the baggage room.

As the train lumbered out of the depot, the fireman craned his neck, looking back. Jerking on the cord, he gave Petty a *toot-toot* for a virtuoso performance. "Son of a gun's a kick in the ass," he said to the engineer. "Moves so fast he's like a blur."

In the warm, smoke-layered baggage room, Petty whipped out a copy of the St. Louis *Globe-Democrat*. His bushy eyebrows crinkled as he frowned at the still-wet front page.

"Rotten, low-down Spaniards!"

Three railroaders in blue denims slouched in oak chairs around the cast-iron pot-bellied stove, sipping black coffee and puffing on cheroots. Stationmaster Perry Drinkwater flicked ashes on the floor and shifted his weight in his creaky chair.

"Now what?" he demanded in his whiskey voice.

"They blew up one of our battleships!"

"Lemme see that!"

The front page was splashed with stories about the *Maine* disaster. All of Havana had been rocked by the blast, and all the lights in the city blown out, as the shattered hulk of the battleship rose partly out of the water in its death spasm, then sank, carrying more than 200 officers and men to the bottom.

The air in the baggage room turned blue with apoplexy.

"The nerve of those scalawags!"

"Over 200 sailors killed!"

"Dying in the harbor, without any warning – from some

bomb planted by those no-'count Spaniards!"

"Wouldn't seem so horrible if they got themselves killed in some roaring sea battle where they had a fighting chance."

"For sure."

"You know it."

"Check and double-check."

"They oughta *know* we'll do something to even the score."

"Don't they know something like that will bring us into the war?"

"Maybe that's what they *want!*"

"That's what they want, they'll *git* it!"

"Petty," Drinkwater rasped, "fetch me my snake medicine."

From the lacquered oak cabinet in the chief's office, Petty brought forth the flagon of Jack Daniel's and a glass tumbler. The stationmaster filled the glass to the brim, fixing his eyes on the amber fluid – usually with fondness, but this time he didn't really see it. His brain was in a whirl and his hands trembled with rage. Then he proceeded to drink the tumbler dry, downing the whiskey in great gulps, pausing now and then to mutter obscenities.

The news detonated similar emotional outbursts across the nation. In Washington, a fuming Teddy Roosevelt, Under Secretary of the Navy, clipped on his pince-nez, dipped his pen and scribbled to a friend, "I would give anything if Pres. McKinley would order the fleet to Havana tomorrow." The frenetic excitement hatched such wild rumors that by the evening of February 17 the chief of *The Associated Press'* bureau in Washington felt compelled to send out a categorical denial on the ticker:

```
THE CRUISER NEW YORK HAS NOT BEEN ORDERED TO
HAVANA; CONSUL-GENERAL LEE HAS NOT BEEN
ASSASSINATED; THERE IS NO CONFERENCE OF THE
CABINET; CONGRESS IS NOT IN SESSION TONIGHT,
BOTH HOUSES HAVING ADJOURNED AT THE USUAL
```

HOUR UNTIL TOMORROW; PRESIDENT MCKINLEY DID NOT GO TO THE CAPITOL, AND THE SITUATION IS DECIDEDLY QUIET.

All in vain. Hearst's *Journal* offered a $50,000 reward for evidence in the matter. Joseph Pulitzer of the New York *World* dispatched a tug to Havana to learn the "truth." Circulations of both newspapers zoomed. By February 18, the *Journal's* had soared past the dizzy one-million notch.

U.S. Navy diving crew at work on the *Maine* wreck in 1898.
(courtesy the United States Navy Archives)

That night in Pacific, Missouri, Petty's bushy eyebrows knotted and vexation spread over his face as he read aloud from the St. Louis newspaper: "All available information indicates the sinking was due to an accident."

The railroaders greeted that pronouncement with scorn and derision.

"Just listen to that!"

"They 'spect us to *believe* it?"

Drinkwater, flicking ashes on the floor and demanding

ardent spirits, erupted like a bullfrog in a millpond: "Bullcrap! Bullcrap! Bullcrap!"

Some U.S. naval experts conjectured that perhaps a mine, somehow torn loose from Havana's coastal defenses, had struck the ship. Others speculated that a spark might have ignited a seepage of coal gas, triggering the explosion in the ship's forward magazines.

Every night in Pacific, the mail train snorted through and the porters flung off the bundles of newspapers that carried more news on the Cuban imbroglio. And Petty did his little act, with the fireman sending back a *toot-toot*. In the baggage room, Petty held up the February 24 newspaper and cleared his throat.

"Hey, how about this?" He read aloud a story headed: "Belief Grows the Sinking Was Not Due to Accident." Evidence pointed to an external explosion.

Almost in unison, the railroaders heaved profound sighs of released tension: thank God somebody was getting the story *right*, finally.

" 'At's more like it."

"A blind man could see that."

"'Bout time they wised up." Most Americans assumed that in some way the Spanish government had machinated the disaster, whether by torpedo, planted bomb, or whatever. But a few Americans suspected that jingoes in the United States may have blown up the ship to embroil the United States in the war between Cuban rebels and their detested Spanish overlords. Another theory, plausible enough, was that Cuban rebels did it for the same reason. To this day the mystery has not been solved to everyone's content.

On February 25, boggled by the staggering workload of the administration's plan to enlarge the navy, the hot-headed Roosevelt got his big chance to slash red tape. John D. Long, the fatigued Secretary of the Navy, groaned, stretched and said he desperately needed a little rest. "You're in charge for the afternoon," he told Roosevelt. When the door closed behind the departing Long, Roosevelt rolled up his sleeves, taking no pains to hide the Cheshire cat grin that suffused his face like a sunrise.

Next day, when Long came back to his office, he found to his dismay that "the very devil" had seized Roosevelt while he was at the helm the previous afternoon. The acting secretary, busy as a sorcerer's apprentice, had dispatched a torrent of cables and telegrams, directing ships, ordering munitions, and supervising naval maneuvers. He had even sent messages to Congress asking legislation to recruit sailors in vast numbers. But Roosevelt's most audacious action was the cablegram he had fired off to Commodore George Dewey, then in Hong Kong:

```
SECRET AND CONFIDENTIAL. ORDER THE SQUADRON,
EXCEPT THE MONOCACY, TO HONG KONG. KEEP FULL OF
COAL. IN THE EVENT OF DECLARATION OF WAR SPAIN,
YOUR DUTY WILL BE TO SEE THAT THE SPANISH
SQUADRON DOES NOT LEAVE THE ASIATIC COAST, AND
THEN OFFENSIVE OPERATIONS IN PHILIPPINE
ISLANDS. KEEP OLYMPIA UNTIL FURTHER ORDERS.
```

* * * * *

In Pacific, harumping to get his co-workers' attention, Petty read a story in the March 8 paper. It announced that Congress was about to pass a bill giving the President $50 million with which to prepare for war. A staggering sum, indeed.

Ticketman Roger Peabody, a lean, lantern-jawed man who parted his black hair in the middle, was appalled at such profligate spending. He grabbed the paper to verify the figure. His eyes bulged and he let out a slow whistle.

"Fifty million frogskins!" he exclaimed in disbelief.

Baggageman Jack McDougall, balding and burly, looked over Petty's shoulder in wonderment. "That'll buy a lot of peashooters," he said.

"They want war," Drinkwater said, his deep voice ringing out from whiskey-loosened tonsils, "we'll *give* 'em war!"

* * * * *

The court of inquiry into the *Maine* tragedy announced the result of its investigation with a report on March 21. Its finding: the battleship "was destroyed by the explosion of a submarine mine, which caused the partial explosion of two or more of the forward magazines." But the court was unable to fix the blame. However, no member of the court imputed it to the Spanish government, "except through want of precautions against such action."

Members of the Navy Court of Inquiry on board the U.S. Light House Tender Mangrove, in Havana Harbor, Cuba, March 1898. Seated around the table are (left to right): Captain French E. Chadwick, Captain William T. Sampson, Lieutenant Commander William P. Potter, Ensign W.V. Powelson, Lieutenant Commander Adolph Marix.
(courtesy the United States Navy Archives)

In Pacific, Petty burst into the baggage room and let a bundle of newspapers drop to the floor with a crash, jolting the railroaders out of their torpor. Now that he had gotten their attention he read the big story in the March 27 paper: President McKinley had decided to inform Spain that "hostilities in Cuba must cease."

The railroaders snorted their utter contempt for the President's mild-mannered reproof.

"Good night, nurse!" Peabody said.

"Ol' McKinley's addled as an egg if he thinks them damn Spaniards will pay him any mind," McDougall said. "I've seen better heads than his on a glass of beer."

"There's only one thing them varmints can understand," Drinkwater said. "Somebody who can whip the socks off 'em. Petty," he roared, jabbing a commanding finger in the direction of his office, *"nerve tonic!"*

* * * * *

In his inaugural address in 1897, McKinley had vowed: "We want no war of conquest. We must avoid the temptation of territorial aggression." But now his peace efforts were bucking open defiance. Senator Shelby M. Cullom of Illinois ranted: "It's time we grabbed some colonies of our own…We *must* get hold of additional property even if we have to start a war for it!" McKinley's most savage critic was Roosevelt, who sneered: "McKinley has no more backbone than a chocolate éclair." At a formal state dinner, Roosevelt bared his teeth and shook his fist at McKinley's chief advisor, Senator Mark Hanna of Ohio. "Damn you!" he bellowed. "We'll have the war for the freedom of Cuba in spite of you and your gutless bunch!"

McKinley, who had served in the Union army during the Civil War, explained his aversion to turning loose the dogs of war and plunging the nation into a bloodbath: "I shall never get into a war until I'm sure that God and man approve. I've been through one war. I've seen the dead piled up, and I don't want to see another."

But the country had made up its mind that the Cuban mess must be cleaned up once and for all. McKinley, putting his trust in diplomacy, was denounced as weak. Knuckling under to terrific pressure would have been the easy way out for him. But McKinley chose the hard way. Knowing he risked political destruction, he pushed ahead with his efforts to negotiate – despite the fire-breathing newspapers, a hysterical nation, an agitated Congress, and even rabid members of his own Cabinet. But now, from day to day, the President, stunned by the failure of the goal of peace he had announced at his inauguration, lived on the ragged edge. The strain was taking a fearful toll. His face grew haggard and his eyes became dark-circled and sunken. He found it difficult to get any sleep, even when he took narcotics in a desperate effort to snatch a little rest.

In Cuba, the stormy sounds of revolution crashed and rolled like Wagnerian thunder. For four centuries Spain had flown its tragically symbolic red-and-gold colors over the island – red for blood and gold for greed, some would say. And now the big Caribbean domain had been a hotbed of revolution for three-quarters of a century. Eight bloody but brief rebellions had broken out between 1823 and 1855. Then came the ninth, known as the Ten Years War, 1868-78, an agony that brought the nation to its knees in total exhaustion. Many Cubans had died – and Spaniards, too – but the oppressed islanders' passion for "Cuba Libre" did not die.

A few years after the Ten Years War – in 1883 – a small revolt aptly named "the Little War" crackled across the island. Now came an arduous time of waiting, as the struggle for freedom bound up its wounds and nurtured its sinews and gathered its strength for the big one. And in 1895, when the iron clangor of uprising No. 11 resounded over the cane fields and towns and jungles, it was a sockdolager.

Boiling pillars of black smoke by day and red blazes of fire by night signaled the passage of rebel bands. Many plantation owners paid heavy bribes to escape ruin, and others demanded succor from the Spanish. A fierce-looking rebel chieftain shook his fist at a planter. "You may have five hundred troops to guard your place," he said, "but I will find a way to destroy it sooner or later."

For some strange reason, renowned artist Frederic Remington, assigned to Cuba by Hearst's *Journal*, apparently failed to see any disturbing signs. In January 1897, William S. Bowen of the New York *World* had written: "A very real reign of terror prevails throughout the rural districts." Yet in that same month, Remington sent a telegram to Hearst:

```
EVERYTHING IS QUIET. THERE IS NO TROUBLE
HERE. THERE WILL BE NO WAR. I WISH TO
RETURN.
```

Hearst wired back:

```
PLEASE REMAIN. YOU FURNISH THE PICTURES.
I'LL FURNISH THE WAR.
```

Nevertheless, Remington packed up his easel, palette and paint pots and went home. But he was fated to pay another visit to Cuba in June 1898, as a member of the press corps with the American Expeditionary Force.

A book chronicling the Spanish-American War written
by Richard Harding Davis and illustrated by Frederic Remington

Under the Spaniards' *reconcentrado* policy, a forerunner of concentration camps, Cubans were driven from their homes and farms and herded into cities. Little or no provision was made to feed, clothe and house them. All Cubans outside reconcentrado zones were deemed rebels and shot on sight.

Hearst's *Journal* and Pulitzer's *World*, pulling all the stops in their frenzied rivalry for increased circulation, published a raft of blood-curdling stories from Cuba. Hearst assigned twenty correspondents to Cuba and hired ten dispatch boats to rush back their stories.

Famed Red Cross worker Clara Barton, horrified by news stories of starving Cubans, sailed to Cuba with a shipload of food and medicine. Barton had nursed in Civil War camps, and then traveled to the front for the German Red Cross during the Franco-Prussian War of 1870. Later she organized the American Red Cross. Now, at age 77, she plunged into the Cuban imbroglio – and said she saw a large building in Havana containing over four hundred women and children "in the most pitiable condition possible for human beings to be in and live." She added: "Massacres in Armenia seemed merciful by comparison."

The spunky Barton was destined to return to Cuba with the American expedition.

When Senator Edward J. King returned from Cuba in January, 1898, he described the tragic conditions in the big island to House Speaker Thomas B. Reed, who replied: "If God Almighty allowed these people to starve, I think we in the United States can."

But few Americans shared Reed's case-hardened opinion.

* * * * *

"Listen to this," Petty said, kicking the stove to get some attention. From the April 4 paper, he read, "'President McKinley is reported as saying he still hopes there will be no conflict.'"

That joggled the railroaders out of their languor. They almost choked with fury.

"Done it again, dammit!"

"Acting like a rabbit – letting himself be spooked by them Spanish four-flushers!"

"If he had a brain, he'd be dangerous."

And Drinkwater needed some soothing syrup.

* * * * *

One evening, as war fever gripped the United States, a friend met Roosevelt storming away from the White House.

"Do you know what that white-livered cur up there has done?" Roosevelt demanded, his neck flushing with choler. "He's prepared *two* messages for Congress – one for war and one for peace – and doesn't know which one to send in!"

But events were moving fast, and McKinley would be caught up in their momentum.

* * * * *

"Here we go again," Petty said, and read from the April 20 paper: "'Ultimatum to Spain; the President will notify her that she must get out of Cuba or be put out.'"

"McKinley's finally showing a little ginger."

"Better late than never."

Two days later, the tension heightened.

"Get a load of this," Petty said, and recited from the April 22 issue: "'The war has come; Spain refuses to receive our ultimatum…The South Atlantic Squadron at Key West is expected to start for Havana today to establish a blockade of Cuban ports.'"

McDougall grabbed the paper to read it for himself. "That'll give them high-and-mighty Spanish hombres something to chew on," he said.

Drinkwater's belly quaked with laughter. "Betcha them fancy-pants horsethieves don't know whether to shit or go blind! Petty – *celebration water!* How's about a little moisture, anybody?"

* * * * *

On April 23, having determined to ask Congress for a formal declaration of war, McKinley issued his first call for volunteers, 125,000 of them.

On the same day, Spain formally declared war against the United States, despite indications a-plenty that most of the Spanish people were already bone-weary of the seemingly endless revolutions in Cuba, and above all wanted no military contest with the Yankee colossus. Spain's declaration announced "the people of North America...have exhausted our patience and have provoked war by their perfidious intrigues, by their treacherous acts, and by their violations of the law of nations and international conventions." Spanish hubris went so far as to predict: "The struggle will be short and decisive. The God of victories will grant us as brilliant and complete a victory as the right and justice of our cause demand."

A day later, early on Sunday morning, McKinley called Navy Secretary John D. Long to the White House. When they emerged from their conference, the following cable was dispatched to Commodore Dewey in Hong Kong:

```
WAR HAS COMMENCED BETWEEN THE UNITED STATES
AND SPAIN. PROCEED AT ONCE TO PHILIPPINE
ISLANDS. COMMENCE OPERATIONS AT ONCE,
PARTICULARLY AGAINST THE SPANISH FLEET. YOU
MUST CAPTURE VESSELS OR DESTROY. USE UTMOST
ENDEAVORS.
LONG
```

Next day – Monday, April 25 – McKinley asked Congress

for a joint resolution recognizing a state of war. By a voice vote the same day, both House and Senate approved the resolution, which stated that "war has existed since the 21st day of April," the day the navy began blockading Cuba.

* * * * *

In the Pacific the following day, Petty stalked into the baggage room, holding up the newspaper to show the big bold headline: WAR FORMALLY DECLARED BY CONGRESS.

"Now for the fireworks!"

"Gonna be a knock-down, drag-out."

"Spanish fur's gonna fly for sure."

A couple of days afterward, Petty brought in another bombshell. "This'll curl your hair," he said as a preface to reading from the April 28 paper: "'Four ironclads and two torpedo-boat destroyers sailed for the United States yesterday from Spain.'"

Drinkwater shook like jelly, nearly strangling with delight: "Looks like our navy's gonna be up to its ass in alligators!"

Some time before this, Petty had made up his mind that he would want to get into the mix-up, if and when the United States decided to punish Spain for her dastardly action in sinking the *Maine*. But he hadn't breathed a word about enlisting to his co-workers yet. This time, however, finally had come to make the announcement.

"Reckon I'll hitch up," he said.

Peabody pulled out cigarette paper and a sack of Bull Durham from his shirt pocket. "Congrats, ol' boy," Peabody said. "Didja hear that Hampton from over Sedalia way is organizing a volunteer company?" He rolled the cigarette and twisted the ends.

"Pete Hampton?"

"The same. Friend of yours?"

"No, but I know who he is. Who's jining his outfit?"

"I am, for one."

"Bully for you, Roger! Anybody else I might know?"

Peabody touched his cigarette to the pot-bellied stove to light it. Even though the weather was warming up with the advance of spring, the stove was kept hot with red coals for boiling coffee. He blew a smoke ring, then ticked off several names on his fingers.

"Them's some good ol' boys," Petty said. "Reckon they'll make jim-dandy soldiers. Wouldn't mind doing my time with you fellas."

"Then do it, ol' pardner."

"Where do I hook up?"

"Jefferson Barracks is where our company is."

Petty turned in his written resignation, picked up his final check, and hopped the train to St. Louis to spend a few days with his mother before going off to fight a war. He also wanted to see a certain girl with honey-blond hair and eyes of China blue.

It was a fateful delay, because if he had gone at once to Jefferson Barracks he would have arrived in time to muster in with his friends in the 3rd Missouri Volunteers – which never left the States.

Chapter 2:
Hue and Cry

Mrs. Petty's face went white as she poured her son a cup of coffee. Her hand holding the metal pot began to shake as if with ague. She jammed it back on the cookstove. Her voice quivered in dismay.

"What? Enlist?"

For a moment she stood there, mechanically wiping her hands on her apron, staggered by fearsome recollections. She had been a mere snot-nose brat hiding in a barn as the War Between the States seesawed across Shiloh's churchyard, but the carnage of those two endless days was seared in her memory forever. She well knew the fate of young soldiers in war's crucible. And now her boy – a soldier.

She sat down and let her gnarled hands rest on the red-and-white checkered tablecloth – rest like two dumb, suffering animals. From under her yellow headscarf, wisps of brown hair drifted, framing her stricken face. The early sun flooded the kitchen through gingham curtains. It lighted up the breakfast table, glinting on the ceramic vase stuffed with the blue-and-white roguery of Johnny-jump-ups. But now a veil had passed over the sun. The brightness had gone out of the day.

"Oh, Alfred, you ain't got a woodpecker's notion of what you're sticking your noodle into. You're nothing but a fool, a precious fool!"

Grits and sausages steamed in flower-decorated crockery. Petty forked man-size dollops onto his plate. "Look, Ma, my mind's all made up. No use trying to change it. I've *decided!*"

She stared at him, distraught and baffled, not knowing how to handle the situation. "You could be…" Her voice trailed off. "…*killed!*"

Petty chewed for a moment, savoring Ma's cooking. "Man, them's good vittles."

"Well?" she demanded. She wasn't going to let him change the subject.

For some reason the look of acute concern on her face struck his funnybone, and he couldn't help venting a little snicker. "Everybody's gotta die some time," he said. "Might as well do it now and get it over with."

"That ain't funny!"

"Well, *somebody's* gotta teach them cuss-fired Spaniards a lesson, and I wanna help 'em do it…Got any more 'pone?"

Lifting the square tin pan off the stove, she scooped a big chunk of nicely browned cornbread onto his plate. Her voice quavered with foreknowledge of the futility of this argument. "You shorely put me in mind of your Pa – get a bee in his bonnet, and stick his neck out, and there's nothing a body could ever do to bring him to his senses. God rest his soul!"

For some minutes they ate their vittles in silence, but Ma only picked at her portions. Now and then her tired brown eyes shot a blank look at her big son, and she wondered at the inscrutability of God's purposes, that He should give her this new tribulation after so many almost unbearable woes in past years.

Petty cleaned his plate with a chunk of 'pone, popped it into his mouth, and then wiped his mouth with the back of his hand. "Ma, I'll be *all right.*" He yawned and stretched lazily, then rose to his feet. "Jess don't *worry*, will ya?"

He walked to the door, took his slouch hat from the coat

tree, and clapped it on at a rakish angle.

"Where ya off to now?"

"Slop the hogs is all."

"I already done slopped 'em – before you were outta bed."

"You could've let me do it."

"You can water 'em. I 'spect they're powerful thirsty by now."

Swinging open the gate in the white picket fence, he detoured through the small peach orchard. The trees were still ablaze with pink blossoms and droning with bees. Spring had come a little late this year. White clouds sailed across the dome of azure. The air smelled as pure as heaven, except for an occasional stink wafted from the hog pen. For a long time Petty stood there in the splendor of the vernal season with an ache in his heart. He was thinking how hard it is to do the thing you believe in when someone you love, who is older and probably wiser, thinks you are making a mistake.

Finally, shaking his head in perplexity, he poured a can of water into the top of the cylinder to prime the pump. Briskly he joggled the handle up and down, and water gushed from the iron spout into the hogs' drinking trough.

Later that morning, which was a Saturday, Petty clapped on his straw boater, wheeled his Columbia out of the barn and cycled the six miles down the road to the whitewashed buildings of the dairy farm where Dorothy Swan lived with her parents. Since Petty's house had no telephone, he had written to her a few days earlier, saying he planned to enlist, and wanted to see her.

She greeted him in a yellow housedress, with her blond hair done in a coiffure drawn up to the top of her head, with bangs in front.

Petty batted his eyes playfully. "You're not a bit hard to look at," he said. "Ready for a spin?"

Her laughter tinkled like wind chimes. "Wait'll I get my bloomers on."

"Bloomers?"

"You'll see."

In a few minutes, she flounced back gaily, wearing a divided pink skirt lavishly decorated with frills, a garment type originally designed by a certain Mrs. Amelia Bloomer.

Dorothy whirled on her toes. "Got 'em by mail order from the wish-book. How do you like 'em?"

"Ain't those diddlywhackers a mite on the daring side?"

"Oh, Al, don't be silly. A girl can hardly ride a bike in those clumsy skirts. Lordamercy!"

Dorothy had packed a basket with chicken sandwiches, Cheddar cheese and a jug of applejack, chilled by hanging overnight on a rope deep in the well. Petty slung the basket over his handlebars and they pushed off, he on his Columbia, she on her Enchantress.

Cotton-bale clouds sailed through the ceramic blue. Jackrabbits fled in great bounds at the approach of the cyclists. For many miles they pedaled along roads lined with telephone poles, their wires traveling in mighty swoops from pole to pole. A delicious breeze blew, cooling them by fanning the perspiration on their bodies. The wind, blowing through the wires, moaned softly, hauntingly. Yellow-breasted meadowlarks sang their hearts out in the grass.

A farmer in straw hat and bib overalls, red bandana hanging from his hip pocket, waved to them as he trudged behind his horse-drawn plow, turning up a curl of dark loam.

They whipped past a carriage drawn by horses with shiny coats. An elderly woman's face froze in horror at the spectacle of Dorothy's breeze-ruffled bloomers, a garment still rare in rural Missouri. "Scandalous!" she hurled after them.

They stopped near a creek, where weeping willows shaded a green bank and a moss-tufted stone bridge leaped over the green gulch.

"How about this?" Petty asked.

Dragonflies zapped over the sun-lit water, meeting one

another and mating in mid-flight, while water-striders took the pedestrian route.

"Couldn't be lovelier," Dorothy said.

They consumed the sandwiches, cheese and applejack with the gusto of appetites sharpened in the fresh air. For a long time they talked – about the war, their families, mutual friends, themselves. Petty reached his arms out to bring Dorothy closer, and they found that their bodies hungered for each other. The war suddenly seemed far away.

* * * * *

On April 29, Secretary of the Navy Long cabled Admiral William T. Sampson that the four Spanish armored cruisers and two torpedo-boat destroyers, last reported somewhere on the Atlantic, might be steaming for the east coast of the United States, probably "for the purpose of inflicting what injury they could upon our coastwise cities and towns." The Spanish fleet and its unknown whereabouts afflicted many a citizen with a bad case of the jitters. About May 13, someone reported sighting the Spanish fleet off Sandy Hook, New Jersey, an alarming report that would, however, prove spurious. But General Nelson A. Miles frantically telegraphed his apprehension to the chief quartermaster in New York:

```
REPORT AT ONCE ANY INFORMATION ABOUT SPANISH
WAR-BOATS ON OUR COAST. GIVE FULL
INFORMATION. HOLD TRANSPORTS UNTIL FURTHER
ORDERS. ACKNOWLEDGE.
```

At that moment, the 71st New York Infantry, bound for Tampa, was already loaded aboard transports at Bedloe's Island, overwatched by the Statue of Liberty. But the soldiers were hastily debarked and re-routed south by rail.

Up and down the coast spread the hue and cry. In some

New England coastal cities, citizens hustled their valuables inland for safekeeping. Telegrams and letters from coastal cities swamped the War Department, demanding that mines be placed in all rivers and harbors and guns be installed all over the map. Influential people tried to goad the administration into adopting a perilous tactic – scattering the naval forces. Item: millionaires with summer mansions on Jekyll Island, Georgia, demanded that warships be stationed nearby to guard their real estate.

Meanwhile on the far side of the world, as dawn's first light glimmered on April 30, Dewey's squadron of four cruisers and two gunboats steamed boldly into Manila Bay, which was defended by shore batteries and ten Spanish warships.

Lithograph showing the Battle of Manila Bay

As a Spanish shell exploded directly over his flagship, the *Olympia*, Dewey uttered his famous order, "You may fire when ready, Gridley," and the bombardment began. During a half-day's shelling, the American warships destroyed or knocked out of action the shore batteries and the ten Spanish ships, with only one fatality among the Americans: a black-gang engineer who died of a heart attack.

In the Monday morning papers, the whole country got the news of Dewey's triumph and went wild with jubilation. Bells rang, whistles blew, and there were a myriad rousing renditions of the national anthem. When night fell, college students built bonfires on campuses across the country, and fireworks glittered in the dark skies over every city and town.

And McKinley appointed Commodore Dewey an acting rear admiral.

* * * * *

In Pacific, the railroaders festooned their offices with red, white and blue bunting. McDougall sauntered in, hung up his straw boater and green blazer, and clapped on his denim railroad cap. "They've declared a holiday to celebrate," he said.

Petty handed him a newspaper. "You just noticed?"

"Betcha they ain't celebrating in Madrid."

"More like sackcloth and ashes," Petty said.

McDougall, skimming the paper, stopped at an item. "Says here the factories making flags put on night shifts and still can't handle the demand for 'em."

"Looks like a banner year for flag-makers," Petty quipped.

McDougall smiled. "When ya going in?"

"Tomorrow's the big day. Woulda gone sooner but wanted to go home and see Ma before I left."

"Better stir you stumps if you're gonna catch up with Peabody. He took off five days ago. I'd go myself, if I wasn't saddled with a family. Cuppa coffee?"

"Naw!" Drinkwater interrupted with a volcanic roar of disapproval, waving his hands in protest at McDougall. Rising from his chair, he lurched into the office to get his jug of creature comfort. "Let's give this young soldier some *gunpowder* to prime his cannon!"

Pacific and St. Louis were blazing with flags, as were most of the other cities and towns across the nation. On New York's Fifth Avenue, St. Patrick's Cathedral displayed a 40- by 35-foot flag between its tall spires. It was said to be the largest flag ever hung in the city. Every night at New York's Knickerbocker Theater, where "The Bride Elect" was playing, the chorus "Unchain the Dogs of War" drew rafter-ringing ovations. In Texas, the governor stationed his whole force of Rangers on the Mexican border to repulse any possible invasion by "Spanish sympathizers." In Georgia, the governor said he personally would lead his state's militia into combat.

Young men and a sizeable number of the over-the-hill gang flocked to recruiting stations. Even some superannuated Civil War veterans, decrepit in body but intact in courage, tried to "go for a sojer."

Secretary of War Russell Alger had monumental problems to overcome – but very little time to devote to them. Alger probably was a distant relative of Horatio Alger, author of boys' success stories. In fact, he had lived the life of an Alger hero in his extraordinary rise from poor orphan to high positions of wealth and influence. But each day now, his office was invaded by at least a hundred persons whose prestige warranted personal interviews, a distraction that consumed nearly the entire day. It was maddening.

"By Godfrey," the harassed Alger fulminated to an associate, "some of these pains-in-the-ass who want commissions, or some other favor, are even hounding me at my house before breakfast. And others are haunting me there even after midnight!"

Sundays and the tattered remnants of the evenings were

relegated to administrative work. Thus America plunged into a war to which the Secretary of War found it impossible to devote much more than his spare time.

Bizarre ideas surfaced in the news media, like strange creatures from the bottom of the sea surfacing when a dredge is hoisted up. William "Buffalo Bill" Cody wrote a newspaper article boasting how he could clean the Spanish out of Cuba with 30,000 Indian warriors. Hearst's *Journal* proposed that whopping athletes such as heavyweights Jim Corbett and Bob Fitzsimmons, baseball star Cap Anson, grid luminary Red Waters, and hammer-tosser Jim Mitchell be enlisted in a regiment that would so daunt the Spanish "by their mere appearance" that they would hoist the white flag.

Frank James, ex-outlaw brother of the notorious Jesse, suggested that his wild-and-woolly experience with guns and horses be put to good use by assigning him the command of a company of cowboys. Martha A. Shute, secretary of the Colorado State Board of Agriculture, announced plans to form a cavalry troop composed wholly of females. Six hundred Sioux Indians reportedly were itching to tomahawk Spanish scalps. It seemed that everybody was trying to get into the act.

However, there was a small minority of dissenters. Though submerged by the nation's impetuous rush toward war, they stood their ground, bravely if not easily. Item: in Kansas City, a cobbler who had the audacity to hang crepe on his door with the sign, "Closed in memory of a Christian nation that descends to the barbarity of war," was besieged by a mob.

In the general intoxication over the victory at Manila, President McKinley on May 8 ordered General Miles to take 70,000 soldiers and capture Havana.

Miles, avid for glory and never bashful about his own military exploits, would have been elated. But years of Indian campaigns had sobered some of his formerly reckless ardor. He knew that no sizeable army could enter the fray now, or for some time. Grudgingly, he told McKinley the nation hadn't enough ammunition for 70,000 soldiers to fight a single battle, and the arsenals couldn't turn out enough on short notice. McKinley revoked his order.

* * * * *

Petty had gone home again briefly to see Ma again and pick up some traveling clothes. Now he felt he had postponed his departure long enough. The time had come to say goodbye. Heavy-laden satchel in hand, he stepped to the door, taking his hat from the coat-tree. Then he hesitated, seeing Ma just standing there, wiping her hands on her apron, her tired eyes brimming with tears. With a desperate little rush, she was in his arms, hugging him, kissing him on the cheek. When she spoke, her voice grated hoarsely.

"Take care and hurry back."

"Don't worry, Ma, I'll be back. Goodbye, Ma."

Petty felt an ache of sorrow. He wasn't at all confident he would see Ma again. The future was a faraway landscape buried in the clouds.

* * * * *

Jefferson Barracks was a panorama of flags and platoons of soldiers, marching briskly and belting out cadence-counts. Petty found the small cubicle of an officer he had been told to look for. A mustachioed officer with bifocals on his nose sat at a battered wooden table awash with papers, his pen scratching quick notations on one paper after another. Pausing, he glanced up. "Yes?"

Petty stepped toward the table. "Cap'n Hampton?"

"You're looking at him." He resumed his notations.

"This where I hitch up?"

Hampton shot another glance at Petty. "Sorry, boy, we're full strength now. Filled the last vacancy a couple days ago. No room for more."

It took Petty a moment to find his voice again. "Know any other companies taking on rookies, Cap'n?"

Impatience flickered across the captain's face. "Same goes for all the others. Full to the brim. Sorry, boy." He shook his head and plunged back to work.

For some seconds Petty just stood there, feeling like an idiot, stupefied by the captain's words. He cursed himself for being so tardy. Not for an instant had it crossed his mind that McKinley's call for 125,000 volunteers would be filled before he had a chance to climb aboard the wagon. With shoulders beginning to sag, he slipped out of the office, shambled away from the stir and color of Jefferson Barracks, then deadheaded on the next rattler back to Pacific.

Slowly he clumped up the wooden steps of his boardinghouse. Sandy McCracken came banging out the screen door on his way to work – bartending in a fancy saloon. The dandy of the neighborhood, he sported a shiny top hat, brown cutaway, yellow waistcoat, yellow-and-brown checked trousers and black leather boots.

At the sight of his forlorn neighbor, he stopped short, walking stick poised in air. "Hey, what happened? You look lower than the ring around a Scotchman's bathtub."

Petty didn't feel like laughing. "Couldn't get in, Sandy. They're jam-full."

"Gee-whillikers, that's rotten." His walking stick made a quick *ratatatat* against the iron railings. "Hey, wait a sec! What's-his-name was telling me they're signing up a few volunteers in the regulars!"

"Regular army? Where 'bouts?"

"Post Office in St. Looey. Some of the regiments are below maximum, is the reason. Could use a few rookies to fill the holes, the man said."

"Much obleeged, pardner!"

"Keep the change."

As Petty took off one way down the street, McCracken sauntered the other way, swinging his walking stick, yelling over his shoulder, "Hope you get a break!"

This time Petty resolved he wouldn't dawdle. He caught the first train to St. Louis, then swiftly legged it to the building at Third and Olive. Luckily, McCracken's information was correct. That very day, May 19, Petty took his physical, repeated the oath of allegiance, and signed up for three years, or the war's duration.

From the post office, Petty and some other recruits were sent out to Jefferson Barracks for processing. More and more volunteers checked into "The Barracks" every day. At last, after much chafing with impatience over the seemingly endless delays, Petty and many other comrades climbed aboard a train bound for Atlanta.

"*B-o-o-a-r-r-d-d!*" And now they were on their way, reveling in the sounds of movement: the clickety-clack of the rails, the feverish chuffing of the stack, and the occasional haunting whistle-wail. They gloated at the countryside now blooming in the high tide of spring. The sun shone warm and the air wafted through the open coach windows smelled sweet, even though fine soot from the stack left a thin layer of smut on everything.

Furiously, like an enormous beast, the train pounded across the blue-grass meadows of Kentucky, rattled past the grandeur of Lookout Mountain in Tennessee, and lurched through the red-clay hills of Georgia to an overnight stop in Atlanta. About noon the next day, they steamed onward again, en route to Tampa, now in a longer train of fifteen coaches packed with ebullient soldiers.

"Tampa, here we come!"

"On to Cuba!"

"Remember the *Maine* – to hell with Spain!"

In a little over a month, nearly all the 125,000 volunteers of the first call, together with the regular units, were mobilized at Tampa, Mobile, Chickamauga Park, and Washington.

But the army had colossal problems to overcome. When war was declared, it had less than 30,000 officers and men in uniform. Most of this hard core of veteran regulars had fought in the Indian wars, picking up many tricks of guerilla warfare, but precious little about fighting in massive, coordinated campaigns. Capping the army's troubles, there were shortages of practically everything – tents, cots, blankets, knapsacks, cartridge belts, canteens, hats, leggings, shoes. The only uniforms available were fabricated of heavy blue wool, hardly suitable for an ordeal in the sweltering tropics. Worse yet, the federal arsenals had none of the modern smokeless powder.

Meanwhile, on May 25, an expedition sailed from San Francisco, bound for the Philippines.

But the Cuban expedition's departure was being stalled by the War Department's lack of preparedness, plus the dread of exposing inexperienced and unacclimated soldiers to the hazards of a Cuban campaign during the rainy and fever season. In fact, the War Department had just about decided to pigeonhole the Cuban campaign until fall. Especially when Surgeon General George M. Sternberg, an expert on tropical diseases who had long resided in Cuba, divulged his alarming conclusion: an invasion any sooner than October would bring on an appalling death rate of up to 50 per cent – from yellow fever alone.

Suddenly came the momentous news that Admiral Pascual Cervera's fleet, its whereabouts up to this time a nerve-racking mystery, had taken refuge in the harbor of Santiago de Cuba, on the southeastern coast of the big Caribbean island.

A few days later Admiral Sampson cabled Washington with the even more electrifying report that his warships had bottled up the enemy fleet in Santiago harbor, but could not enter and destroy it because of hazards from forts and mines guarding the tortuous entrance of the huge, landlocked body of water. The very names of the Spanish warships echoed with a sonorousness that made one think of the rumble of distant thunder, or cannon. They were the armored cruisers *Cristobal Colon, Almirante Oquendo, Infanta Maria Teresa,* and *Vizcaya,* and the *Furor* and *Pluton,* torpedo-boat destroyers.

Several days later, Sampson dictated another cable to Washington:

> BOMBARDED FORTS AT SANTIAGEO, 7:30 TO 10 A.M. TODAY, JUNE 6TH. HAVE SILENCED FORTS QUICKLY WITHOUT INJURY OF ANY KIND, THOUGH STATIONARY 2,000 YARDS. IF 10,000 MEN WERE HERE CITY AND FLEET WOULD BE OURS WITHIN FORTY-EIGHT HOURS. EVERY CONSIDERATION DEMANDS IMMEDIATE ARMY MOVEMENT. IF DELAYED, CITY WILL BE DEFENDED MORE STRONGLY BY GUNS TAKEN FROM FLEET.

Cervera's *Almirante Oquendo*

Cervera's four cruisers were reputed in some quarters to be the best vessels of their class in the world – four or five knots faster than American battleships and more powerful than American cruisers. In reality, they were in abominable shape. But as long as they remained afloat, Spain held a potentially murderous weapon.

Since Dewey's annihilation of the Spanish fleet in Manila Bay, Cervera's fleet in Santiago harbor remained virtually all of Spanish naval power that was still afloat. If Cervera's fleet could be captured or destroyed, Spain's power for offensive warfare would be wiped out. And the Spanish army in Cuba, chopped off with a meat axe from all reinforcements and supplies, would be doomed. The Americans would only have to wait for it to die on the vine.

Now the army was being asked to perform the somewhat bizarre role of helping to destroy an enemy fleet. On the evening of June 7, Secretary of War Alger dashed off the following telegram to General William R. Shafter, who had been given command of the Fifth Army Corps, at Tampa:

```
YOU WILL SAIL IMMEDIATELY, AS YOU ARE NEEDED
AT DESTINATION AT ONCE. ANSWER.
```

Without waiting for an answer, the overwrought Secretary of War wired Shafter again:

```
SINCE TELEGRAPHING YOU AN HOUR SINCE THE
PRESIDENT DIRECTS YOU SAIL AT ONCE WITH WHAT
FORCE YOU HAVE READY.
```

Shafter replied:

```
I WILL SAIL TOMORROW MORNING. STEAM CANNOT
BE GOTTEN UP EARLIER.
```

The military juggernaut was being set in motion. Full speed ahead, and damn the torpedoes.

Chapter 3:
Chaos at Tampa

The train disgorged Petty and his fellow recruits in a Tampa where the wildest confusion held sway. The town and its environs of normally 10,000 people on the west coast of Florida were now swollen with 20,000 restless soldiers.

Some three and a half centuries earlier here at Tampa Bay, Spanish conquistador Hernando De Soto had launched his epic journey through *terra incognita* in the north. Now it was a kind of turnabout, for this same bay was a staging area for an invasion by *norteamericanos* into a Spanish dominion to the south.

Tampa was picked as the springboard for the American expedition because it was the nearest port to Cuba with room for a large camp.

But the encampment was a Gordian knot of befuddlement. One writer called Tampa "the focal point of one of the worst mix-ups in our military history." Teddy Roosevelt, arriving with his Rough Riders and unable to obtain food for them for twenty-four hours, termed it "a scene of the wildest confusion." Other observers offered variations on the same theme. Everything the army needed – food, uniforms, weapons, ammunition – was in short supply or nonexistent.

Not a single regiment was fully equipped. Many soldiers

had no GI equipment at all. Only one government arsenal was manufacturing war materiel. So the government had to rely on private manufacturers, who seemed far more interested in milking fat profits from shoddy supplies than in doing right by their country.

Only a single rail line ran into Tampa. Both freight trains and troop-carrying coaches funneling into Florida from other parts of the United States had to compete for space on the continuously-congested Tampa spur. Some regiments hijacked trains from other regiments to transport them to Tampa. And arriving regiments often discovered that all their equipment – artillery, rifles, munitions, uniforms, medicines and provisions, horses and mules – were stranded in boxcars up to one hundred and fifty miles away. Some volunteer regiments had to spend twenty-four to forty-eight hours idling in Tampa town streets and sleeping on sidewalks until word of their arrival reached the proper authorities, who told them where to camp.

Military camp at Port Tampa City during Spanish-American War:, 1898
(courtesy Tampa-Hillsborough County Public Library System)

Luckily Petty and his fellow arrivals had been earmarked at Jefferson Barracks for regiments already bivouacked at Tampa. Now they were allowed to choose the company they wanted to serve in. Petty, assigned to the 13th Infantry, strolled down the dusty streets of "Tent City," flicked sweat from his brow with the back of his hand, then picked Company H at random. He had left all his friends back at Jefferson Barracks with the 3rd Missouri Volunteers. It no longer mattered which company he served with, so long as it was headed for Cuba. Weren't they all comrades in arms?

Next morning, after breakfast mess, the bugler blew assembly. As they fell in, First Sgt. James O'Neill's teeth worked on a chaw of "baccy." O'Neill, about thirty-five years old, had short-cropped brown hair with a gray fringe around his ears. Masses of brown freckles sprinkled his pink Irish skin. His uniform owed its neat creases not to an iron, but to having been pressed under his mattress.

"All you new men," he bellowed, "when I call off your name, form a line over here...*Agnew!*"

"Yo!"

"Well, *move* it! *Ball!*"

"Hyar!"

"*Binkli!*"

"Present, sergeant."

"'Present, sergeant'? Whadda we got here, some goddamn kinda grammer perfessor?" O'Neill said, in pretended crankiness. A stream of tobacco juice splattered the dust. "C-I-E-S...Lordamercy, how do ya pernounce that?"

"Cieslewicz," replied the soldier of that name.

"Gesundheit! *Donovan!*"

"Yo!"

When all the new men were lined up, O'Neill marched them to a supply building at "route step" – the only maneuver that ignorant rookies fresh off the train could be expected to perform, since they weren't obliged to keep in step. As they filed through the building, quartermaster corpsmen issued them shoes, campaign hats and heavy blue-wool shirts and trousers.

Petty fingered the fabric of the wool shirts he had just been issued. "Hey, what's the deal? We going to Cuba or Alaska? Shouldn't we get khaki or something?"

A sergeant glared. "Take it or leave it, buster!"

As it turned out, Petty often didn't have that much of a choice anyway. By the time his turn came, all the shoes, trousers and hats that would have fit him had been exhausted and he had to make do with his civilian shoes and trousers and old slouch hat, all of which had seen palmier days.

Each solder also drew a steel bayonet and scabbard, a canvas-covered tin canteen, and lastly an ammunition belt, box of cartridges and a bolt-action, .30-caliber Krag-Jorgensen, a Danish-designed rifle with American improvements. The clip held five cartridges. With one cartridge in the firing chamber, and wearing a full belt containing one hundred cartridges, a soldier in the field had one hundred and six rounds to face the enemy with.

Petty hefted his Krag, admiring its size and weight and feeling confident he could hit anything he aimed at. A rifle was no novelty. Ever since he could remember, there had always been one or more squirrel rifles or other firearms hanging over the mantle. As a tad of only six years, alone at the edge of the woods, he had rested the long barrel of his father's cap-and-ball rifle in the fork of a small tree to steady it, and bagged his first squirrel.

* * * * *

The morning sun was throwing off heat like a furnace when the new men in Petty's company assembled in the sparse shade of some rickety pine trees for their first rifle class. Their instructor was Ludwig Seufert, a banty, blond-haired corporal with an imperious air toward rookies. Levity soared to a rowdy crescendo.

"Hat-ease!" Seufert hollered, then added after the noise had simmered down somewhat: "I don't mind telling you I didn't volunteer for this job."

But Petty's mind was all concentration, oblivious to everything else, as he demonstrated to another soldier how to snap the cartridge clip into the rifle. As the hubbub died away, Petty's full-toned rustic voice lingered in the air.

"Lemme show ya something else. When you aim your rifle, don't *pull* the trigger. Jess *squeeze* it, gently. Like this."

As Seufert, watching incredulously, did a slow burn, Petty sighted his rifle on a distant clump of palmettos and squeezed the trigger. The hammer clicked on the empty chamber. Seufert's jaws worked silently at what he considered a brazen affront to his authority. Arm extended, he pointed directly at Petty, and words came out of his mouth like Gatling bursts.

"*You*, soldier! What's your name?"

"Who, me?"

"Yeah, you!"

"Petty, sir."

Seufert kept his arm and finger extended, pointing straight at Petty, like a weapon. "Don't call me *'sir'*! Don't you even know how to answer when a noncommissioned officer speaks to you? What the hell's your full name, goddamn it?"

"Petty, Private Alfred C."

"Okay, Petty, Private Alfred C., now get this." He dropped his arm. "And all you other rookies, too. *I'm* doing the instructing here. And I don't want any dumb-ass greenhorn who *thinks* he knows something about a rifle fouling up some other dumb-ass greenhorn. So just forget everything you think you know. We're gonna start all the way from the beginning. There are three ways to do something."

Seufert ticked them off on his fingers.

"The right way, the wrong way – and the army way. We're gonna do it all the army way."

Seufert picked up his rifle and flipped it to port arms.

"Now the first thing to remember is, this is a *rifle*, not a *gun*. In the army, anything you raise to your shoulder and fire is a rifle. A gun is strictly an artillery weapon. Any questions so far?"

That was too much for Petty to resist. In a loud voice that carried an air of mock innocence, he asked, "Corporal, can I tell you about the time me and Pa went pheasant hunting with a *shot-rifle?*"

The soldiers cracked up, and the red-faced Seufert made a mental note that this wisenheimer would have to be dealt with. Sandbagging him with extra duty might knock some sense into his head.

"Petty, if you don't shape up," Seufert said, "you and me are gonna have to go to the hospital for an operation."

"Operation? Why so, corporal?"

"To have my Number 10 brogan extracted from your ass!"

That quite broke up the gathering.

Each morning, they were drilled with their rifles, learning all the movements in the manual of arms. They also learned how to field-strip their weapons and reassemble them. Some learned how to do it blindfolded. On a "dry-fire" range, they went through the motions of loading, aiming, firing, and ejecting shells. But they were never allowed target practice with live ammunition. Ammunition was too scarce and precious to waste on the firing range.

Each afternoon, they were drilled in the basics of military formations, marching, and deploying on the battlefield. They trained in the blistering sun, as temperatures approached 100 degrees in the shade, drenched with sweat in their heavy wool uniforms, bullyragged by their merciless drill sergeant: "You clowns march like a buncha appleknockers with the hives."

"Oh, God!" someone anguished.

The sergeant heard that. "Your soul may belong to God," he said, "but your ass belongs to me!"

Marching in formation wasn't Petty's forte.

"Count cadence...COUNT!"

The soldiers roared in unison: "HUP, TOOP, THREEP, FO-AH...HUP..."

"By-the-right-flank – HO! Left-flank – HO! Petty!" the sergeant screamed, "for Chrissakes, get in step! Don't you even know left foot from right?"

"Sorry, sarge."

"Jug-eared tanglefoot," the sergeant muttered under his breath. "Count cadence...COUNT!"

Petty vowed to keep one eye cocked on the man on his left, Fay Ball, so he could instantly follow his cue. This was an error. So now and then he had to suffer more abuse for executing commands a particle on the tardy side.

For weeks in that hot summer sun they drilled in the dusty wastes, chanting: "I-had-a-good-home-and-I-*left*-it...*Left*, right *left*!" Their evaporating sweat left white efflorescences of salt on the shoulders of their blue shirts.

Seufert had charge of appointing some of the work details. One Monday at reveille, he faced the company, clipboard at the ready.

"Petty!"

"Yo!"

"Front and center!"

Seufert snapped out several other names. Grudgingly, the men whose names were called lined up in front of him. "Report to the mess sergeant for KP," he told them. A chorus of groans sounded from the detail. "Dismissed! All you other men, fall out and police up this area. All I wanna see is asses and elbows!"

Tuesday, as the soldiers lounged around their tents after breakfast, Seufert appeared again with his clipboard.

"Petty!"

"Yo!"

When Petty and the other unlucky soldiers had lined up,

Seufert said: "Report to Corporal Thompson at company headquarters for latrine detail. Dismissed!"

Wednesday also, Seufert jotted Petty's name on his list.

"Report to the officer of the day for guard duty," he ordered the detail.

It seemed to Petty he was catching more than his fair share of fatigue duty. Thursday morning, instead of returning to his own tent after breakfast, he strolled into Fay Ball's tent, half a dozen tents down the line.

"Seufert's got it in for me," Petty said. "Every morning without fail, he puts me on his shit list."

As Petty sat on a cot and talked with Ball, he could peer out beneath the rolled-up tent flap and watch Seufert start to choose men for a work detail. Seufert stalked into Petty's tent, emerged, glanced again at the soldiers in the vicinity and seemed a bit puzzled. He then picked his detail from the men close at hand.

"Didja see that?" Petty said. "That ringtailed sharpshooter is gunning for *me* again!"

At assembly, Seufert called out: "Petty!"

"Yo!"

"Where the hell were you an hour back?"

Petty had trouble keeping a straight face. "Over yonder, corporal," he said, gesturing down the line of tents.

"After noon mess, report to the supply sergeant."

This time it was a job unloading cases of canned beef from boxcars in Tampa. Petty knew he was getting an unfair shake, but figured he would just have to weather it. If he complained it would only stir up a hornets' nest.

Along the tracks, dozens of soldiers were unloading boxes of supplies from boxcars, then transferring them into wagons, each of which was hitched to four mules. The mule-wagon caravans then plodded through the sandy streets of Tampa, winding toward the army camp a mile away.

After the men had worked for two hours in the hot sun, the

corporal in charge of their detail, a seamy-faced old regular, said, "All right, take ten," and the men gratefully sank to the ground in the shady side of the boxcar. Conversation drifted into speculation on what might lie ahead in Cuba.

"Them Spanish soldiers," Petty said. "Betcha they ain't no great shucks at scrappin'. Look what ol' Dewey did to their navy."

"We'll massacre 'em," said another recruit.

"Listen," the corporal said, raising his index finger for emphasis. "Don't *never* underestimate the enemy. First rule of war. What the hell you lame-brain Johnny-come-latelies know about war? Hell, you ain't dry behind the ears yet!"

His scorn was affable, so the rookies accepted his criticism without offense.

Moments later, the corporal's thoughts flickered back to the task at hand. His lined face twisted into a wry grimace and he spat in disgust.

"If this supply mess is any tip-off to the fixes we'll be messing with in Cuba, we could lose this war before we ever get organized."

"It's that bad?" Petty asked.

"Bad? We couldn't be in worse shape if the damn Spaniards was running the show! Up in New York and Chicago, they just cram the stuff in boxcars and send 'em rattling off to Florida. Like as not, a train can't get no closer 'n twenty-five miles from Tampa because the tracks is all jammed up. Hear tell they got a thousand loaded boxcars just rotting on sidings from one end of Florida to the other – some as far back as Carolina even – *hoo-hee!*"

"Piss-poor way to run a railroad," one rookie said.

"Probably ain't the railroaders' fault," Petty said. "You don't know the crap we have to mess with."

"That ain't the worst of it," the corporal added. "They don't even send no invoices. And forget to put tags on the cars to show what's in 'em."

"They got no tags, how ya tell what's in 'em?" somebody asked.

"That's the stumper. Only way to tell is bust 'em open and have a look-see. I've seen officers and men tear-assing up and down the tracks like crazy with crowbars, busting open car after car – fifty to a hundred cars maybe – just trying to latch onto whatever their outfits need. Like as not, they never find it. Just the other day they finally sniffed out five thousand rifles that some of the regiments was needing in the worst way. Whole trainload of uniforms and crap just up and disappeared completely for ten days – then popped up on a siding thirty miles up yonder."

Loading horses onto railroad cars at Port Tampa during the Spanish-American war (courtesy the State Library and Archives of Florida)

The corporal spat again. "Look at the artillery and all – we'll be needing 'em soon as we hit the beach. Scattered in hundreds of cars on sidings from hell to breakfast. Guns on one siding, gun mounts on another, shells somewheres else. Carloads o' meat is rotting on sidings way upstate while some of the outfits down here only gets hardtack!"

"We're getting more 'n hardtack," Petty said. "But that rotten sowbelly they dish out is making a lot of the guys as sick as a dog." He scowled in rueful remembrance. "Had the trots myself yesterday."

"Fella says they even had some ol' boys *die* from this rotten grub," another soldier said.

"Helluva note," Petty said. "Jine the army to fight Spaniards – and get scragged by your own cooks!"

The corporal shook his head sorrowfully. "I been in the army eighteen years, and I ain't never seen the likes of this before."

"Who's ever in charge," Petty said, "don't seem to know diddley-do."

The blame for the monumental foul-up may not be possible to fix on one person. But it might be mentioned that a vital part of the quartermaster operations at Tampa was assigned to a major who, according to correspondent Stephen Bonsal of *McClure's Magazine*, "was never observed to draw a sober breath" during his assignment there.

Bonsal, who did not identify the miscreant major, wrote:

The fact that this man had a great "pull" was fully appreciated both by his superiors and his subordinate officers, and on all sides his weakness was treated with much consideration...Finally he was attacked with delirium tremens, and ran day and night like a maniac up and down the corridors of the hotel, insulting or assaulting every man or woman he met with. Only then it was decided that the major had gone a little too far even for a man with such a powerful "pull"; he was placed in arrest, and two officers were detailed to make a formal report upon his condition. In a few days there came from Washington a telegram, ordering the major to report to the War Department at once…A few days passed, and when we were expecting to hear that, thanks to his "pull," the major had escaped a court-martial, we read in the Official Gazette of the army that he had been promoted to high rank in the volunteer army, and ordered to assume even more responsible duties than those which he had failed to perform at Tampa!

Despite all the shortages, Lieutenant-Colonel Roosevelt managed to wangle new rifles, smokeless powder, tropical uniforms and other amenities for his Rough Riders. Roosevelt had left his position as Under Secretary of the Navy, vowing he was not about to sit out the war at any rear-echelon desk job. He had helped organized the cavalry outfit from as assorted a bunch of characters as ever slapped leather. Newspapers found it difficult to satisfy the public's interest in him and the Rough Riders, and the public rarely deemed it necessary to scold Roosevelt for his flamboyant and literally cavalier methods.

But the rest of the army weltered in a sorry state of unpreparedness and confusion.

Except for those fortunates billeted at the magnificent Tampa Bay Hotel, the encampment – with its sand and mosquitoes and millions of devilishly-persistent flies – was hardly a pleasant place. According to correspondent Richard Harding Davis of the *Journal*, the town itself was "chiefly composed of derelict wooden houses drifting in an ocean of sand." Many of the sun-bleached buildings were occupied by cigar-makers, many of them Cubans in exile. Shops catering to the tourist trade often displayed baby alligators in their windows. Cuban and American flags hung in front of every restaurant and cigar-shop and many private homes. Ankle-deep sand swamped the wooden sidewalks and filtered into doors and windows.

"Just met the unluckiest rookie in this here camp this morning," Fay Ball said to Petty, as they sweated out a chow line. "A real hoodoo."

"Howzat?"

"First day in camp yesterday, he buggered his hand with his bayonet, got bit by a tarantula, sat on a big ants' nest, found a snake in his boot, stepped on an alligator, and went on sick call with a dose of malaria."

A smile crept over Petty's face. "Was he bragging or complaining?"

"Dunno, but he said he felt like a dirty deuce in a new deck."

"Speaking o' gators," another soldier put in, "you ain't gonna believe this, but over in one of Company C's tents the other night when the boys was sleeping, one of them big ugly sumbitches comes up smack dab in the middle of the floor. Right up through the sand! Sumbitch was eight feet long! Fella said he must been tunneling for water."

"Helluva place to tunnel," Petty said. "They got more booze in that outfit than they got water. Not sure I believe it, neither. Some of them boys is as windy as a tree full of hoot-owls."

* * * * *

The palatial Tampa Bay Hotel, constructed by railroad tycoon Henry B. Plant, became the officers' quarters. Covering six acres, the labyrinthine building loomed against the sky as a strange apparition of Moorish-style architecture. Seen from a distance, it seemed to rise alone from the encircling desert like a castle in story-land or, as someone said, "an enormous strawberry shortcake." The great five-story pile of red brick was crowned with thirteen silver minarets, for the thirteen months of the Moslem calendar. Three sides of the building were flanked by gingerbread verandas oscillating with hundreds of rocking chairs.

The lavish interior was an amazing conglomeration of

statuary, overstuffed sofas, glass prisms, and potted palms. The floors were covered with 30,000 square yards of crimson carpet emblazoned with blue dragons. The hotel contained 511 rooms. It also had a gaming casino, a swimming pool, and some enormous public rooms into which division and brigade staffs moved their offices. Correspondent R.H. Davis said the hotel was so big one could work up an appetite just by "walking from the rotunda to the dining room," where such luxuries as steaks, eggs, ice cream, ice water, highballs, and Scotch whiskey garnished the bill of fare.

In the evenings, the full moon rose over the rustling palms, pouring its bland yellow light on white blooms of oleanders and the soaring, dream-like architecture. Lines of incandescent bulbs glittered on the verandas where stalwart sun-tanned officers rocked and talked and smoked. There was many a back-slapping reunion of old comrades and shipmates from far-flung army posts and naval bases. In the garden, while a regimental band played waltzes, officers and war correspondents danced under whispering palms with ravishingly-gowned and heavily-perfumed ladies, some of them Cuban senoritas who had fled Havana.

The hotel was a pleasure dome as sharply contrasted with the terrible struggle to come as was the gala ball on the eve of Waterloo.

Those lucky enough to be lodged in the hotel regarded it as a beautiful oasis in the desert, and they scratched their heads trying to figure out why Henry Plant had ever built such a many-splendored edifice in such isolation. But they thanked their lucky stars he had. All the high-ranking military men and their staffs were quartered there, as were 89 press correspondents and artists, and 14 foreign military attachés. Among the correspondents were Julian Hawthorne, son of novelist Nathaniel Hawthorne; Stephen Crane, who created a literary sensation with his Civil War novel, *The Red Badge of Courage*; and the already-mentioned dapper R.H. Davis of

Hearst's *Journal*, about whom the archrival New York *World* commented in a mischievous jibe:

> *Mr. Davis has had his portrait published as a war correspondent attired in a Norfolk jacket with twenty-four pockets, golf trousers, cavalry boots, hat and gauntlets, a field glass, a notebook, a revolver, a cartridge belt, and a practicable flask. In fact, no war correspondent on the stage has ever surpassed the equipment of Mr. Davis when facing the camera.*

General William Rufus Shafter had been assigned to command the Fifth Army Corps, which would make up the Expeditionary Force. He parted his gray hair in the middle and wore a bushy, drooping mustache. In the Civil War, he had won the Medal of Honor in the savage battle of Fair Oaks, Virginia. Later he acquired the moniker of "Pecos Bill" for his audacious exploits while fighting Indians in the Southwest. Now, after 27 years of army service, he was 63 years old, weighed some 315 pounds, and was tormented by gout and other ailments.

Time drowsed on during seemingly endless days while top brass were planning the next move. Correspondents on the spacious verandas kept the rockers going as they speculated on all imaginable aspects of the impending invasion. Davis called it the war's "rocking chair period."

While the hotel became the hub of the social whirl for the elite, with balls and garden parties and receptions, social activities of the enlisted men were somewhat less elegant.

At reveille on May 30, Sergeant O'Neill of Company H shifted his quid and announced some good news: "All regular army men will fall in at company headquarters at 2 o'clock to get their pay."

A squall of cheers and whistles rent the air.

"Hat-ease! Rookies who haven't served a full month won't

get their pay until the end of the next payroll period."

To the agonized groans that erupted from the rookies, O'Neill retorted sharply: "Army regulations. Dismissed!"

That afternoon, poker games sprang up like mushrooms after a spring rain. Bottles of dago red and John Barleycorn appeared as if by legerdemain. Some were smuggled in by civilian scalpers from Tampa who had circled the army payday on their calendars.

Quarrels over cards by juiced-up soldiers led to a few dust-ups with their resulting black eyes, bloody noses and livid contusions – all perfectly normal phenomena on a soldiers' payday. Not to worry. But suddenly inside a plain wood-frame building, headquarters for one of the regiments, where the stakes in a wild and woolly game were escalating to new heights, some pie-eyed hothead took offense – "Goddamn crimp artist!" – and fired a shot at the soldier who had offended him.

That was carrying things a bit too far, even for an army payday.

As Petty and others collected at the scene, hospital corpsmen hefted the wounded man onto a stretcher and packed him off to an army doctor. A tense silence wrapped the compound.

Without warning, a mass of tight-lipped soldiers burst onto the scene, shoving bystanders out of their path. Ripping the door off its hinges, they stormed into the building, ejected its stunned occupants, then smashed windows, pitched tables and chairs outside and started booting planks off the walls, In a short span, they so thoroughly demolished the building that barely a slat remained standing. Minutes after their arrival, they cleared out of the shambles, having avenged the wounding of their comrade and the insult to their regimental dignity.

The soldier who fired the shot had fled the scene before the avengers arrived; otherwise their wrath would have descended principally on him. Petty overheard one soldier say to another: "That crazy ol' Pribble shouldna been playing cards at all. He was so drunk he didn't know whether he was afoot or a-horseback."

One day early in June, a newsboy from Tampa trotted into camp, hawking extras.

Somebody bought a copy. Others avidly read over his shoulders the story of how navy Lt. Richmond Hobson and his daring bluejackets had sailed the collier Merrimac into the mouth of Santiago harbor, intending to scuttle it and cork up Admiral Cervera's fleet for good. Torpedoes were strung alongside, wired to the bridge, and detonated. In the riot of Spanish fire that greeted their approach, a fateful shell crippled the rudder assembly and thwarted them from steering the sinking ship into position. Plunging into the water, they were captured and taken aboard the Spanish flagship, their mission a failure. But Cervera, to the surprise of many Americans, extolled the courage of Hobson and his men and sent an officer under a flag of truce to assure Admiral Sampson that they were safe and would be well cared for.

"Damn decent of Cervera," Petty said.

"Aw!" another soldier protested. "Sumbitch probably figured he'd catch hisself a double dose o' hell from us if he don't watch hisself."

Now the waters of Tampa Bay were choked with the hulls of thirty-two idle transports. All were stubby, aged, single-stackers from coastwise service. Some were from the Great Lakes, and some were sidewheelers. Each had a large number painted on its bow. Though these ships left much to be desired, it may be that they were the best obtainable in the stress of the emergency. The army had bought some of the ships and chartered the others. To get the chartered transports, the government had to promise the owners two and three times the standard freight rates.

All were skippered by civilians, who acted as if they couldn't care less about the whole business.

Soldiers preparing to embark for Cuba at the docks in Tampa
(courtesy The Library of Congress).

The Tampa port was hardly suitable for embarking thousands of soldiers. For one thing, only two ships could lie alongside the wharf at a time. And the nine-mile, single-track rail line linking the harbor and Tampa town was a hurly-burly. The situation was not improved when Henry Plant, the hotel builder, gave his commercial impulses a free rein by running excursion trains of sightseers in and out of the port.

Meanwhile, General Shafter held conferences day and night in attempts to untangle the logistics snarl – in vain. The worst was yet to come.

Chapter 4:
Expedition Against Cuba

The confusion and fury rose to an even higher pitch when the expedition started loading its wagons, weapons, animals and supplies aboard the transports.

All told, 952 horses and 1,336 mules were crammed aboard. The horses were artillery horses and wagon teams. They didn't include any cavalry horses, which were being left behind. There simply was no room for them. The cavalrymen were by turns aghast and apoplectic.

"Without our hosses? That's plumb loco!"

"Anybody send troopers off to fight without their hosses," another said, his neck flushing with choler, "ain't got enough brains to pound sand down a rat-hole."

Also loaded were 199 wagons, seven ambulances, sixteen light field guns, four 7-inch howitzers, four 5-inch siege guns, eight 3.6-inch mortars, a Hotchkiss rapid-fire cannon, a dynamite gun and four Gatling guns. As often as not, guns went on one ship and ammunition on another. Because everything had to be shuttled down the single rail line to the port, the little railroad was a madhouse on wheels. Loading was not finished until early June 7.

Now the soldiers could start embarking.

Someone erroneously had calculated that the ships could

carry 27,000 men. When the truth came out, that they actually could carry only about 17,000, the anxiety to find a place on board rose to a frenzy, as many units obviously would have to be left in the lurch.

In the 13th Infantry's compound, a messenger trotted up and down the rows of tents, summoning all regulars to the assembly area.

Minutes later, when the regulars scattered back to their tents and started packing, Petty buttonholed Sergeant O'Neill. "What now?" he asked.

O'Neill chomped on his chaw, grinned and danced a jig. "Gonna get on the boats!"

"How 'bout *us*?"

A horsefly incautiously alighted on the ground close by and was zapped by an amber jet. "Rookies'll stay here."

The sun was riding high, but to Petty the earth suddenly seemed drowned in darkness and desolation.

"You mean we *ain't going?* We're gonna stay in Florida?"

"You figured it – all by yourself. Congratulations."

"But *why*, sarge, *why*?"

"You guys ain't been drilled long enough – and besides, there just ain't room enough on the boats for everybody. Somebody's gotta get the shitty end of the stick, and it ain't gonna be the regulars. Not if I can help it."

Petty felt sick enough to die. So did the other rookies. Agonized groans emanated from their wretchedness.

"This ain't what we hitched up for!"

"Leaving us behind, to rot in this stinking Tampa!"

"What a low-down deal!"

"We been *betrayed!*"

About noon, the skylarking regulars marched away, loaded down with packs and horseshoe-shaped blanket-rolls, bound for Cuba and glory in the war against Spain – abandoning the heartbroken rookies in the sandy, fly-blown wastes of Florida.

During the embarkation, simple confusion became chaos

compounded. Roosevelt and Col. Leonard Wood were determined that the Rough Riders would not be left behind when the expedition started. When they were finally told that it would depart the next morning, they were ordered to go to a certain track to meet a train. "We went to the track, but the train never came," Roosevelt recalled. "Then we were sent to another track, to meet another train. Again it never came." However, they found a coal train and took possession of it. Its conductor, "partly under duress and partly in a spirit of friendly helpfulness," transported the Rough Riders down to the quay.

Wood commanded the Rough Riders, while the charismatic Lieutenant Colonel Roosevelt was second in command. Leonard Wood was one rugged soldier. A soldier and a half, is more accurate. Tracking Indians in the Southwest, he received the Medal of Honor in the Geronimo campaign, and distinguished himself as the only white man who could tire out an Apache on the trail.

But now there was no place the Rough Riders could find specific information as to what ship they would sail on. Finally, Wood was informed: "Get any ship you can which is not already assigned." With no by-your-leave, Wood pirated a small motor boat, which enabled him to taxi out to where the transport *Yucatan* was anchored and commandeer it for his troops. This transport was something less than a luxury liner. Roosevelt, in a letter to his friend Senator Lodge, called the *Yucatan's* below-decks area a "Black Hole of Calcutta."

Soldiers in the 13th Infantry, Petty's regiment, managed to find an empty train with an antique wood-burning locomotive. Dispensing with needless ceremony, they dragged a sleeping engineer out of bed and put him to work. At 10:30 a.m., the regiment steamed jubilantly to the wharf, cheering wildly as they discovered that they had beaten the 21st and 24th regiments.

Suddenly, in Washington, came Admiral Sampson's telegrams saying he had discovered Cervera's fleet in Santiago harbor, and had disposed his warships in front of the narrow entrance. But Secretary of the Navy Long feared there was a chance Cervera might escape from the Santiago bottle. Swift action seemed imperative. On the evening of June 7, after regiments had been embarking all day at Tampa, Alger and McKinley sent the aforementioned wires to Shafter ordering him to sail at once with whatever troops were on board.

Shafter issued a general order: "All who are not on board the transports by daybreak will be left behind." The terse command was like throwing gasoline on a fire.

The palatial Tampa Bay Hotel, where the correspondents were quartered. (courtesy the City of Tampa, Florida)

The wee-hour tranquility of the Tampa Bay Hotel was ruptured at 2 a.m. on June 8 when correspondents were ordered to embark on the *Segurança*, the headquarters ship. William Dinwiddie of the Washington *Star* described the commotion:

A motley assembly scurried through the hotel in canvas hunting suits, in white ducks, in the brown fatigue clothes of the army, and even in immaculate shirtfront and patent leathers. Six-shooters, machetes and belts full of ammunition circulated through the halls...along with canteens, rolls of blankets, binoculars, kodaks and pouches filled with notebooks.

Shafter, trying to embark as many soldiers as possible and still comply with orders to sail immediately, rushed too many troops to the port at once. The embarkation erupted into a monumental stampede. Some regiments, dreading they would be left in the lurch, grabbed other regiments' trains – more than once at gunpoint. Because of this overeagerness, many regiments reached the port in the wrong order for boarding.

Now thousands of yelling, cursing soldiers were churning about on the waterfront. It was one temper-busting, unholy mess.

"Hell won't be no more crowded on the last day," one frazzled old soldier said, "than this wharf is right now."

Largely without guidance from top brass, somehow the regiments squeezed into the ships, dumping their baggage into jumbled heaps in the holds. By 4 o'clock on the afternoon of June 8, they finished loading. The signal was given and the transports began to breast the waters of the bay toward the gulf. Just then, a consternating telegram:

```
WAIT UNTIL YOU GET FURTHER ORDERS BEFORE YOU
SAIL. ANSWER QUICK. R.A. ALGER, SECRETARY OF
WAR
```

A telegram bounced back to the War Department:

```
MESSAGE RECEIVED. VESSELS ARE IN THE STREAM
BUT WILL BE ABLE TO STOP THEM BEFORE
REACHING GULF.
```

About 8 p.m., a torpedo cruiser charged down the bay and a sailor bawled through a megaphone: *"Return to Port! Three Spanish cruisers within three hours' sail of the offing! Return to port!"*

A long silence ensued. Then some impatient soldier loudly hooted his contempt: "What a buncha crap!"

The alarm had been raised because an American vessel, the converted yacht *Eagle*, thought she saw some Spanish warships on the night of June 7 near Nicholas Channel, on the route to Santiago de Cuba.

With stacks belching torrents of dark smoke, the convoy's naval vessels steamed full ahead to Nicholas Channel to hunt for the strangers.

The navy didn't know for sure that all of Cervera's ships were blockaded in Santiago, or that none had managed to escape. It had to check out the *Eagle's* report before it could allow the transports to go to sea. It would have been too risky to dispatch troop-laden transports, even though convoyed by warships, across the sea to Cuba as long as there was doubt.

Meanwhile off Santiago, navy Lt. Victor Blue boated ashore from one of Sampson's blockading ships. Slipping through enemy lines, he scrambled up a lofty hill to get a good look at Santiago harbor. Making his way back to the coast, he reported to Sampson that Cervera's six warships were still boxed up in the bay.

Also, the quick navy sweep of Nicholas Channel disclosed no hostile ships.

Meantime the transports sweltered for several days in the stagnant air of Tampa Bay. The soldiers were given landing drills in the ships' boats and sometimes shore liberty. Some spent their liberty on Port Tampa's "Last Chance Street," a naughty avenue packed with gin mills and whorehouses.

One day about sundown, some regulars from Petty's regiment drifted back into camp.

"What gives?"

"Just got a little ways down the bay and they got orders to go back."

"What the hell for?"

The regulars only shrugged. "Typical army."

Two days later, the regulars started packing again. And suddenly came the heart-stopping announcement: Rookies would go along too! Piercing whistles and wild cheers yawped from the ecstatic rookies. The reason why they now were being allowed to go along was never explained to them, but they couldn't care less. Only one thing mattered – they were sailing to Cuba to fight against Spain.

"We ain't gonna rot in Florida after all!"

"And put up with all that stupid marching and KP and guard duty!"

"And never see the war!"

It was the happiest day of their lives.

In fact, the reason for taking the rookies was that Shafter decided to profit from the delay by stuffing as many more troops into the transports as they would hold. He packed them in until the ships were loaded far beyond their official carrying capacity, when reckoning the impediments of war already loaded. He crammed soldiers in until one might think the ships' seams would burst.

Aboard the *Saratoga*, carrying Petty's outfit, were 38 officers and 636 enlisted men, consisting of the 13th Infantry and some other contingents. Had the long-awaited hour of departure arrived at last? It seemed so.

"All hands are aboard, cap'n," a gimpy merchant sailor reported to *Saratoga's* ruddy-faced skipper.

"And the troops?"

"All troops are embarked, sir."

Through the hot muggy air from down the long bay tootled a series of falsetto whistle-wails – some kind of signal, obviously, for the skipper gave a gruff order: "Make all preparations for getting under way."

"Aye-aye, sir."

"Stand by to get under way! Look sharp on those lines! Cast off all lines! One-third speed ahead!"

"Aye-aye, sir."

Clang-clang.

Petty felt the *Saratoga* shudder as its engines pounded, moving it down to an assigned station in Tampa Bay.

"Stand by the anchor…*Let go!*"

The chain thundered out the hawsehole. Now *Saratoga* and the other ships would have to await the momentous hour when all could go to sea together. That meant more seemingly endless waiting for the thousands of soldiers growing ever more impatient at delay after delay.

The big day was June 14: the navy finally decided the convoy could start again. Aboard the transports, besides the horses and mules and war materiel, were 815 officers, 16,072 enlisted men, and numerous civilians, including 30 clerks, 272 teamsters and packers and 107 stevedores.

When the headquarters ship *Segurança* fired a small rollaway deck cannon and hoisted the blue peter, a signal flag, anchor winches began to grind in unison, winding up the clanking chains. Engines began to pound and labor, and funnels vomited clouds of black smoke. Lusty cheers resounded from thousands of throats as the decks of the transports quivered with waving hats. One after another, the thirty-two transports began to steam slowly toward the far blue edge of the open sea.

"Check that!" somebody shouted. Behind, on the receding horizon of jumbled port structures, the most imposing building on "Last Chance Street," for some unexplained reason, was erupting in smoke and flames, almost like a farewell salute to the departing transports.

Ready or not, the armada – so ill-prepared and so heavy-laden, but buoyed by such wild surmise – was moving toward the enemy. It was the largest armed force ever to leave United

States soil, and it was the jump-off of the most reckless adventure in American military history.

The 17,000-man invasion force was sailing for a Cuba dominated by nearly 200,000 Spanish soldiers. The expedition was throwing down the gauntlet against odds of better than ten to one.

Chapter 5:
Rust-Bucket Armada

Like a school of leviathans, the thirty-two barnacle-crusted transports lumbered down the channel and sailed out of Tampa Bay on their rendezvous with destiny. Outside the roadstead, the ships maneuvered into position until they were ranged into a formation of three long columns, southbound.

For hours Petty leaned on the rail or strolled the decks of the *Saratoga*, watching the enormous convoy plow the blue sea toward Cuba, watching the Florida coastline fade in the distance. A poignant sadness came over him as he mused how very possible it was that he might never again feast his eyes on the towns and cities and fields and hills of America. Even the dreary "Tent City" and sands of Tampa seemed imbued with a certain charm.

The day was fading, too. Pinpoints of light began to twinkle on the receding Florida shore. They seemed to Petty not unlike the lights of St. Louis when seen from miles away.

His thoughts drifted back to the days that used to be. He remembered Ma's care-lined face; his younger days in Tennessee and Arkansas and southern Illinois; hunting in the woods with Pa, a burly, gray-shocked man in blue overalls, ever chomping on an unlit stogie, a flask of corn on his hip ("To prevent snakebite," he would say with a sly wink.) and later, croppin' shares in the cotton. When Alfred was only 7, Pa's health began to fail. Doc said he had consumption.

His family loaded the spring wagon with all their tools and pots and blankets and grub and shooting irons, then hitched up ol' Maude, the mule. After tramping through southern Illinois, they rode a rickety ferry across the Ohio into Kentucky, then larruped contrary ol' Maude on the rest of the weary road into Tennessee.

All ardently hoped the crispy air of Pa's native Tennessee would work on him the cure he prayed for. But less than two years later, Pa's tortured wheezing ended with a death rattle, and he was buried in the churchyard.

For a year, young Alfred had been picking cotton, working in the fields the same endless hours the big boys and full-grown men worked. Ma had been left with seven young'uns, three of them younger than Alfred, and she needed everybody's willing hands to pitch in and make ends match. There was never time for Alfred to go down to the schoolhouse to get some larning.

When the long day in the field was done, and he had stuffed his ravening gut with cornporn, hominy grits, dumplings and apple cobbler, he was dead on his feet and only too ready to collapse onto his straw-filled tick.

But Sundays and rainy days granted a boon of precious leisure. Ma began teaching him the Three R's, though there were too few books in the house to serve as texts. But one musty old volume was garnished with etchings of Civil War scenes. The one he liked best showed General Philip Sheridan after his celebrated twenty-mile ride from Winchester, galloping among his defeated Federals at Cedar Creek, waving high his slouch hat, shouting, "Turn, boys, turn – we're going back!" As everyone knows, they counter-attacked and won a famous victory.

Alfred would never tire of perusing the curious expressions, mixed admiration and surprise, on the soldiers' upturned faces. He could almost hear Sheridan's voice ringing out, rallying his heavy-hearted troops. The picture etched itself indelibly in his green memory.

When Alfred was 12, the family hitched up poor aging Maude to the wagon again. After riding a ferry from Memphis across Big Muddy, they trekked into Arkansas. A year later, having mastered reading and writing, Alfred got his first job as a railroad telegrapher, work that in time transferred him to depots in Kansas and Missouri, and even to bleak railroad shanties in Indian Territory. It was a proud profession – pounding the brass key, sending the *dit-dit-dah-dit* out on the wires, quicker than scat, helping to direct rail car traffic across a continent.

Good times and hard times. Somehow even the hard times were mellowed by time and distance.

Most often he thought about the lovely Dorothy, and his heart ached with longing to hold her in his arms again.

At last, consigning his reveries to some other time, he quit the rail and climbed down the ladder into the hold. Ventilation was so poor you could cut the stink with a knife. Some of the rowdiest Company H comrades were playing poker, sitting cross-legged on the hatch that sealed the opening to the cargo hold below, surrounded by garbage cans overflowing with trash.

Petty stared around at the tiers of slapdash wooden bunks, five or six high, rising from deck to overhead. Most of them were occupied by their tenants, as the transport offered little room for its crowded soldiery to move about. There was barely enough room to walk in the narrow aisles between tiers.

"Ain't enough room here to swing a cat," Petty said.

"It ain't much, but it's *home!*" a solder said with a mock-insane chuckle.

"Hey, pardner," the dealer asked, giving the cards an expert shuffle, "wanna take potluck?"

A bit of sport might be just the thing to relieve his

homesickness. "Why not?"

"Whatcha been doing up there?"

"Jess watching the ships is all."

"You seen one, you seen 'em all."

Another soldier threw up his hands in the position for aiming a rifle. "The only thing I wanna see," he said, "Is a Spaniard – when I'm squinting down my gun barrel."

By degrees his comrades' devil-may-care nonchalance chased away Petty's feeling of sadness.

Unknown to everyone on board the transports, the Marines had landed in Cuba four days before, on June 10, and were locked in combat at Guantanamo Bay.

Watched over by the guns of the *Oregon*, *Yosemite* and *Marblehead*, 600 Marines hit the beach and ran into savage resistance from the Spanish. Day and night the fighting continued as the small band of Leathernecks desperately defended its beachhead.

On the same day that the big convoy was sailing out of Tampa, correspondent Stephen Crane, writing for the New York *World*, was at Guantanamo with 200 Marines and 50 Cuban rebels as they assaulted a ridgeback under a sun so hot Crane thought it would "melt the Earth." Scrambling to the top, they came under heavy fire from a big thicket on the far side, a thicket alive with the loud popping of enemy Mausers. Crane wrote: "Along our line the rifle locks were clicking incessantly, as if some giant loom was running wildly, and on the ground among the stones and weeds came a dropping, dropping rain of rolling brass shells."

The five-hour battle for Cusco Hill proved the key to the capture of Guantanamo Bay, an invaluable prize for the navy. It offered a base for the fleet, sheltered waters for coaling, and a handy cable station.

* * * * *

Aboard the *Saratoga*, someone spotted the impeccably-groomed Lt. Thomas M. Anderson, Jr. climbing down the ladder into the hold, and shouted: "Ten-HUT!"

Dropping their cards, the soldiers hopped to their feet and stood at attention. Most of the soldiers in the bunks remained where they were.

"Hat-ease! Forget that kind of formality while we're aboard ship. Now I want you men to police up this area. It looks like a damn pig-sty."

To Petty, it seemed the young lieutenant's order lacked a vital ingredient.

"Sir," he ventured in what he considered was a properly deferential manner, "the garbage cans are running over. Don't you think you oughta get a garbage detail to empty 'em first?"

Anderson jumped as if shot. "Ten HUT!" he barked.

Petty snapped to, rigid as a soldier on parade. Anderson slowly looked him up and down with unconcealed disdain, taking in his seedy civilian trousers, worn shoes and slouch hat. *A sorry-looking example of a soldier*, Anderson thought.

"What's your name, soldier?"

"Petty, Private Alfred C. – sir."

"Now get this, Petty. You *never* question an officer's order. Understand?"

Everyone in the hold, cardplayers and bunk occupants alike, were dead silent, taking it all in.

"That remark was damned insolent," Anderson continued. "Whether you know it or not. See that it never happens again!" Anderson pointed his index finger at Petty as if he were pointing a Colt .45. "When an officer gives you an order, you *jump!* And no backtalk. Got it?"

"Yes, sir!"

There was something about Petty that made Anderson's dander continue to rise. "I could have you court-martialed for insubordination! Who the hell do you think you *are*? What kind of crap are you trying to *pull*?"

"Which question do you want me to answer first, sir?"

As the other soldiers busted out laughing, Anderson's neck took on a fiery tinge.

"None of your snotty remarks! How long have you been in the army, soldier?"

"'Bout four weeks, sir."

"*Four weeks* – and you still haven't learned to never argue with an officer? What kind of soldier *are* you?"

"Dunno, sir."

"Well goddamn it, you sure as hell better find out!" As Anderson continued his harangue, his face waxed red. He perceived that the cardplayers were making heroic efforts to keep from disintegrating. Also, scattered catcalls and horselaughs from the peanut gallery were adding to his sense of discomfort. When he finished tongue-lashing Petty, he climbed back up the ladder, pausing for a moment to say, "Next time I come down here, I want to find this shit-pot as neat as a bandbox! You men all got that?"

"Yes, sir!" everyone chorused.

"Or else I'll have all of you scrubbing the decks with toothbrushes!"

As Anderson disappeared through the hatchway, the stifled amusement exploded in gales of laughter.

"Wow, Petty, he really raked you over the coals!"

"Hooooo-eeeeee! Boy, has he got your number!"

"You'll never get a stripe in this man's army – 'cept with a horsewhip!"

Petty felt sure he had learned his lesson: he would fare better in the future if he obeyed all orders without volunteering any advice.

At night, contrary to strict orders, every ship was sailing along with all her light blazing. Regimental bands blared out popular songs such as "Banks of the Wabash" and "The Girl I Left Behind," wafting the heart-tugging melodies across the dark waters in the enchanting evening hours.

For some unexplained reason, the tugboat *Captain Sam* deserted the convoy on its first night out.

The *Yucatan*, carrying the Rough Riders, had been converted from a freighter, and the army had commissioned a civilian contractor to install bunks. He and his men used cheap, green lumber and precious few nails to do the job. On the first night out, when the cavalrymen climbed into their bunks, many bunks collapsed and the hapless troopers had to spend the rest of the voyage sleeping on deck.

Dawn found the rust-bucket armada crawling along at six or seven knots over a smooth, sparkling sea. The last ship in the convoy was the *Segurança*, carrying General Shafter, the headquarters staff and the 1st Infantry.

Later that day, heaving past the Tortugas, the transports were joined by their navy escort: the battleship *Indiana*, the cruiser *Detroit*, the gunboat *Castine*, and other smaller vessels. Two torpedo ships, *Ericson* and *Rodgers*, joined the convoy after it doubled Key West. The screen of gray warships guarded the three columns of black-hulled transports fore and aft and on both sides. Shafter had decided to move the convoy at the speed of the slowest ships – a schooner freighted with hogsheads of fresh water and a sidewheeler towing a landing barge. Speed seldom exceeded six knots.

The navy had issued precise orders on the formation the transports were to maintain: columns were to be 1,000 yards apart, with 400 yards between ships. But the ships were commanded by arrogant civilian captains who loathed navy regulations and showed little – if any – respect for convoy requirements. Soon the convoy was spread out over thirty to forty miles of sea, and the formation became ragged and hardly recognizable as a formation.

O'Neill, leaning on the rail, squinted off into the distance at the spectacle of the transports making fools of themselves. "They call that a formation?" he roared, punctuating his scorn with a stream of tobacco juice arcing overboard.

Petty's eyes puckered as he studied the brilliant horizon. "Navy boats seem to be having an uphill fight trying to keep the dam transports from going six ways from Sunday," he said.

"Knot-head skippers couldn't find their way to first base!" O'Neill said. "I've seen better formations in a herd of jackasses. Come to think of it, there ain't that much difference.

Aboard the *Segurança*, correspondent R.H. Davis licked a pencil tip and scribbled: "The gunboats were like swift, keen-eyed, intelligent collies rounding up a herd of bungling sheep."

The air was warm and balmy and a gentle breeze rippled the water. Petty had never been to sea before. In fact, he had never even seen the ocean before. But now he reveled in the lovely mornings, marvelous with the intense blue of tropic seas. The moving transports flushed out occasional exaltations of flying fish, and now and then a leaping dolphin or porpoise. Sometimes Petty watched an old moss-backed sea turtle paddling purposefully along, and wondered to what strange destination its reptilian brain might be navigating.

In the evenings, he watched the red sun slide behind the dark horizon and the lights began to glitter on the ships for miles ahead and astern, while regimental bands played ragtime.

Colonel Wood of the Rough Riders wrote to his wife: "...Hard it is to realize that this is the commencement of a new policy and that this is the first great expedition our country has ever sent overseas and marks the commencement of a new era in our relations with the world." Roosevelt also wrote home: "...It is a great historical expedition, and I thrill to feel that I am part of it." Roosevelt added that he was astonished that the Spanish were not attempting to interfere with the convoy, as some of the slower vessels were lagging dangerously far behind the escorting warships. He also expressed "fear" they might find Santiago captured before they could get there.

As the three-column convoy straggled across many miles of sea, with many ships lagging behind, some others came close to collision. The *Yucatan* nearly ran down the

Matteawan. The hospital ship *Olivette* nearly smacked into the drifting water schooner, which had broken its towing hawser.

The *Gussie*, with 300 cantankerous mules aboard, had to make a canteen stop at the Bahamian island of Inagua to re-fill the old sidewheeler's water tanks, to quench the mules' whopping thirst. Again the water schooner snapped its towline and the *City of Washington* was sent back to retrieve it. Some hours later, the *Leona*, carrying two cavalry regiments, vanished behind, and the convoy had to halt until the laggard ships could catch up.

Petty wrote to his mother, not knowing when or where he could post the letter: "Dear Ma, Everything is fine. Some of the horses died and they dumped them overboard yesterday, and now we can see their dead bodies floating all over the sea... You would not believe how big the ocean is."

On the fourth day out, Petty wrote to Dorothy, "Sweetheart, some of the guys got awful sick, but I am all right..." He told her what had happened:

In the rough seas of the Bahama Channel, a navy gunboat creamed up to *Saratoga* with a sailor in white duck standing on the bow, wig-wagging frantically. The gunboat cut its speed until it was pacing the transport. Someone on the gunboat bellowed through a megaphone, and *Saratoga's* engines stopped.

Below, as the throbbing engines went silent, Petty and the others fixed each other with curious stares. Then they pounded up the ladder and crowded the rail.

"What's up now?"

"Ain't got the foggiest."

Sergeant O'Neill, chomping furiously on his quid, charged up. "Okay, I want some volunteers *right now!* Four men with strong backs and weak minds! You, you, you and you! Let's hit it!"

O'Neill pushed through the crowd, with Petty and the other "volunteers" scampering in his wake.

In the makeshift sick bay, they wrapped blankets around two delirious, flush-faced soldiers, and hauled them onto litters. Struggling up the companionway with their heavy burdens, they followed O'Neill to the rail.

"Lift 'em in the boat – *careful!*"

Three of *Saratoga's* sailors standing in the lifeboat reached out with helping hands. Rusty davits shrieked as the boat was lowered to the heaving, foam-flecked indigo. Oars flashed as the boat lurched toward the *Olivette*.

Boats from some of the other transports also were converging on the hospital ship. Hoisting the prostrate forms of the fourteen invalids from the bobbing small boats to the *Olivette's* rolling deck was a ticklish proposition, but was accomplished without accident.

The lifeboats returned to their transports, engines started up and the convoy began to move again.

"What's wrong with those guys?" Petty asked O'Neill.

"Doc says typhoid."

Roosevelt wrote again: "We are well within the tropics, and at night the Southern Cross shows low above the horizon; it seems strange to see it in the same sky with the friendly Dipper."

The torrid sun beat down on the ships, heating them up so that below-decks temperatures ranged up to 110 degrees. The soldiers cursed the heat, and griped about not having enough water to bathe in and hardly enough for drinking. The *Miami* had only twelve toilets for 1,000 soldiers. The food was abominable. The canned, or "embalmed," beef that the army had relied on so heavily as a field ration seemed to spoil as soon as the cans were opened.

From time to time the convoy was joined by tugs from Key West that had been chartered by newspapers or press associations. Finally the original 89 correspondents were almost doubled, and the number of press boats nearly matched the number of major ships in Sampson's fleet. Hearst's *Journal* had ten boats with the convoy, the New York *Herald* and *The Associated Press* each had five, and the New York *World* had three. The Chicago *Record* and the New York *Sun* each had one.

Hearst and his retinue sailed aboard a big steam yacht, *Sylvia*, flagship of his flotilla. Chartered from Baltimore Fruit Co., it was equipped for a tropical cruise with plenty of ice and other luxuries. It had a darkroom for photographer J.C. Hemment, and a printing press on which Hearst planned to print Cuban editions of the *Journal*.

Aboard the *Segurança*, Shafter pondered the impending campaign. He had to study the problems in punishing heat and amid the distractions presented by foreign attachés, Cuban generals, clerks, secretaries, waiters, seven war correspondents, the divisional staffs and 500 soldiers, all jumbled together on the confined headquarters ship.

Landing an inexperienced army on a steep, enemy coast would be perilous enough. And the foreign attachés volunteered gloomy opinions of the expedition's chances thereafter. One, a French major, predicted inevitable disaster.

Glumly, Shafter perused some accounts of invasions of Cuba by foreign powers and their invariably disastrous outcomes. One chronicled the British expedition of 1741 under Lord Vernon, which landed at Guantanamo with 5,000 men, aiming for Santiago. Though the expedition met with only meager resistance from the Spanish, some 2,000 men died in the horrendous ordeal. Finally, an utter failure, the expedition was abandoned – only forty miles from its starting point, and still sixteen miles from Santiago, about where the Americans would land at Daiquiri. Shafter also knew that in 1801 Napoleon sent an army to Santo Domingo where in parallel tropic conditions a ghastly two-thirds of the soldiers succumbed to yellow fever.

"With knowledge of these previous expeditions before me," Shafter later wrote, "you can imagine the feelings with which I entered upon that campaign. I have had yellow fever myself, and I knew just as well before I landed as I do now that within three or four or perhaps five weeks (it came sooner) that many would be prostrated with disease...If I could get to Santiago before the men gave out, well and good. If not, we were gone...I determined to rush it."

* * * * *

"Land ho!" the lookout called in a stentorian voice.
"Where away?"
"Three points off the starboard bow!"
Cuba!
"That's it!" yelled a soldier on the *Saratoga*, his eyes shining with eagerness as he stared hard at the dim blur on the horizon.
"Times I wondered if I'd ever see it," Petty said, thinking of his vain attempts to join the 3rd Missouri, and of how he almost missed the boat at Tampa.
"Hot-diggety!" yelled another, throwing his hat in the air and dancing a jig. "I can already see the damn Spaniards – skedaddling for the hills!"
Why the fast Spanish torpedo boats that plied these waters didn't attack the convoy remains a puzzle. The scattered, dawdling transports would have made big, fat targets, almost impossible to miss.
Suddenly the sun traveled rapidly across the sky – the ships were changing course to round the stern, gray slopes of Cape Maisi, easternmost point of Cuba. The cobalt blue ocean garnished with whitecaps had now gentled down to a placid sea of emerald and turquoise, absorbing its new colors from the coral reefs off Cuba. As they bore to the south, the dim cape disappeared below the horizon. Again they swung on a new course, heading west.
A long blue line of mountains rose above the horizon. As

the ships approached, the mountains lifted ever higher. Now they soared upwards – an emerald landscape filigreed with silver streams cascading into the sea. The mountains reminded Roosevelt of Montana. Correspondent Stephen Bonsal thought of Japan. To Petty, they seemed not unlike the beautiful green mountains of Tennessee, where he once lived.

Nearing the shore, they heaved past a small beat-looking jetty. This was Daiquiri, where 7,000 soldiers would disembark. Farther, they cruised past the small cove of Siboney with its scatter of huts where Petty's outfit, among 8,000 additional troops, would land. Atop some backdropping hills, small blockhouses perched like sentinels. Still farther west, they skirted past the narrow entrance of Santiago harbor, where Admiral Cervera's fleet lay boxed in.

Three miles off shore, the armada presented the Spanish with a show of force, as the transports in single column, flanked by battleships and cruisers, plied past. Not a shot was fired. Far to the north the peaks of the Sierra Maestra – the "Master Range" – leaped pristinely in the red rays of the morning sun, like mountains in a dream. Several miles off shore, the transports dropped their hooks, screened from the enemy by the warships.

Behind the gray warships rose the forbidding shores the soldiers had come to assault. Sailors line the rails of the warships, cheering the soldiers on the transports, their voices ringing across the water, and the soldiers returned the huzzahs. Press boats scurried about, looking for copy, like small terriers on a hot scent.

As the cruisers and battleships slowly steamed within effective range of the forts guarding the harbor, orders sped to the gunners: *"Main batteries commence firing!"*

Fascinated, Petty and his comrades watched the warships lumber past the harbor entrance two miles away, their turrets vomiting clouds of smoke and belching thunder as they probed the enemy hills with shellfire. For Petty and most of the others on the transports, the ear-splitting cannonade was the first time they had ever heard guns fired in anger.

Sometimes the high-powered shells walloped an ancient fort, which blossomed in slow motion with rubble and dust. Now and then the Spanish lobbed a shot from camouflaged shore batteries. Smoke roiling from the enemy guns betrayed their positions. In minutes, the warships silenced each with one or two well-placed shots. Spanish batteries failed to score a hit on the American warships, missing their targets by anywhere from a few hundred yards to a quarter of a mile.

U.S. Sailors watching the battle from the deck of a ship.
(courtesy U.S. Navy Archives)

Past the Santiago forts, then farther to the west, the warships shelled the coast as they loafed by. Later they circled back for another pass, sledgehammering Daiquiri and Siboney and many other points along the coast, to confuse the enemy as to where the Americans would land. The following morning, *Saratoga* and many of the other transports and some of the warships upped anchor and ramped back to Siboney and Daiquiri. Dropping their anchors, they began preparations for landing troops.

No one aboard the transports yet knew that the Marines had already won their beachhead at Guantanamo.

Aboard the *Segurança*, E.J. McClernand, assistant adjutant-general to Shafter, issued a general order that read in part:

All troops will carry on the person the blanket roll (with shelter tent and poncho), three days' field rations (with coffee ground), canteens filled, and 100 rounds of ammunition per man.

The Commanding General wishes to impress officers and men with the crushing effect that a well-directed fire will have upon the Spanish troops. All officers concerned will rigidly enforce fire discipline, and will caution their men to fire only when they can see the enemy.

And now the supreme moment of the voyage to Cuba – the transports were clearing their decks, making ready to disembark thousands of soldiers via small boats onto the sandy beach at Daiquiri, where an iron-ore pier jutted into the water. The Americans were about to land on enemy soil. Time was an iron dictator, and General Shafter had vowed to rush the army to Santiago "before the men gave out." The invasion was on!

Chapter 6: Invasion

With his tatterdemalion band of 4,000 rebels, General Calixto Garcia departed his camp near Holguin, bound for the coast for a secret meeting with General Shafter and Admiral Sampson. This was the same rebel general later immortalized in Elbert Hubbard's famous essay, "A Message to Garcia."

Many of Garcia's soldiers were barefoot, half-starved and armed only with machetes. On their five-day forced march through a wild spell of downpours ripped with lightning bolts, they crossed the high passes of the Sierra Maestra, arriving at El Aserradero on the coast, twenty miles west of Santiago, on June 19.

Under clearing skies on the afternoon of the next day, two navy longboats carrying thirty men shoved off from the *Segurança*. The party consisted of Shafter and Sampson, their aides, correspondents and foreign attachés. At El Aserradero, they glided into a small, scalloped cove flanked by rugged hills, while the rusty-hinge squawks of seagulls filled the air. Ecstatic Cuban rebels dashed into the surf. Their cries of joy and greeting resounded in the cove like a wild comber breaking on the sand. Seizing the Americans, they carried them bodily to the beach, then dragged the longboats after them.

Guides led forth two small, scrubby mules to enable

Shafter and Sampson to climb up the steep, mile-long trail to Garcia's field camp. One disrespectful observer noted that Schafter's diminutive mule "almost disappeared from view" as the huge-caliber general was hoisted onto its back.

Below Garcia's camp, the indigo sea stretched far away. Above and beyond, the jungle-matted mountains climbed up and up through a thin haze to banks of dazzling white clouds.

As the Americans approached the camp, a burly six-foot-four man with crossed bandoliers on his chest loomed in front of a palm-thatched hut. The Americans correctly assumed the imposing figure to be that of the legendary rebel general. Garcia's shaggy white hair betrayed his age, nearly 70. A neat goatee and a long, drooping mustache ornamented his face. Between his eyebrows a tuft of cotton issued from a wound that had never healed. Some twenty-four years earlier, about to be captured by the Spanish and fearing he would be tortured, he fired a pistol upward from under his chin. The bullet tore out through the middle of his forehead. But the skill of a Spanish surgeon saved his life.

"Buenos dias, caballeros," Garcia said. With a courtly wave, he ushered the visitors into the hut.

After introductions by a Cuban interpreter, Garcia motioned Shafter to a sturdy box doubling as a chair. "Por que no se siente usted?"

"Don't mind if I do."

Several other boxes and a wooden table were brought forth, but there weren't enough boxes to go around. Most of the party had to remain standing. The hut was packed and Shafter felt stifled in the heat and closeness. His thick wool uniform aggravated his discomfort.

Garcia tapped his head, then pointed at Shafter's white pith helmet. "Por que no se quita usted el sombrero?"

Comprehending, Shafter doffed his helment. His ruddy face steamed with sweat. "It's awfully hot," he croaked weakly.

Garcia shot him a look of concern. "Usted no tiene buena cara," he said. "You should take better care of yourself," the interpreter translated.

"I'm so tired," Shafter said, heaving a great sigh. "Utterly exhausted. And I've got a million things to do."

Garcia asked Shafter what he thought of the stormy weather they had been having for the past three days.

Shafter sizzled at the mere thought. "I sure hope this goddamn rain is making the Spaniards as miserable as we are!"

Garcia cocked his head, listening to the interpreter, then nodded in agreement. "Espero."

"But I guess they're more used to it than we are," Shafter added.

The amenities dispensed with, they got down to business. Shafter explained that the American objective was to capture both the city of Santiago and Cervera's fleet. Shafter's ruddy face tightened with lines of determination, as he remembered his exploits in the Southwest many years ago. Perhaps too many years go. But, as "Pecos Bill," audacity had always been his watchword. The best chance for success, he told Garcia, would lie in an all-out assault.

"Give me the map," he said to an aide, who unfolded the well-worn document on the table.

They bent over the chart. Garica, pointing to locations with the tip of his machete, advised Shafter to land his troops at Daiquiri, sixteen miles east of Santiago, and Siboney, six miles closer, because relatively few Spanish were defending those villages. And their beaches offered the best landing sites close to Santiago. Garcia traced routes on the map, showing where he would post rebel units to support the American landings. And he marked a sector west of Santiago where he said he would station 3,000 other Cubans to block any Spanish reinforcements trying to enter the city.

"General Garcia," Shafter said firmly, "I want you to send a large force of your men to demonstrate at Cabanas – right here, just west of Santiago bay," he pointed, for the benefit of all the conferees. "To hoax the Spanish into thinking we'll land our troops there. To reinforce the hoax, I'll send three or four transports to Cabanas with orders to simulate landing preparations. Is all this clear?"

When Garcia and the interpreter nodded vigorously, Shafter felt certain the rebel leader understood the plan. He turned to Admiral Sampson. "Sir, will you kindly explain to General Garcia your role in this little drama?"

Sampson pulled the box he was sitting on closer to the table, then moved his finger along shorelines on the map, showing where his warships would bombard prior to the actual landings at Daiquiri and Siboney.

"My guns will extinguish any enemy strong-points and interdict the advance of any hostile forces toward the invasion beaches. To begin with," he added, and indicated a point on the map, "we'll create a fuss over here, to coincide with the simulated landing at Cabana. Do any of you gentlemen have any questions?"

At Daiquiri, a small peninsula offered some protection from the strong southeast trades, which in summer drive a heavy surf onto the coral reefs.

"Here at Daiquiri," Shafter said, indicating the town, "I'll land a regular army division under…uh, let's see…General Lawton, and the volunteer cavalry division under, of course, General Wheeler. They'll be ordered to close in on the Spanish at Siboney. Then we'll use Siboney as the main beachhead. It's a lot closer to Santiago."

"Caramba!" Garcia said, and indicated through the interpreter that he thought it was an excellent plan. "Hasta la vista!" he said, as the conferees adjourned and exchanged salutes.

Soon after the Americans returned to the *Segurança*, a squall that had been threatening for some time descended in force. After it blew on past, the Americans watched in astonishment as a water-spout began to take shape far out on the eerily-lit sea. The spinning dark column, growing thicker and thicker, stretched from the strange sea to the weird dark clouds like some gargantuan umbilical cord. All around the spout, the sea boiled like a caldron. Someone on a transport cried out in alarm: "It's coming toward us!"

As if on cue, the battleship *Indiana* cut loose with half a dozen big shells. The last one struck the water column and exploded. From fifteen feet above the waves, the column collapsed into the sea. The upper part of the twisting spout was slowly sucked up into the clouds. An hour later, a sudden rain pelted ships and sea.

Restlessly, General Shafter, his mind burdened with staggering problems, prowled the *Segurança* decks. Summoning his adjutant, he dictated an order: absolutely no news correspondents were to go ashore with the first assault waves.

An hour later, correspondent R.H. Davis, spiffily togged out in white shirt, silk scarf, tailored riding breeches, field boots and sun helmet, confronted Shafter, waving a copy of the order he had ripped off the bulletin board.

Davis, who had covered the Greco-Turkish War in 1897, was the most illustrious war correspondent of his day and probably the most dapperly dressed. He was writing for Hearst's *Journal* at a salary of $3,000 a month.

"General," Davis said. He spoke quietly, but smoldering anger resonated in his voice. "This order directs that none but fighting men will be allowed in the first boats of the landing party. That shuts out reporters."

Shafter fumed inside but tried to mask his irritation: damn reporters think they have a right to challenge everything. "My good sir, I'll need all available space in the boats to give my troops as much firepower as possible in the initial assault. If I let a hundred reporters go along, that means sacrificing the space for a hundred riflemen. A hundred rifles could mean the difference between victory and disaster."

"General, sir, I understand why you can't let all the reporters go along. But certainly you could make an exception for me. Perhaps you don't understand. You see, I'm not a mere reporter – I'm a descriptive writer."

That did it with Shafter. "I don't give a good goddamn *what* you are!" he exploded. "I'll treat you all alike!"

Furiously, Davis ripped the copy of the order into shreds, flung the pieces overboard, and then walked off in a huff.

From that time, Shafter's image suffered to some degree in many dispatches from American reporters and, as might be expected, fared worst in those from Davis.

As the red sun rose from the gunmetal blue sea on June 22, five warships glided toward shore – the *New Orleans*, *Wasp*, *Hornet*, *Vixen* and *Scorpion*. At 9:40 a.m., the *New Orleans* hoisted the blue peter as the signal to the gunners on all the ships: *Starboard batteries commence firing.* The big guns opened up, enveloping the warships in coiling smoke as they plastered the countryside around Daiquiri. Shells bludgeoned the cliffs and rocketed into the trees, uprooting great palms and ripping up the ground, raising tumbling clouds of dust and debris. They tore tin roofs off houses, sending some of the corrugated sections spinning to phenomenal distances. Waves of cheers resounded in the air. "It was the grandest sight I ever witnessed," wrote one observer.

For twenty minutes the cannonade continued. Not a single enemy gun answered the fearsome barrage. At 10 o'clock, Shafter ordered that the blue peter be raised on the *Segurança*, the pre-arranged signal to cease fire.

Under clouds of smoke hovering over the scene, the beach seemed deserted. A few fires were burning, smoking up the town. An old pier and several gondola cars used for hauling iron ore to the pier were blazing merrily. The Spanish apparently had torched them, then cleared out before the American bombardment.

Painting of the *Indiana* firing her 13-inch guns

Steam launches from the warships were assigned to tow small navy boats loaded with soldiers up to the beaches. The army had had little experience in amphibious operations and had obtained only four shallow-draft vessels for landing craft. And two of them had gotten lost on the voyage from Tampa. Now Shafter had to gamble on the navy's small boats.

The command was given, and suddenly soldiers were donning haversacks, horsecollar blanket-rolls, cartridge belts and canteens. With rifles slung on shoulders, the men slid down ropes to the boats bobbing and leaping alongside. Soldiers shoved off from the transports, pushing the boats away with oars, and the launches began to tow the strings of heavily-laden boats toward shore. They snaked through clouds of gray smoke still hanging over the water, then ran through the tumbling surf until they crunched onto the sand. A great shouting arose as the first soldiers jumped out of the boats and touched solid ground. The time was about 10:25 a.m.

A tattered Cuban youth emerged from somewhere, waving a white flag and yelling in English: "Yanquis! Come on! The Spanish have gone!"

Breaking combers roared and hissed while more Americans landed, struggling to shore through the white water.

"Viva Cuba Libre!" they yelled when they saw the young Cuban.

"Vivan los Americanos!" he shouted, and his face was ecstasy.

Now several tiny figures could be seen scaling the crag hundreds of feet above the shore, making their way toward a small blockhouse on the crest – Capt. J.J. Crittenden of B Company, 22nd Infantry, and four of his men. Below, more and more soldiers watched the climbers. Suddenly atop the peak the Spanish flag came down. Moments later the Stars and Stripes fluttered against the blue, whereupon a tremendous cheering and shouting arose, punctuated by brazen bugles and shrieking steam whistles from ships for miles around.

Now, boat after boat delivered soldiers to the ore pier. Some of the earlier arrivals had found a bucket and managed to quench the flames with seawater. The pier was so high that to reach it the arriving soldiers had to leap from the heaving boat at the precise moment it rode a surging wave-crest – a tricky feat.

Two black troopers attempting to land on the pier were crushed between the boat and pilings and drowned. Corporal Edward Cobb of Richmond, Va., and Private John English of Chattanooga, Tenn., were members of the 10th Cavalry, which with the 9th Cavalry would weather savage combat in the days to come. The 9th and 10th, organized from black soldiers of the Union Army who stayed in service after the Civil War, had become legendary as the "Buffalo Soldiers" who fought Indians and outlaws and helped carve out America's western empire.

Invasion

The 9th U.S. Infantry arrives at Siboney Beach

Although the transports had been ordered to stay clustered off Siboney and Daiquiri, some had scattered far out to sea during the night, or even vanished completely. Many valuable hours were frittered away while steam launches towing strings of empty boats went searching for their assigned transports. One transport, the *Knickerbocker*, carrying 600 soldiers assigned to spearhead the advance, got lost during the night and didn't show up until late afternoon.

Into the evening the debarkation continued, until 7,000 Americans had gone ashore at Daiquiri. Not a single shot was fired at them.

"It was great luck for us," wrote correspondent George Kennan for *Outlook* magazine, "but it was not war."

In the commandant's residence at Daiquiri, the Americans discovered 8,000 rounds of Mauser ammunition. They also found an unfinished letter in which the local commandant assured General Arsenio Linares, the commanding general, that he was "abundantly able to resist any attack at Daiquiri, either by land or sea."

American general officers, surveying the network of rifle pits and stores of ammunition, whistled softly in amazement, and were rather inclined to agree with the Spanish commandant. But Linares apparently had ordered him to pull back to Santiago.

Cuban scouts said the 200 Spaniards at Siboney also were gone, having scattered that morning at the onset of the naval bombardment.

Shafter now ordered Brigadier-General Henry Lawton, commander of the 2nd Infantry Division, to march into Siboney. Lawton at once sent two brigades on the trail with orders to "Keep marching until dark." Lawton was the man who, decorated for bravery at Atlanta in the Civil War, later captured Geronimo after a 1,300-mile chase through the Southwest. He was a big man, six-four, and wore a gray mustache.

Soon after 8 o'clock of the following morning, Lawton's high-spirited soldiers entered Siboney – unopposed except for a few shots fired at long range – and found coffee and tortillas still roasting over campfires. The Spanish, reported by Cuban scouts as having decamped, apparently had come back. Spoils of war included some casks of wine and half a dozen locomotives, which the Spanish had sabotaged by damaging vital parts.

Siboney's capture gave the Americans a good beach for landing troops and supplies half a dozen miles closer to Santiago.

The capture came at an opportune moment. The rising truculence of the surf had forced Shafter to break off landing operations at Daiquiri before all the troops could go ashore. He promptly ordered the transports to proceed to Siboney and discharge their remaining troops.

Conditions were worse at Siboney, as there was no pier at all. Rocking idly, the transports awaited their turns to disembark soldiers. Hundreds of scavenging gulls filled the air with their harsh squawks as the vibrating steam launches jockeyed strings of boats alongside the transports. Sergeant O'Neill pushed to the rail where Petty and others were watching the show.

"Petty?"

"Standing by, Sarge."

O'Neill leaned on the rail and jetted yellow juice into the sea. A gull dived after it. "You'll stay on the boat."

Petty let out a groan from the depths of his soul. "Sarge, that was like a kick in the guts."

Only a short distance away, the mountains and jungles of enemy country lifted from the foam-swept beaches, and the boats were creeping alongside the transports, and the decks were crowded with soldiers ready to disembark, and the ecstasy of combat was maybe only minutes away, and Sarge was telling him he couldn't go. *Couldn't go? Oh, Lord!*

"But *why*, Sarge? Why *me*?"

"Why *not* you? You somebody special? Damnit, you're not the only man who hasta stay behind. We're leaving some regimental property on the boat. Some of you rookies'll have to stay here and guard it, so them sticky-fingered merchant sailors don't steal us blind."

"Please, Sarge, lemme go ashore. I *gotta* go! Please!"

O'Neill, seeing the misery in Petty's face, worked frantically on his quid. "Okay, boy, you win. Good luck – but don't tell *nobody* I made an exception for you, ya hear?"

Rapture spread over Petty's face as he stammered his gratitude. This was the third time he had nearly missed the boat. First, arriving at Jefferson Barracks too late for the 3rd Missouri Volunteers. Second, when the transports had made their abortive start. And now this.

Suddenly the word all had been waiting for from top brass came down like an electric current, galvanizing everybody: at once, hundreds of jubilant soldiers began spilling over the rails, dangling on ropes or grabbing handholds wherever they could, dropping into the heaving boats. Some let go too soon and crashed down hard as the boat lurched upward on a wave. Some waited too long and fell many feet as the boat sank in a trough. Soldiers' lubberliness was a butt for sailors' jibes.

When a string of boats was packed with soldiers, the steam launch racketed shoreward, snaking the boats behind. Soon the water was dotted with bobbing convoys, roller-coastering toward shore.

Petty, letting his lungs expand with the wind and the smell of salt spray, roared in exultation: "Let 're go, Gallagher!"

"Too many guys in this boat!" someone hollered. "Water's spilling over the edge!"

"I'm *sitting* in water!"

"All this rocking makes me sea-sick!" complained another. "Watch out – I'm gonna urp!"

As the boats dipsy-doodled through the combers and grated onto the sand, the soldiers jumped into the hissing foam and splashed to shore.

To defend Santiago, General Arsenio Linares had available 19.000 crack troops to throw into the lines. And the seas, favoring the Spanish defenders, were rolling the most ponderous since the arrival of Sampson's blockading squadron early in the month.

If Linares had ordered several thousand soldiers to dig in on the limestone cliffs dominating Daiquiri and Siboney, and wait out the bombardment, he could have turned the American landings into a slaughterhouse. For some reason, he had neglected this. Instead, his soldiers merely blew up some installations and pulled back toward Santiago.

As Shafter had ordered it, several transports sailed off to Cabanas on the far side of Santiago bay to fake landing preparations there. Possibly this ruse confused the Spanish and helped to hamstring any resolve they may have had to defend Daiquiri and Siboney. So the American invaders captured the beaches with the loss of only two men, and those by pure accident, not enemy action. This amazing good luck was not lost on correspondent R.H. Davis, who wrote: "God takes care of drunkards, sailors and the United States."

Now for the animals: from the transports up to half a mile from shore, the horses and mules, some blindfolded, were shoved into the sea. These animals were nearly all artillery horses, wagon teams, and pack mules. Cavalry horses had been abandoned in Florida.

Many panicked when plunged into the ocean. Most headed for shore. But, as some were blindfolded, and sea-swells were high enough to obscure the coast from view of others, they started thrashing in all directions. Some headed out to sea. Frantic teamsters cruised about in small boats, trying to snatch off blindfolds and herd the bewildered animals toward shore. They talked encouragement, patted them reassuringly, and tried to keep their muzzles above water. Often when a towrope was tied to the halter, an animal lost its panic and began swimming after the boat. Sometimes five or six swam behind one boat, linked by halters, with a leather-lunged teamster egging them on.

But many still floundered helplessly. Someone had an inspiration: buglers on shore blew "Stable Call" and "Assembly." Many horses responded: hooves flailing, they surged in the direction of the familiar clarions. But not all were rescued. Some began swimming in circles until they drowned. Some swam out to sea and were lost. One horse was glimpsed two miles from shore, swimming in the direction of South America. In all, scores of horses and mules were drowned, dotting the blue sea with their carcasses.

Most of the half-drowned and exhausted animals that made it to shore required several days to regain their strength, a delay destined to cripple the transfer of rations and supplies to forward positions.

In a railroad roundhouse at Siboney, soldiers from the 22nd Infantry came across the half dozen locomotives the Spanish had sabotaged. But some of the men had been railroaders. By cannibalizing parts from several engines, in mid-afternoon they had one engine ready to roll. Four soldiers climbed into the cab. One jerked triumphantly on the whistle-cord, and the wildly tooting engine ground out of the roundhouse and snorted down the track, touching off a volley of cheers.

As the sun plummeted behind the mountains, the shades of night closed in on the invading army. Campfires blazed in the darkness. The soldiers hung their clothes over their fires to dry. Later, they cooked bacon and coffee in tin pans and munched on hardtack.

On the distant ships, soldiers still impatiently waiting their turns to go ashore were tantalized by the spectacle of the campfires twinkling like strings of diamonds against the jet velvet hills, and they feared they were missing part of the adventure.

In the blinding glare of naval searchlights, boats kept ferrying in more and more soldiers, who celebrated their landings with howls of triumph. On shore they found some of the earlier arrivals dancing naked around campfires in the random rains, or yelling with abandon as they plunged into the surf to revel in their first bath in a week.

Petty and Fay Ball were among a dozen soldiers clustered by a huge bonfire, where some were drying clothes on sticks and branches placed near the flames, when a corporal from the Signal Corps Detachment loped up.

"Hey, any of you guys seen General Shafter's aide, Colonel McClernand?"

Nobody replied in the affirmative.

"If you do, tell 'im we now got the whole letter translated."

"What letter?" Petty asked.

"The one the Spanish general left – saying he wouldn't have no trouble holding off the Americans."

Petty and Ball unpacked their blanket-rolls. Pounding stakes into the ground, they rigged their shelter-halves to form a two-man dog-tent, with open end facing the ocean. They spread their rubberized ponchos on the rain-soaked ground and laid their blankets on top. Now, with heads propped up on pillows made by tucking shoes under blankets, they watched the huge yellow moon climb up from the deep purple sea and shine on the invasion fleet. Hardtack and bacon and coffee lingered as a pleasant warmth in their bellies.

"Solid comfort," Petty said.

"Snug as a bug."

"Lookit that ol' moon. Sure don't get as big as that back home."

From the black shapes of the transports, etched starkly on the moon-dazzled sea, a faint chorus of song – "Camp Town race track five miles long..." – was wafted from soldiers waiting their turns to pile into small boats and head for the beach.

"Doo-da, doo-day," Ball echoed loudly. "Ain'tcha glad we're so lucky to come to Cuba?"

"Betcher ass we are. I almost didn't make it. Sarge was gonna leave me behind on the boat to guard some ol' regimental property. Aw! – I'm not supposed to say nothing about that. Forget it, will ya?"

"Sure...whaddya speck we'll do tomorrow?"

"Shafter'll think of something, I reckon."

"Wonder how soon we'll go on the attack?"

"Good God, you crazy galoot, how the hell should I know?"

"I wasn't *asking* you. I was just wondering."

"Well, move over, will ya? You're taking too much room,"

As they watched some noisy new arrivals land on the beach, Petty said: "Whaddya think about the Spanish commander at Dackery leaving a letter saying he wouldn't have no trouble holding us off?"

"'At's a kick in the pants. I can just imagine ol' General

Shafter saying, 'Hey, boys, this Spanish general says he won't have no problem keeping the Americans out of Cuba. He must know what he's talking about, or he wouldn't be a Spanish general.'"

Petty chipped in: "'No sense fighting when, by the word of a Spanish officer and a gentleman, it wouldn't be no use. Might as well go back to the boats, boys, and call the whole war off. Save us a lot of trouble.'"

They laughed themselves silly at their fantasy of the American Expeditionary Force being hornswoggled by a letter.

"After we knock the stuffin' out of 'em," Petty said, "we'll say, 'Hey, we got a little letter to deliver. It's from your ol' general at Dackery. Says he won't have no trouble holding us off. Only thing is, before he even finished his letter, he took off like a bat out o' hell – so he wouldn't get his ass shot off!'"

Petty, when he finally caught his breath, added: "Some of these Spanish generals are sure gonna have their asses in a sling by the time this war's over!"

In the next instant they froze in horror as the inky silhouette of something very like a spider, a gigantic spider all of a foot high, loomed just behind their feet, against the backdrop of moonlit sea. In yet another instant, it scuttled into their tent. They apparition struck them with such terror that they stampeded through the rear flaps, almost collapsing the tent.

"Good God!"

"Biggest goddamn spider I *ever* saw!"

"Don't never wanna see no bigger, that's for sure. Didja see which way it went?"

"Naw! Too busy getting the hell out. 'Spect me to draw a map?"

For some minutes they squatted on the ground several yards from their tent, discussing the terror. Gradually their rapid heartbeats began to slow down.

"Aw, gimme a match," Petty said. "I'll see if it's still

hanging around."

He struck a light and peered into the tent. Whatever it was had vanished to parts unknown.

"'s okay now," he said, blowing out the light. "Must've gone somewheres else. Might as well crawl back in and try to get a little shut-eye. Probably have a big day tomorrow."

But there was little sleep that night for these thousands of American soldiers camping their first night on enemy soil, consumed with feverish speculations on what tomorrow and the other momentous days to come would hold in store.

Chapter 7:
Confusion Compounded

At daybreak, with the nighttime chill yet lingering in the air, Petty stepped over to a squat palm tree where he and Ball had tossed their jackets on the duff. As he picked up his jacket – "*Yeeeeoww!*" – the nocturnal monster scuttled from under it, now materializing in all its garish daytime shades of red, yellow, orange and black.

Petty stood immobilized, eyes bulging, "What the hell *is* it" he demanded of a passing soldier.

"Land crab. Jungle's crawling with 'em. Don't fret your gizzard. It's harmless."

"You can have it – free of charge! We like to jump out of our skins when it scooted into our tent last night."

Morning revealed the beachhead inundated with waves of white shelter tents. It seemed that almost everywhere among the tents, wherever there was a bit of room, soldiers were boiling coffee and cooking bacon. Even the hardtack, they found, was made more palatable when heated over a fire. Wandering about were a scattering of Cuban rebels slaking their curiosity about American military equipment, and some ragged and forlorn refugees begging for food. At some distance in the background rose a collection of thatched huts and an iron railroad trestle. A grove of rustling coco palms rambled across the flat bottom of the Siboney ravine.

Among the tents an officer walked, hollering through a megaphone: "By order of the Commanding General, all drinking water will be boiled! All drinking water will be boiled!"

"Boil our water!" Petty said. "Little tin cups is all we got to boil with. What kind of jigamaree is that?"

"They want us to boil it," Ball said, "they oughta give us some big pots to do it bang-up proper."

"Well, let's get some on the fire for coffee, anyway. Gimme them rocks and I'll grind us some beans."

Meanwhile in the cavalry camp, an electric tension stitched the air. Cuban scouts had warned Maj.-Gen. Joseph "Fightin' Joe" Wheeler, commander of the cavalry division, that Spaniards were entrenched at Las Guasimas, named after its riotous growth of guasima trees. Not a village, it was merely the point where two trails joined. The bewhiskered Wheeler, now in his sixties, had been an Alabama congressman at the onset of the war with Spain. In the Civil War, the feisty bantam had won his laurels while harassing Sherman's supply lines all the way from Atlanta to Nashville. In that war, infantry had never pushed ahead of his cavalry, and now he was not about to let it happen in Cuba.

With the brigade divided into two columns, the right-hand column, formed of 1st and 10th Cavalry units, took the valley trail. The left column, composed wholly of the Rough Riders, followed the Santiago road. The early slanting sun cast long shadows as it illuminated the two advancing columns. They followed roughly parallel routes less than half a mile apart, but soon lost sight of each other because of the dense tangles wrapping the hills.

It is an elementary military axiom: when the enemy's positions and strength are unknown, it is of cardinal urgency to get those facts. Neglecting essential reconnaissance could mean jeopardizing a large force by marching it blindly into a trap.

Recall Custer at the Little Big Horn. But now Wheeler and Wood and Roosevelt and their men were traipsing up the jungle trails to Las Guasimas with no such elementary precaution. And they ran smack into a buzz-saw: hundreds of enemy Mausers starting popping.

"Bushwhackers!"

A frenzy of slugs thrashed the branches around them. The Mauser bullets zipped by with their peculiar *whit-whit* or *z-z-z-z-z-eu* sounds, and struck some of the troopers with gruesome thwacks. It was a terrible time of dusty death in the sunny thickets.

Capt. Allyn Capron Jr. fell, mortally wounded. Sgt. Hamilton Fish, playboy scion of a famous New York family, slumped dead, a bullet through his skull. Other troopers fell, dead or wounded. Several troopers did some wild shooting, inadvertently firing into Americans in front of them, causing some of the American casualties.

Messengers raced back to Siboney with word that the Rough Riders urgently needed help. (Later the troopers would vehemently deny that they had needed any assistance.)

The Hotchkiss cannon seemed to draw enemy fire like a magnet. Troopers scattered from its proximity as if from the plague. A reporter said Col. Leonard Wood remained calm under fire but Roosevelt "jumped up and down" in his frenzy to keep his troopers advancing. Although correspondents are supposed to be noncombatants, R.H. Davis was seen firing with a rifle he had taken from a wounded trooper.

As General Wheeler watched his cavalrymen lunge toward the Spanish breastworks, and caught glimpses of some of the Spanish fleeing in the direction of Santiago, he temporarily forgot himself. Turning to his aides, the old Confederate warhorse yelled in jubilation: "We got the damn Yankees on the run!"

Miles away at Siboney, Petty and thousands of other Americans heard the crackling fusillade echoing in the hills

Confusion Compounded

and envied their comrades who were tasting the joys of combat.

A final count showed that 964 Americans fought in the Battle of Las Guasimas, routing an estimated 1,500 Spaniards. Sixteen Americans were killed and 52 wounded.

On the battleground of Las Guasimas – Americans going to the front.
(Harper's Pictorial History of the War with Spain, Vol. II)

General Lawton, his face livid, stalked into Wheeler's camp and shook his finger in Wheeler's face.

"General, you provoked a needless fight that could have turned into an American disaster!"

"General Lawton, sir, don't you think a quick victory would give the folks back home something to cheer about?"

In relaxed moments, the two generals addressed each other as Hank and Joe. This was not one of those moments.

"Give the folks back home something to cheer about!" Lawton echoed in exasperation. "General, this is a military campaign, not a political campaign! And we'll have no more grandstand plays for the folks back home! Is that clear?"

"General, sir, I don't know how the hell we're going to win this war if we don't tangle asses with the enemy a few times."

"General Wheeler, *I* was given command of the advance, not you. And, by God, I'm going to *keep* in command – even if I have to post a guard to keep you and your troops in the rear!"

Later, Wheeler's ruffled feathers were smoothed down when Shafter sent a message of congratulations – with a warning not to start any more fights without specific orders.

In Santiago, someone asked one of the Spanish soldiers who had so hastily decamped from Las Guasimas if the Americans had fought well.

"Well?" he replied. "Caramba! – they tried to catch us with their hands!"

"When we fired a volley," another said, "instead of falling back, the Americanos came forward. Madre de Dios, that is not the way to fight, to come closer at every volley."

The day after the battle, some ragged Cuban refugees driven out of Santiago by the hope of finding something to satisfy their hunger, drifted up to American advance posts. They reported that *La Espana*, a Santiago newspaper, announced that morning that the Americans had been repulsed at Las Guasimas with heavy losses. This rather baffled the refugees, because they had seen the Spaniards fall back, and now here they were eye-witnessing the Americans pressing on after them. Shafter wrote to General Miles in Washington: "Reports from Spanish sources from Santiago say we were beaten, but persisted in fighting, and they were obliged to fall back."

As the Americans consolidated their advance positions beyond Las Guasimas, Shafter grappled with the immense problems of getting supplies on shore and organizing the base camp.

The beachhead pullulated with men and animals as the army tried to get itself together in the infernal heat, which often topped 100 degrees. Sudden downpours drenched the soldiers, animals and supplies, compounding the general misery. Horses that had been confined too long in the ships' dismal holds, then exhausted themselves on the swim to shore, languished and died. Wagons taken apart when loaded at Tampa now had to be re-assembled on shore. Civilian laborers collapsed in the heat and soldiers had to do their jobs. The beach was littered with jumbles of ammunition boxes, crates of stores and bales of forage. But much remained unloaded. Doctors had been landed without their medical paraphernalia. Field guns were being trundled forward on the trail before their ammunition was located. Salt pork and hardtack were in fairly ample supply, as well as sugar and coffee. But there were acute shortages of onions, potatoes and tobacco. Some units received too many rations, others not enough. Confusion seemed the order of the day.

What with the miserable food, accursed heat and oppressive wool uniforms, scores of soldiers were coming down with sicknesses of one sort or another.

Shafter still had a mountain of supplies to bring ashore. But for some reason – sheer orneriness, some said – the ships' captains weren't cooperating.

"Lookit them ships way the hell out there," Sergeant O'Neill snarled, gazing at the horizon dotted with tiny vessels. His neck flushed with ire. "Some of 'em must be fifteen or twenty miles out – just sailing around way out there all day, burning government coal. Them puddinhead skippers are supposed to be under *military* orders, but how the hell do you communicate with 'em?"

"Beats me, Sarge," Petty said, concealing his amusement at O'Neill's rising dander.

"If we had a real berserker of a general," O'Neill continued, "he'd damn sure communicate with them bastards. He'd order 'em to get their mangy asses back here, and he'd see that their anchors kept 'em here, and he'd appoint a signal officer to wig-wag orders. Only way to communicate with 'em now is, somebody's gotta chase all over creation in a rowboat to find 'em. All that food and stuff out there – goddamn it, we need it *here!*"

"Ain't no pier to unload the stuff on," Petty said, his belly quivering a trifle.

"That's what I *mean!* Shafter oughta assign a port captain and get these buggers off their asses and start building one! Hell's fire, better fetch it in a dab at a time in rowboats than not a all, like right now."

"Maybe they're scared they might hit a rock if they get too close," Petty said, half-strangled.

"Hell, them rum-guzzling flat-heads would rather leave us starve than scratch the paint on their pretty boats. Yellow-belly toss-pots! If we had anything better'n a blubber-butt general, he'd order somebody to build a wharf, pronto. Most sickening mess I've ever seen or heard of! Never thought I'd seen anything worse'n Tampa, but here it is! Fat old slob just sits on his ass in his tent all day. Nobody knows what to do because they ain't no orders coming down. Nobody's in *command!* Nobody's *in charge!*"

Petty suddenly suffered a violent fit of coughing.

"Better do something about that before it gets any worse," O'Neill said.

Petty was saved from embarrassment by a sudden development: some of O'Neill's intemperate remarks had been overheard by a gray-templed, jut-jawed first lieutenant, thirty-eight years old, a veteran of campaigns against the Apache and Sioux. Grimly, he strode up to the group.

"Ten-HUT!" somebody said, and all popped to.

"Hat-ease," the lieutenant said. *"Except you, sergeant – you remain at attention while I'm talking to you!"* He fixed O'Neill with a glare that bored into him. His voice had the edge of a Wilkinson sword.

"Why the hell did you come to this war if you can't stand

the gaff! Plenty of men would've been glad to take your place. War's always been this way. Did you expect to see the Old Man standing out here with a book in his hand, telling these mule-skinners how to handle their outfits? *Did you, sergeant?*"

"No, sir!"

"The fat old man you talk about is going to win this campaign. When he does, this'll all be forgotten. Now we'll have no more of that seditious talk. Got that, sergeant?"

"Yes, sir!"

"Any more of that mouthing-off and I'll have you court-martialed for trying to incite a mutiny!"

With that, the lieutenant stalked away. When he had passed out of earshot, the crestfallen O'Neill demanded: "Who the hell's that flannel-mouth?"

A gray-haired old corporal shook with repressed laughter, then let out a whoop. "Didn't you recognize the man, Jim? That's none other than ol' Blackjack Pershing hisself! Better watch your step when he's around. He can be meaner'n a bear with piles."

John J. Pershing was the lieutenant's name – the man who one day would lead raids into Mexico after Pancho Villa and later command the American Expeditionary Force in France during World War I.

Pershing, however, evidently had some feelings akin to those of the sergeant he had chewed out. For he scribbled in his diary: "Everything was in the direst confusion. No one seemed to be in command and no one had any control over the boats, transportation nor anything – and it was only by the individual efforts of the officers of the line that order was brought out of chaos, at least a semblance of order."

Correspondent Davis, another acid critic of the logistics situation, wrote that the transport captains acted with an arrogance and obstinacy for which they deserved to be clapped in irons, adding:

I was on six different transports, and on none of them did I find a captain who was, in his attitude toward the Government, anything but insolent, un-American, and mutinous, and when there was any firing of any sort on shore they showed themselves to be the most abject cowards and put to the open sea, carrying the much-needed supplies with them.

"I'm so hungry I think I gotta tapeworm," Petty said. "Let's take a gander at the jungle and see if we can find some groceries on the trees."

Petty and Ball found some mango trees, and carried hatfuls of the leathery-skinned fruit back to their tent.

"Better not eat that stuff," O'Neill said. "Or you'll soon be laughing on the wrong side of your face."

"Hell, we already done ate a belly-full," Petty said.

"They'll give ya the craps."

"Them Cubans eat'em. Seems like that's all they ever eat."

"They can't afford to be too particular. Besides, they're *used* to 'em."

"What's wrong with 'em? They taste so good I can't believe they'd mess us up."

"Don't ask me. All I know is they're giving a lot of the boys some bad cases of belly-ache and turkey trots."

"Well, what *can* we eat in this stinkin' jungle?"

"Them coconuts are okay. Limes, too. Here, try this one."

Tasting it, Petty burbled with ecstasy. "Man, I'm just a-hurting for some more of those!"

Sure enough, Petty and Ball suffered as a result of their indiscretions with the mangoes or from whatever cause. At any rate, O'Neill had predicted it.

One day some small boats floundered through the angry sea toward the beach at Siboney, carrying General Garcia and some cohorts. They were being ferried in from the transport *Leona*, which had picked them up from El Aserradero on the far side of Santiago. Pitching and tossing, the boats were obviously in difficult straits.

"Let's give 'em a hand!" someone hollered.

Petty and scores of other soldiers dashed into the surf, seized the gunwales and steadied the boats as best they could while the Cubans slipped overboard and struggled toward shore. Many seemed so weak that only with help could they stay on their feet in the rip-currents that sucked around them.

"Hey, señor," Petty said to one, stretching out his hand, "grab a hold."

Many were almost naked. Most were armed only with machetes.

"These jaspers are in bad shape," Petty said, "Dunno how they're ever gonna do much fighting. They looked starved. Who's the big guy? Lookit the *size* of him!"

"Must be General Garcia."

"He don't look like he's missed too many meals."

Assembling on shore, Garcia and his men promptly vanished into the jungle on some unexplained mission of their own.

A day later, Petty wrote letters to Dorothy and Ma: "We helped Gen. Garcia and some of his rebels come ashore yesterday. They are a sorry looking bunch but I do not suppose they can help that." In his mother's letter, he added: "Gen. Garcia's soldiers are as skinny as a starved deer but he is something else. He looks like he ate a lot of your good cooking."

* * * * *

Shafter's crucial dilemma was how to get through the awesome terrain with a force large enough to overcome Santiago. For the ten miles from Siboney to the outskirts of Santiago, only a few abominable roads staggered through the wild tangles. The main road was only a dirt trail that warped up and down the slopes – here knee-deep in muck, there fording streams without bridges. Ironically named El Camino Real, The Royal Highway, it was first constructed almost 300 years earlier. Beyond Las Guasimas, the trail moseyed two miles to a village called Sevilla, where Shafter set up his field headquarters.

One day Shafter and his staff, reconnoitering west of Sevilla, picked their way up the lofty hill called El Pozo ("The Well"), named after the war-gutted hacienda huddled at its base.

El Pozo – a pen and ink drawing by William Glackens for the October 1898 issue of *McClure's Magazine*

To Shafter's left, or south, humped the coastal bluffs hiding the sea from view. To the north, four miles away, crouched the menace of El Caney village, said by Garcia's men to be a Spanish stronghold. Directly in front, the trail zigzagged west, down and through a rolling landscape quilted with primordial jungle, a dense rainforest stuffed with banyans, ceibas and mahogany stands. Majestic royal palms soared above the green mat. A thousand yards ahead, the Aguadores River flowed across the trail. Several hundred yards farther, the San Juan River streamed across it.

Some of the hills ringing the jungle basin were crowned by blockhouses, small forts from which the Spanish could signal to one another with flags, or by heliograph – bouncing the sun's rays off a mirror. Each blockhouse rose two stories, the lower commonly of fieldstone, the upper of wood. Some were ringed with trenches, rifle pits and barbed wire.

Beyond the jungle rose a chain of knolls known as San Juan Heights. The highest was crowned with a blockhouse, whose design reminded some observers of a pagoda. Beyond this ridge, Shafter could make out the calcimined walls of Santiago's barracks and hospital gleaming in the sun. Through field glasses, he could plainly see some Red Cross flags on the hospital roof.

General Linares, having forfeited a splendid chance to turn the American landings on the beaches into a disaster, had pulled his forces back to San Juan Heights.

But now, time and disease would become his ever-stronger allies in his struggle with the invaders.

Chapter 8:
Spoiling for Action

Impetuously, the giant fist of the Colossus of the North had hurled a raw, largely-unblooded army across the sea, into the miasmatic jungles of eastern Cuba.

So green the island. So blood-red the crop for harvest. So many years had trouble been brewing. Long had Americans sympathized with the hapless islanders' passion for "Cuba Libre." But the Spanish overlords denounced the *Yanquis* for sticking their noses into something that was none of their damn business. Now was the time for the big showdown, the shoot-out at high noon between Uncle Sam and the Spanish Bandido.

Now, the towering adventure – 17,000 men against Cuba. More precisely, against the Spanish ogres and their uniformed minions, nearly 200,000 all told, who dominated the anguished island.

Jamming onto the beaches, forcing into the jungles, the 17,000 had thrown down the gauntlet in their brazen challenge to the high and mighty sovereigns of the island. The military objective: Santiago de Cuba, and the fleet of Admiral Cervera, corked in by Admiral Sampson's fleet. Could Cervera escape from the bottle? No man knew. At the bottom of the bottle, fortified Santiago lay coiled like a scorpion's tail.

Look back and remember: the sheer audacity of it all! The

hasty conception, abortive birth and untimely growth of the headlong enterprise. All the daylight tribulations, nighttime labors, ten thousand maddening details. All the things that had to be done (and so many left undone): orchestrating the whole combine, setting up the camps, mobilizing the army, procuring food, clothing and munitions, sailing across the sea in a crazy armada, gambling everything on the big stake, winner take all.

Everything fouled up and helter-skelter. Rotten food, the wrong uniforms, ammunition and supplies that couldn't be found. Almost everything needed was in short supply or nonexistent. One thing there was never a shortage of: problems. "We need more problems," Petty grumbled, "like Custer needed more Indians."

The worst was yet to come.

The broiling sun flared down on the invaders from out of a washed-out blue sky punctuated with vultures and buzzards – a bad omen any way you looked at them.

Opposing the 17,000 Americans were 36,000 Spanish soldiers in Santiago province. Some 19,000 of those were garrisoned at Santiago. The rest were dispersed in half a dozen encampments. The remaining 160,000 Spanish troops in Cuba were posted near Havana.

Spoiling for action, the Americans idled on the beaches and in the jungle fringes, harassed by clouds of mosquitoes, flies and gnats. The soldiers oiled their rifles with sowbelly grease, fondled their ammunition, fried their grub, fed and watered the animals. They gawked at the warships and transports loafing far out on the blue horizon. They splashed into the surf to grab the small boats as they wallowed in, to lift out the boxes and crates and sacks containing the hundred sundries vital to an army on the road to combat.

The road to Santiago.

* * * * *

"Hey, give us a hand here!" Corporal Seufert yelled. "Hey, Petty!"

Petty had just come off one detail and was flaked out on the sand, just starting to slide into a doze. Groggily he raised himself on an elbow. "Who, me?"

"Yeah, you! Who the hell do you think I'm talking to, the general?"

"Why *me*?"

"Why *not* you? Somebody give you special privileges? Goddamn it, get your insolent ass over here on the double. And don't gimme no lip!"

Petty scrambled to his feet. "Okay, Corp. Just asking."

Seufert's gray eyes blazed. "You buckin' for a court-martial?"

"Not this soldier. Coming big and pronto."

They splashed into the water to drag a navy launch up onto the sand. A sunburned Marine jumped out and said he had a message for General Shafter from his commandant. While somebody ran off to fetch the general's aide, soldiers clustered around the Marine as he told how it had been at Guantanamo. One episode struck Petty so vividly he knew it would never fade from memory:

"One afternoon the sun started getting a little dim," the Marine said. "I looked up. Seemed like a cloud was passing by. Cloud kept moving. Pretty soon I seen it was no damn cloud a-tall. It was a goddamn whole mess of buzzards. They went to work on the dead bodies of about 400 Spaniards that we had polished off in three days' fighting. In twenty-four hours, stinkin' buzzards picked 'em all clean as a hound's tooth. You could lift up a skeleton by the belt – that's all that was left of his uniform – and shake his bones." The Marine made a motion of grabbing a belt with his fist and shaking it. "And they would rattle."

The soldiers on the beach had nothing much to kill but time. But they wrote intent letters to the folks back home. All about how it was so far on the road to glory in the holy war against Spain, the war to liberate Cubans who had had it up to here with Spanish villainies. Yet that may have been a secondary motive for many Americans. For many, the biggest thing pulling them may not have been compassion for suffering Cubans. Novelist Sherwood Anderson, who soldiered in Cuba at age 17, put it this way: "Our hearts did not ache for the people of the island of Cuba. Our hearts ached for adventure."

Seventeen thousand men – fresh-faced kids and leather-skinned veterans, all together going after Linares, going to kick his butt and make him let the Cuban people go. Young and old, black and white, clowns and sobersides, from Marine to California, from Minnesota to Texas and the territories.

The dogs of war, fanged and slavering, had been turned loose and were loping down the road of destiny and fate.

The road to Santiago.

But Cuba, it was now becoming clear, was a crazy place to fight a war, with its hazards of disease – yellow fever, malaria, and a witches' brew of other distempers and contagions lumped together as "Cuban fever." Instead of the chance of merely getting creased by a bullet (a hero's proper wound), there were chances galore of coming down with fever or dysentery, maybe cashing in the ol' chips. Where's the glory in that? And all that godforsaken jungle and mountainous terrain to be put behind you before you even get to Santiago. The so-called roads were beyond belief. How in blazes do you bring up your wagons? And field guns? Crazy as a quilt. Nutty as a chinkapin.

In fact, because of the abominable roads, Shafter would have for actual use as artillery support, when the chips were down, only four batteries of antiquated field guns, four to a battery. A mere sixteen field guns to go against fortress Santiago, whose defenses were stiffened by the formidable guns of Cervera's fleet.

* * * * *

Two shadows flickered among the trees. A dead branch cracked underfoot. *Hark!* The sentry's rifle barrel glinted in the moonlight. *Click* – he cocked his weapon.

"Halt! Who goes there?"

"Friends," Petty said. He and Fay Ball were tramping back to the beach after exploring the jungle.

"Advance, friends, and be recognized."

They stepped into the clearing.

"Give the password."

"Uh… Remember the *Maine* – to hell with Spain!"

"Give the *correct* password!"

"Oh, all right, goddamn it – Remember the *Maine*."

"Pass, friends."

"Probably bucking for a stripe," Petty muttered.

* * * * *

The road to Santiago. And somewhere ahead, the terrible menace of Krupp cannon and Mauser magazine rifles.

The trail the expedition would travel cut through dense stands of trees braided with nets of vines, rioting here and there with red bougainvillea. Other flowers, some may have been orchids, glowed like spots of pale fire or flickered like yellow cats' eyes. Through the jungle's evil beauty, through the swampy stench of rotting vegetation and gassy miasma and darkness, rambled the road to Santiago, the winding, winding trail to Santiago.

Like a fuse burning hot and smoky, sizzling to the powder keg of San Juan Hill.

Chapter 9:
Ordeal: The Road to Santiago

General Shafter hoped his face didn't betray his anxiety. "Who, and how many?" he asked.

"General Pando, weeth 8,000 hombres," said the rebel scout.

Shafter blanched under his florid tan. *Pando with 8,000 men!* This ominous chunk of intelligence rocked him like a bombshell, forcing him to a crucial decision: he would have to attack without waiting for the reinforcements now sailing from Tampa.

Pando was driving his 8,000 regulars on a forced march from Manzanillo to reinforce the Santiago garrison and thus ease the pressure on the city. Pando's column, the Cuban scout added, also was bringing supplies on pack-trains and beef on the hoof for beleaguered Santiago. He was said to be fifty-four miles from the city, pressing on at twelve miles a day, which was good time in that terrain for an army complete with supply train. At that rate, he would arrive on July 2 or 3, four or five days hence.

On top of San Juan Hill crouched a low farmhouse with red-tile roof and broad eaves. The Spanish had turned it into a fort, or blockhouse, by cutting loopholes in the wooden walls and reinforcing the walls with breastworks of broken stone, earth and sandbags. Atop this blockhouse floated the blood-and-gold colors of Spain. Now American observers with spyglasses on El Pozo Hill could see the ridge swarming with Spaniards digging trenches and raising earthworks. Their straw sombreros bobbed in the long pits as their shovels piled the yellow dirt on the side they knew the assault would come. Others, perhaps officers directing the operations, swaggered about the blockhouse or galloped along the ridge on white horses.

Since April, the Spanish had excavated more than 4,000 yards of trenches on the ridge, usually in two or three parallel lines. Now they were feverishly giving them a final beefing-up. General Linares had fixed upon this strategic ridge as his primary defense line for Santiago. It was a natural roadblock in the path of the invaders.

Shafter, feeling sick with dread at the thought of 8,000 enemy soldiers moving in, sent an aide to General Garcia, requesting him to march his 3,000 rebels to the northwest of Santiago and make it as hot as they could for Pando's relief column.

Several days earlier, Petty's regiment and thousands of other Americans had been given the word to advance. Slogging out of Siboney, they followed the old wagon road heading toward Santiago, but it was a tiresome road and they groused endlessly.

"How can it be so hot and so rainy at the same time?"

"El Camino Real – The Royal Highway. What a laugh."

"So who's laughing?"

Many years of internecine warfare had reduced the course to a sad state of disrepair. From Siboney, it meandered up a marshy valley sprinkled with stagnant pools and lagoons, wandering past clumps of royal and coconut palms.

Petty sniffed as they tramped past the scum-laden ponds. "Stinks to high heaven."

A short hike out of Siboney, they stared at seven low

mounds of dirt, each with a crude wooden marker: the graves of seven Rough Riders killed at Las Guasimas.

"Kinda takes some of the glory out of the war," Ball said softly.

Farther, the trail pivoted to the left and writhed across a series of densely-wooded ridges to the crest of the dark green watershed beyond. A light blue haze filled the green gulch. Now they were forced to advance in single file as the trail wound through the up and down terrain matted with vines, brush and trees.

"Hey, Petty," someone hollered, "pull in your ears – we're coming to a bridge!"

It didn't bother Petty. He had been the butt of jokes about his ears as long as he could remember. "Speaking of ears," he retorted, "you seem to be a little short. But I gotta give you credit for one thing – you're really long on mouth!"

The jungle occasionally echoed with a peculiar cooing sound.

"Could be wood cuckoos, or it could be Spanish scouts signaling that we're on our way," O'Neill said. "Cubans say that's the way they pass the word."

Sometimes the trudging soldiers topped a lofty ridge where they could look out over the vast sea of vegetation ahead, which the entire army would have to negotiate. Here and there a Poinciana tree quilted with bright red flowers bloomed against the jade-green jungle. Magnificent royal palms rose above the wild tangle. Vines crept up their trunks as if seeking to drag the regal trees down to the common level.

Between the green hills, off into the shimmering skyey distances dotted with buzzards and vultures, they still caught occasional glimpses of the big black transports and gray warships ranged on the glittering sea.

"Them's our babies," Ball said proudly.

"That's the big message from up north," Petty said.

"They *told* us to go down to this hell-hole and do a job,

and by God we're gonna do it!"

"We'll wrap up them Spanish sonsabitches and send 'em home in a package, C.O.D.!"

From Siboney, Lt.-Col. Joseph E. Maxfield and his crew of four privates escorted a wagon being trundled forward by mules, advancing to El Pozo Hill. The wagon contained the Signal Corps' uninflated observation balloon. Destined to play a tragically unforeseen role in the momentous drama ahead, the balloon had arrived in New York from France on the steamship *Teutonic* in May and was sent deflated to Tampa. In the confusion there, it was lost for several days. But Maxfield and two dozen enlisted men finally tracked it down. At El Pozo, Maxfield and his men finished the irksome job of mending the numerous leaks that had sprung when the varnish melted in the oven-like ship's hold.

Maxfield's face was a gloomy mask. "We've got barely enough hydrogen to inflate it," he said.

Lt. John H. Parker had floated his battery of Gatling guns to shore on bridge pontoons borrowed from the engineers, because he couldn't get hold of any boats. Now Parker and his Gatling crew shoved forward on the trail, their four ten-barreled "coffee-grinders" hauled by mules. The men hollered lustily as they plunged wildly along the downhill sections of the narrow trail snaking through the hills, and turned the air blue with curses during their uphill struggles.

Onward trudged the long procession while the sun streamed through the foliage of palms, lime trees and hardwoods, a tropical rainforest strewn with orchids. Spanish bayonet, a wicked plant with long, sharp leaves, menaced the unwary. Land crabs rustled in the leaves like skulking enemies and clicked their claws in a threatening manner. Some were as big as rabbits. Far in the north loomed the rugged blue cordillera of the Sierra Maestra.

In the six days after the Battle of Las Guasimas, Shafter shifted most of his troops forward to the high ground around

Sevilla, where horses and mules could graze in small clearings. Just west of Sevilla, Petty's outfit debouched into a clearing.

"Sergeant, order a halt," said Lt. William N. Hughes, the company commander.

"Company-y-y-y...*Halt!*" O'Neill roared. "Fall out and pitch tents!"

Wearily, the soldiers dropped their rifles, shucked off haversacks and blanket-rolls and propped up their dog-tents. Cursing, they slapped at swarms of gnats, flies and mosquitoes.

"Hell of a place to camp," O'Neill said, looking for a clear field of fire for tobacco juice. "If the enemy had any starch in him, he could sure do us some damage."

"Then why're we camping here?" Petty asked.

"Lieutenant's got his orders same as we do, even if they don't make no sense. See that ridge over yonder?" O'Neill squirted a yellow stream in the direction indicated. "The enemy could put some cannon up there and plaster us royally from one end to the other. But he's not even making a little demonstration – not even firing rifles."

"Maybe he don't give a rat's ass," Petty said. "Right now, I mean. Maybe he's saving a little surprise for us."

In fact, the reason for the Spaniards' apparent indifference was that they had picked San Juan Heights as the decisive battleground, a choice that could hardly have been better for defense.

Straight ahead, beyond the encamped Americans, the trail pitched down and slashed through the jungle basin drained by the San Juan and Aguadores Rivers. To the right, an old road forked off to El Caney, four miles north, where a large contingent of Americans would fight a raging battle on the same day as the San Juan assault.

Along the muddy trail and in the few open glades around Sevilla, the army camped, plagued by insects and 100-degree-plus temperatures. Buzzards and vultures circled in the brassy sky with the tireless patience of their tribe. Often the soldiers had to step aside into the jungle to let the traffic pass – staff officers and messengers, some on horseback; mule-trains and groaning wagons and Signal Corps men stringing telephone lines. All day long, the pack-trains and wagons, each drawn by six mules, plodded past, going forward to unload and returning for new loads. The trail seldom offered room enough for two wagons or mule-trains to pass. The hopeless traffic snarls, endless delays and utter confusion often worked the most placid tempers into conniptions.

When the sun shone, which wasn't often enough, the soldiers foraged in the jungle for coconuts and mangoes, even though warned against the latter. Or they loafed in the leaf-dappled shade beside streams that burbled through little jungle Edens. They cooked fat pork and beans to eat with their hardtack and sat around bitching about the tobacco shortage. Some soldiers were paying others two dollars for a package that originally cost eight cents. Because of the shortage, some smoked dried grass, leaves, roots, even dried horse manure.

All of the men were supposed to have been issued rations for five days, consisting of a can of "embalmed" beef to be shared by two, a big chunk of sowbelly wrapped in sacking, two handfuls of navy beans, usually carried in a spare sock; two handfuls of unroasted coffee beans, one of sugar, an armful of hardtack, and a few pinches of salt and pepper carried in an envelope.

But because some regimental officers neglected to draw rations for their units, many soldiers were destined to fight on empty stomachs.

This was the rainy season in Cuba, and nearly every day terrific downpours engulfed the expedition, drowning campfires and sending streams of water and mud whipping along the trail. The men could only huddle wretchedly in their sopping tents. The New York *Sun* correspondent wrote: "No man who has not gone over this trail...can understand the suffering of our troops and the heroism with which they bear it." Most bore it in stoic humor. Lieutenant Parker said being in a typical Cuban downpour is "like standing under a barrel full of water and having the bottom knocked out." Petty said: "I don't mind it so much when other men's clothing stinks, but when I can't sleep on account of my own, it's getting serious."

So far, Petty's outfit hadn't heard a shot – except those from the faraway Battle of Las Guasimas – or seen hide nor hair of the enemy. To Petty, it seemed so quiet one might think there was no enemy soldier within a hundred miles. But the Spanish weren't about to make war in the jungle. They had carefully picked the arena. Entrenched on San Juan, they knew the single trail was just about the only approach through the jungle. All they had to do was keep their cannon trained on the exit. It would be shooting fish in a barrel.

One day Clara Barton, age 77, and some of her Red Cross staff hiked the eight miles from Siboney to El Pozo Hill to watch Spaniards digging trenches on San Juan. From El Pozo, officers, attachés and correspondents often had sent reports to the rear, saying the Spanish were busy improving their defenses on San Juan.

"Why doesn't our artillery ever lob some shells at those targets?" Ball asked.

"Shafter must know what he's doing," Petty said.

"I imagine he's got an inkling," O'Neill said.

"He's always staying way back somewhere," Petty said, with an air of puzzlement. "Why don't he come up here and see what's happening?"

"Why don't you ask him?" O'Neill said.

"I'm just saying, it don't make no sense to have him back there, and all us up here, and nobody knows what to do. We just wait and wait, and nothing ever happens."

"I never seen a guy in such a hurry to get shot. When the firing starts, you'll wish you was right back here in this peaceful ol' jungle."

"Pig's eye. Whaddya think I come all the way from

Missouri for? To rot in this stinkin' jungle? I just wanna get it over with."

"You'll get your chance, boy. Don't worry about that. I can feel it in my bones. We didn't come all this way just to crawfish out. There's gonna be a real big mix-up somewhere ahead. We just don't know where or when. Like the gamblers say, 'The die is cast.' That means hell for breakfast, somewhere and somewhen."

"But how we gonna get all the goddamn artillery and wagons up to Santiago? Through all this godforsaken mud and jungle? At this rate we'll *never* get there!"

"Why don't you ask General Shafter? He just might tell you."

O'Neill was not about to get caught in any more loud criticism of the way things were going – not after his run-in with Lieutenant Pershing.

"I can see General Shafter now," O'Neill continued. "'Why, Private Petty, I thought you'd never ask. Well, you see it's like thisaway: Admiral Sampson and General Garcia and I have it all worked out' – and he'll get out his maps and papers and shit – 'Looky here, we've got this little problem of taking Santiago, and a few other little problems that go along with it. You see, we've got all these troops and guns and rations and ammunition and supplies to bring up here and here and here' – he'll be marking on his map – 'to get everything ready for the big show, and then we'll just march into Santiago as pretty as a parade, and take over Admiral Cervera's fleet, too. Now, Private Petty, maybe you'd like to look these plans over carefully and see if you *approve*. And if you *approve*, Private Petty, why, we'll just get on with it. Of course, you understand that all these plans are depending on that General Linares doesn't *mind*. He's the big-shot Spanish general, you know. They say he's a particular bird, with funny Spanish ideas. There just might be something in all this rigamarole that he doesn't cotton to. And if he *minds*, we just might have a few other little problems!"

O'Neill nearly fell down, overcome by his own wittiness.

Only when it was learned that the Spanish were erecting more formidable works near El Caney, which might enfilade the Americans' right flank, did Shafter determine to move without further delay. In fact, the Spanish had done a superb job of transforming El Caney into an awesome fortress. They had also strung a profusion of barbed wire fences on San Juan ridge.

And, hurrying to the Santiago battleground – Pando with 8,000 men!

With a worried frown, Brig.-Gen. Adna Chaffee called on General Shafter. "Marching all our troops down the single trail could be disastrous," he said.'

"What's the alternative?" Shafter asked.

Chaffee took off his campaign hat, fingered the crease, then donned it again. Chaffee's personal trademark was wearing his campaign hat creased from side to side instead of front to back. This was the veteran cavalryman who had won dubious renown for yelling at his troops during a skirmish with Sioux Indians: "Forward! Any man who gets killed, I'll make him a corporal!"

Chaffee pulled out his notebook and pencil and began to sketch.

"We could hack a new path out of the jungle, parallel to the jungle's edge – like this – with many trails slashing out of it to the open meadow. Then our men could fan out before the battle, quickly form for the attack, in other words debouch *en masse* from the jungle – instead of pouring out of the single trail like targets in a shooting gallery"

Chaffee paused, but Shafter remained noncommittal, so he continued, sketching on his pad. "The enemy knows where the trail leaves the jungle and has his guns trained on it. If our men leave cover from a single trail, their bodies will be piled so high they'll block the road."

Shafter was feeling deathly ill from the awful heat and the strain of long hours under pressure. He felt a frantic urgency to get the army on the move. To set it in motion *now*. Delay for anything was anathema. The rains could make transportation of ammunition and supplies almost impossible. And the first signs of yellow fever were cropping up.

And, *Pando with 8,000 men* throbbed in his brain like enemy drums.

"We just can't spare the time to cut new paths," Shafter said, with a noticeable weakness in his voice. "It would give the Spanish more time to reinforce their defenses. We haven't got the *time!*"

General Lawton dropped by, and Chaffee repeated his idea, but was not able to arouse his interest.

Lawton brought up another point. "Before we advance on San Juan," he said, "We certainly should capture El Caney."

"How long will that take?" Shafter asked.

"Two hours," Lawton guessed.

It was a bad guess. It would take nine hours. And because Lawton's men would be pinned down at El Caney for nine hours, Shafter would have to fight at San Juan with only 8,400 men, instead of the 15,000 men he counted on.

On the morning of June 30, as the rising sun raised a mist from the rain-washed jungle, Lieutenant-Colonel Maxfield and Lt.-Col. George M. Derby, chief engineer on Shafter's staff, made their first ascent in the balloon, in an attempt to reconnoiter the terrain ahead.

On this same day, which was the day before the impending battle, Shafter rode again to El Pozo with some of his staff. With red-rimmed eyes, he stared through his binoculars, training them along the San Juan crest, then far beyond to the red-tile roofs of Santiago. In front of him dipped the basin of tangled jungle, where the shallow San Juan River flowed near its far edge. Still farther lay the open savanna that rose gently to the base of the San Juan ridge, where General Linares' men were furiously completing their defenses.

It was obvious to Shafter that the Americans, after wading the river, would have absolutely no protection from enemy fire as they advanced toward the brutal slope.

He felt sick.

Chapter 10:
Moving Up

Petty and many other soldiers had never seen a balloon before and stared goggle-eyed at the great gas-bag of oiled pongee silk. Tethered by cable to an army wagon, it sailed along just above the trees. Two soldiers loped in front, manning guy wires, while the two officers rode in the swaying basket.

"A mighty nice target for the Spanish," Petty said.

The ill-starred use of the observation balloon was only one of several cardinal follies that would cost the lives of an incalculable number of Americans.

That afternoon, Shafter summoned the division commanders to his headquarters and outlined his battle plan. Though exhausted by heat and illness, he gave no evidence of any desire to withdraw from directing operations.

"We'll begin the assault on Santiago tomorrow morning," Shafter said in a hoarse voice that betrayed his suffering, "with San Juan Heights as the main objective. El Caney will be captured to protect our right flank. Hank, that's your job," he said, addressing General Henry Lawton.

"You've got two hours to do it in, and it's vitally important to get it done as soon as you can. Clear?"

Lawton nodded. "Consider it done, Bill."

According to Shafter's reckoning, by the time Lawton's division of 6,500 men had mopped up El Caney in two hours, the other two divisions would be in jump-off positions in front of San Juan. Lawton's division then would back-track to rejoin the main force, comprising General J.F. Kent's first division and Wheeler's cavalry division, to begin the main assault.

With only feeble artillery support, Shafter was preparing to launch his infantry and dismounted cavalry in a mad frontal assault in broad daylight against the implacable guns of San Juan Heights. Yet his orders were received with elation by Generals Lawton, Kent and S.S. Sumner, an old cavalryman who was temporarily replacing the ill Wheeler.

"Reckon it won't be long," Sumner said, "before we'll be having Spaniards for breakfast!"

Perhaps because of such overconfidence, the three generals failed to challenge the most glaring defect in Shafter's plan: dividing the force at the start of a major battle. If Shafter had bypassed El Caney, he could have gone into action on a united front with more than 15,000 men.

* * * * *

Again came the rain. About 4 o'clock in the afternoon, Petty's outfit struck camp and started its advance through the downpour. All over the encampment, soldiers were striking their sopping tents and trudging onto the trail to Santiago. Soaked and miserable, yet high on a sense of adventure, they tramped along, boots sloshing in ankle-deep mud. As rain trickled down their faces, they ogled the enormous balloon hovering over the trees, still dimly visible in the noisy shower.

"Follow the balloon, boys," came the cry, and the word was passed back along the column. Stephen Crane wrote: "The military balloon, a fat, wavering yellow thing, was leading the advance like some new conception of war-god. Its bloated mass shone above the trees, and served incidentally to indicate to the men at the rear that comrades were in advance."

The cavalry led the westward march, followed by the infantry. The long column bristled with rifles and guidons. Behind rumbled the field guns, their mules tugging at long traces as drivers snapped buckskin-thong whips over their heads.

"Cannoneers forward!"

The roaring command rang from some leather-lunged sergeant, urging his men on. Waning sunlight flickered on the polished steel guns as iron-bound wheels wobbled over the muddy road. Wagon trains and pack mules lurched along in the rear of the long column.

For some distance the trail wandered close to the shallow Aguadores River. Wherever it forded the river, it turned into a quagmire for many yards on each side. Cloudbursts had swamped the road, converting long stretches into bogs in which wagons and gun carriages sank to axle-depth. Each vehicle stuck in the mud of nearly every ford. Whinnying horses strained, eyes bulging, muzzles foaming, massive thighs rippling. Hooves plunged in the muck as the animals lunged vainly. Soldiers splashed into the water, tied ropes to the wagons and carriages, and hauled on the lines. Each time a vehicle got stuck, all the other traffic had to stop until it was extricated. Some of the horses suffered bad wounds when their iron collars were jerked tight by sudden jolts over granite boulders in some of the fords.

Only sixteen three-inch field guns were rumbling through the jungle with the expedition. The huge siege guns still lay aboard the transports.

Up and down and through the mud and across the fords, through the green denseness, men and horses and mules shoved and dragged the gun carriages and supply wagons, busting their guts in the rock-ribbed fords and deep mud. Everyone was hot and sticky. And tired, tired, tired. Every burden grew heavier.

Moving Up

It was all one big hullaballoo of blaspheming soldiers, braying mules and whickering horses.

And agonizing wagon wheels.

"Hey, doc, give us a little grease?"

"Sorry, bub, it's all gone. See your supply sergeant."

"Don't never ask *me* for anything, you ornery…"

Late in the afternoon, a battery of four field guns managed to lumber into position on El Pozo Hill.

Along the jungle trail, some of the overeager infantrymen in General Kent's first division were forging ahead, while some of the cavalrymen were falling behind. Thus one division was getting mixed up with the other. An aide dashed up to the head of Kent's column.

"General Lawton's order, sir, halt these men and order them into the brush to let all of the Rough Riders pass by."

Roosevelt's Rough Riders cross a ford a mile from the front
(courtesy National Archives)

Petty, Ball and some others grudgingly stepped aside for a while. As the cavalry passed, Petty said, "Gonna give 'em first crack at the enemy, I guess."

Some distance beyond, the cavalry struck off on a trail to the right that thrust across a broad meadow and soon ushered them into a narrow trail flanked by jungle.

As Petty's outfit resumed its march, the men passed hundreds of Cubans camped by the trail, cooking their evening meal. They grinned ferociously at the passing Americans and yelled, "Santiago!" jabbing their fingers westward, then gesturing with their fingers across their throats.

"God help the people in Santiago if those jaspers ever get in," Petty said.

Elsewhere on the trail, hundreds of other Cubans were on the march, padding along in rawhide sandals with unwieldy bundles of provisions lashed on their backs or teetering on their heads.

Near El Pozo, a hospital corpsman smelled a strong odor and stopped to investigate, and found a spot of newly-dug earth with a human arm protruding from it. He looked up as a Cuban approached, smiling and smoking a cigarette.

"Espanol," the Cuban said, and tapped his machete and made the sign of throat-cutting.

Through the drizzle on the long-winding trail, the procession continued – a pageant of battleflags, officers on horseback, black soldiers and white soldiers, their tin cups clinking against bayonet scabbards; mule-trains burdened with ammunition cases; red-faced teamsters spewing clouds of profanity and cracking buckskin whips over horses dragging heavy wagons.

"Lookit that ol' Southern boy!" a soldier said.

Petty had taken off his shoes, scraped the mud off, tied the shoes around his neck, and was trudging along in bare feet.

"Bet that ol' cottonpicker never owned a pair of shoes in his life 'til he jined the army," another said.

"Hey, Petty," yelled a third, "what the hell you think them shoes is – some new-fangled kind of necktie?"

Moving Up

To the guffaws that followed, Petty retorted: "You peckerwoods got any idea what this mud is doing to leather?"

So cocksure was his answer that before long many of the others also removed their shoes. Now a third of the platoon was squishing along in bare feet. Corporal Seufert noticed the breach of military decorum:

"Platoooon-n-n...*Halt!* Awright, goddamn it, all you meatheads get those shoes back on right now! This ain't no grape-stompin' picnic!"

It wouldn't be long before many shoes would be splitting apart in the mud and water.

By degrees the rain died away, the clouds dissolved, and the wet and glistening balloon soared higher and higher, gilded by the last rays of the setting sun.

The soldiers in the column caught glimpses of the two officers in the basket as they trained their binoculars on the enemy works somewhere in front. The men cheered and hallooed.

"Bully for the balloonists!"

"Hey, colonel, ya see any Spaniards, give 'em a shot for me!"

"Tell 'em we're on the way and we're sorry we're late!"

As darkness fell, the ground crew reeled in the balloon and the officers reported to Shafter that barbed wire had been strung in profusion on the San Juan slopes. Four miles to the north, they could spy a blockhouse at El Caney. Over the hills in the west, they could see Cervera's fleet bottled up in Santiago harbor.

To the enemy next day, the balloon would become not only a gigantic target, but a huge signpost or guidon, pinpointing the position of the American column on the jungle trail. It would be a disastrous blunder. Everyone would agree on that. But nobody could understand why it had been allowed to happen.

Except for the superficial data picked up by the

observation balloon, reconnaissance of the terrain appears to have been woefully lacking. Correspondent Davis wrote: "I cannot find out that anyone reconnoitered the wooded basin before San Juan. I know a man who says he knows another man who told him he did so, but of thorough reconnoissance [sic] there was absolutely none."

Just why Shafter didn't ask Admiral Sampson to turn the colossal guns of the Atlantic fleet on the enemy ridge, well within its range, remains a mystery. Both the *Oregon* and the *Indiana* had 13-inch guns which could throw half-ton projectiles a distance of five miles. Or, if the army had advanced along the coast, instead of through the interior, the fleet could have cleared the approach with a trail of havoc. On any given target area, Sampson's warships could have concentrated a fire of about 100 shells a second, including the small projectiles from rapid-fire guns and one-pounders. Enemy infantry could not have survived, let alone fought, in a field swept by such horrific fire.

For some unknown reason, the Atlantic fleet was not asked for its assistance in these directions.

Perhaps Shafter's primary blunder was in failing to relinquish his command because of incapacity. This huge, ailing, aging man suffered in no small degree both physically and mentally, and this no doubt clouded his mind and affected his judgment.

* * * * *

Into the gathering dusk, the long column continued its tramp. For hours, into the warm, insect-stuttering darkness, the thousands of Americans, with their mules and big-wheeled wagons, labored through the mire, bantering and cursing and singing: "Ta-ra-ra-*boom*-de-ay." Or, sometimes they sang a new rendition of an old song, *There'll be a Hot Time in Santiago Tomorrow*. Now an enormous yellow moon sailed through a rain-washed sky sprinkled with diamond-sharp stars.

Far into the night the soldiers marched. At last, Petty's regiment halted in a moonlit glade. Here they camped, though crowded rather awkwardly. There was no room to pitch tents.

"Pass it around – no lights or fires!"

Groggily they spread their blankets in the wet grass. It was getting chilly, and a clammy ground mist swirled eerily around them, wafting the stench of jungle decay to wrinkling noses. Hardly anyone had much to say. Petty's mind was preyed on by the thought that soon they would come to grips with the enemy, but seemingly no one knew when or where. Or if they did, they weren't letting the rank and file know. All of his other comrades in that dark and dismal jungle were bothered by similar melancholy reflections about the imminence of a desperate struggle.

Some of the romance had gone out of the war.

That evening, General Linares must have realized that his chain of defense was weakest at its most dangerous link, for he rushed two companies of regulars, some Krupp cannon, and sixty volunteers from the city's home guard to bolster the other defenders on the San Juan ridge.

Chapter 11:
Bullets for Breakfast

    Late that night in his tent near Sevilla, Shafter, by the light of a kerosene lamp, scribbled a laconic note and dispatched a messenger. The messenger took it via horseback and steam launch to the *New York*, where he delivered it to a sleepy-eyed Admiral Sampson, who was irked at being aroused at an ungodly hour. The message read:

Camp near San Juan River
June 30, 1898

Sir:
    I expect to attack Santiago tomorrow morning. I wish you would bombard the works at Aguadores in support of a regiment of infantry which I shall send there early tomorrow, and also make such demonstration as you think proper at the mouth of the harbor so as to keep as many of the enemy there as possible.

    "The works at Aguadores" refers to a fortification at a hamlet where the San Juan River spills into the sea. Sampson's fleet, bottling up Cervera's fleet, lay well within shelling range of San Juan Hill. Yet Shafter's message conveyed no suggestion that Sampson lay waste the San Juan fortifications, keystone of the whole Spanish line, to save American lives.

At first light the next morning, the soldiers in the jungle cast off their blankets, shivered in the ghostly mist, and set about building cook-fires. Unlike in other reveilles, nobody seemed to have much to say.

The date: July 1. On this fateful morning, the armies of Spain and the United States would meet in a berserk collision as each summoned up its will, sinew and power of arms in a supreme effort to crush each other at the gates of Santiago. From the works at Aguadores, to the arrogant blockhouse on San Juan, to the big sugar-refining kettle on Kettle Hill, and to the fortress village of El Caney, Americans and Spanish would join in battle on a front almost seven miles long.

As the blood-red disk of the sun peeped over the horizon, shining over the wild panorama of mountains and jungle, Spanish defenders ran their flags up-staff, hoisting them into the red light of the dawn.

In their jungle camp, Petty and the others heard a distant shot resound clearly on the damp air. For some seconds, everyone stood without moving – listening, listening. A few minutes later, another shot rang out. Quickly followed by another. And another. By degrees the sputter of firing swelled into a continuous clangor.

Before dawn near El Caney, four miles away, American cannoneers had moved into position. As the sun rose, they squinted at the town – red roofs, white walls, church towers, and a blockhouse on a knoll, where the Spanish colors had just gone up. With practiced precision, the artillerymen sighted their four field guns on the blockhouse. Soon the slamming of artillery and *crump* of shell-bursts was joining the fusillade that echoed to the Americans in the jungle basin.

Only 520 Spaniards were defending El Caney, but they were well dug in, brilliantly led by General Vara del Rey, and fought magnificently against odds of better than ten to one.

Meanwhile, Petty's regiment wolfed bacon and hardtack,

sluicing it down with black coffee. Messengers galloped up with final orders for the commanders, who at once relayed them to the men:

"Strike camp! We're moving out! You will leave your haversacks and blankets here!"

"Leave'em here?" Petty said. "Son of a Dutchman! Looks like today's the day for our little get-together with the Spaniards."

After piling blankets and haversacks in a heap, the soldiers buckled on cartridge belts and canteens and grabbed their rifles.

"Turn your cartridge belt buckles to the rear!" O'Neill hollered.

"What the hell for?" Petty demanded.

"Ya leave it in front, and that shiny ol' brass buckle will sparkle in the sun and give some Spanish sharpshooter a nice little target to aim at... *Fall in*!"

After the men had grouped, more strident commands: "Ten – HUT! ... Sling – HARMS! ... Right – HACE! ... First file, route step... Forwar-r-r-d...HO!"

The column of soldiers swung down the trail, heading in the direction of San Juan Hill.

Meantime in his headquarters camp near Sevilla, Shafter called for his horse. With the aid of two privates, he hoisted his ponderous bulk into the saddle. Roweling his horse to the top of a nearby ridge, Shafter looked out over the distant terrain, surveying the Spanish positions as best he could from this vantage point. Riding back to camp, he began to feel so faint he nearly tumbled from his horse. Groaning, he gasped to Lieutenant-Colonel McClernand, his chief of staff:

"I'm sick. You know the plan?"

"Yes, sir."

"Then carry it out." He paused, breathing laboriously. "Send Miley forward to keep us informed. I'll join you later."

On El Pozo Hill, Capt. George S. Grimes' battery of four

three-inch field guns had been entrenched in gun-pits the previous evening. Now the cannoneers unlimbered the guns.

The San Juan ridge glinted in the early sun. Grimes swept it with binoculars. "About 2,500 yards," he estimated.

A cannoneer set the range on the gun. "Number one gun – load!" Grimes ordered. "Make ready!"

Another cannoneer slammed the shell into the breech and snapped the block shut. The section chief raised his hand, signaling that his crew was ready.

"Fire!"

The muzzle flared with a shattering blast. A churning cloud of thick, white smoke jetted out, then lifted and hung in a great motionless layer on the still air. In the same moment, orderlies' horses reared and plunged, their eyes wild with fright. In the lee of El Pozo stood a farmhouse, a rambling red-tile building of adobe and brick, now sheltering a detachment of Cuban rebels. Some of the Cubans dashed from the lee of the structure: "Vivan los Americanos!"

It was the first shot fired by the Americans in the battle of San Juan Hill. But Grimes scowled, lowered his glasses, and muttered: "Too short!"

Surging forward, the gunners shoved the piece back from its recoil and slammed another shell into the breach. Grimes, rolling up his sleeves, stepped up to the gun. He squinted along the sights, set them for 2,800 yards and jerked the lanyard. A deafening crash followed. The projectile rushed over the treetops with a roar that soon decreased to a whistle, then suddenly died. In less than three seconds came a distant *crump*.

"Way over, captain! Try 'er again."

After another adjustment, the gun boomed. The shell struck a small building on San Juan and raised a cloud of dust flecked with debris. Gunners waved their hats and cheered. Cubans near the farmhouse yelled, "Santiago!" and gleefully brandished their machetes.

"On target, sir!"

The fourth shot produced a similar result: they knew they had the correct range. Now the gunners went to it in workmanlike fashion, sending shell after shell screeching over the valley, tearing up the Spanish works with geysers of earth and debris. But for some reason the Spanish in the blockhouse and trenches remained seemingly unperturbed. At any rate, there was no answering fire.

Because of clouds of thick smoke spewed by the old-fashioned black powder, it was often several minutes between rounds before the smoke pall drifted away and the gunners again could see the enemy positions. By this time more than a score of Grimes' shells had thundered over the trees en route to San Juan Hill. Still no answering fire came back.

Captain Gette, the Swedish attaché, stared at the ridge in puzzlement. "I should think they would get tired of receiving those. Don't they have any artillery?"

Just then a *boom* broke the silence of the distant ridge: the first Spanish projectile arrived with a devilish shriek, a shell-burst, and the twang of shrapnel scourging the air.

The Rough Riders had halted in the farmhouse yard with the 10th Cavalry, and the hospital corps had set up its quarters there.

The third Spanish shell *blammed* directly atop the farmhouse, smashing through the roof and sowing chaos inside and out. Several men were killed and many wounded. Three Rough Riders were wounded and some of their horses were disabled. In the shelling that continued for several minutes, the Spanish cannoneers also killed two men at the American gun battery and wounded five.

With their hackles up, the American gunners retaliated as best they could. But after each barrage they sent toward San Juan Hill, clouds of smoke from the black powder hovered about their guns for a minute or more, pinpointing their positions and offering a beautiful target for the Spanish gunners.

Correspondent Davis later took pains to find out who had ordered the troops stationed so close to the American guns, and was told by General Lawton that it was by Shafter's order. Incensed at such "stupidity," Davis wrote: "They might as sensibly have been ordered to paint the rings in a target while a company was firing at the bull's eye."

Other Spanish gunners, knowing where the trail threaded the jungle in front of San Juan, were firing in that direction. Shells struck the treetops with terrifying bursts, spraying the Americans below with a rage of shrapnel.

Farther back, not yet under enemy fire, the 13th infantry pushed forward. Now the jungle was so dense it seemed to Petty that an elephant would have been invisible ten feet from the road. They had marched only a short distance from where they had camped, when:

"Company-y-y-y... *Halt!*"

They had to stop because the company ahead had halted, barring the way. They idled in the road a few minutes. Then the company ahead began to advance.

"Forwar-r-r-d... *Ho!*"

Again they moved forward a few yards – and were ordered to halt for the same reason as before.

Although the 13th Infantry hadn't yet reached the zone of enemy fire, they could hear the awesome sounds of combat – crackle of hundreds of rifles, slamming of field guns, and *crumps* of shell-bursts. They plodded past a lone man in civilian clothes astride a large horse, watching the column go by. He wore a revolver on his belt.

"Good luck, boys," the man said, waving his straw hat.

"Who's that?"

"Damned if I know."

It was William Randolph Hearst.

Now, as they thrust into enemy range, shrapnel and rifle slugs began slashing the trees around them. From up forward, hospital corpsmen struggled back along the trail, carrying litters bearing wounded Americans. Many left a trail of blood as they passed. The Spanish had the trail zeroed in. Horrifying shell-bursts raged over the column. Mauser bullets by the hundreds scourged the trees, loosing showers of leaves and twigs. In front of Petty and behind, soldiers were dropping. A dud artillery shell smashed to earth, spraying dirt on the Americans.

"Lordamighty," Petty said, feeling sick. "Nearly caught it that time."

Under the lethal rain, the Americans endured agonies of fear. And supreme frustration: they couldn't see anything to shoot back at. Because of the jammed trail, the rate of their advance bogged down to an excruciating slowness. The only commands Perry heard were "Forward, Ho!" and "Halt!" There was nothing to do but obey orders – and torment themselves with the thought that at any second they might join the casualties.

For two seemingly eternal hours the packed column endured the spasmodic advances and nerve-wrecking halts, all the while under unrelenting fire that they had no way of returning.

Up forward, a small band of Americans burst out of the jungle and spilled into a ragged line on the far side of the San Juan River. Here they could fire up at the Spaniards on the ridge. But the Spanish held the whip-hand: they were well dug in, were firing downhill on the exposed Americans, and knew the range.

Just as the leading battalion of the 71st New York Volunteers debouched from the trail, pouring into the open savanna, a shell exploded in its midst. A dozen men collapsed in a bloody welter. This was too much for the others, who spun around and streaked for the rear, rupturing through other outfits, sowing demon panic. Only when regular officers formed a cordon across the trail were the wild-eyed soldiers reined in. So as not to impede the soldiers pressing forward, they were ordered to move off the trail into the jungle.

Pushing on, the 13th Infantry moved past the 71st men lying in the jungle.

"Time for a siesta?" Petty asked.

"Watch it!" one of the 71st men yelled, ignoring the gibe. "They're shooting low!"

Shooting low? That didn't mean a thing to Petty.

"Seems to me they're shooting to kill," he said. "We been able to figure that out all by ourselves."

"Hey, you're supposed to be *in front of us!*" an overwrought H-Company officer bawled to a 71st officer, who only gazed back in mute stupefaction.

As General Kent hurriedly worked his way up toward the head of the column, he pointed to the undergrowth congested with the prone bodies of the 71st, and said to an aide, "Tell the men to pay no attention to this sort of thing – it's highly irregular."

More than 300, or almost a third, of the 71st New York had never fired a rifle. Yet fate had decreed that this raw volunteer unit, after hours of waiting on the crowded trail, found itself – officers as bewildered as rookies – practically leading the way down an unknown trail under galling fire from an invisible enemy, and took a direct hit from a shell as they dashed into the open.

By this time the men of the 13th Infantry, passing the last of the 71st men, had worked themselves up into bundles of raw nerves.

Meantime, General Vara del Rey's stubborn defense of El Caney was keeping Lawton's division tied down, preventing it from linking up with the main force. And somewhere on the road from Manzanillo, the vaunted General Pando and his formidable 8,000 were closing in.

About noon, Shafter sent a messenger on horseback with a note to Lawton:

General Sumner informs me that he is in need of the assistance of every available man that can be sent to reinforce the centre[sic].

Shortly afterward, Shafter sent another messenger on his way to Lawton with another note:

I would not bother about the little blockhouses, they cannot hurt us.

A few minutes later, Shafter sent yet another note speeding to Lawton:

You must proceed with the remainder of your force and join immediately upon Sumner's right. If you do not, the battle is lost.

Despite this command of extreme urgency, Lawton disobeyed his commanding general by refusing to pull his division out of the El Caney meat-grinder.

Chapter 12:
The Balloon Fiasco

Suddenly Petty saw the balloon again, looming above the trees a hundred yards ahead – a huge target for the enemy to take pot-shots at, easier to hit than the broad side of a barn. On the ground, four privates manned mooring ropes. *What a blunder*, Petty thought. *Any information they get will be more than cancelled by giving away our position.*

In the basket, Maxfield and Derby focused their binoculars, scanning Spanish trenches on San Juan. For some reason, the trenches seemed empty. They spied something else: to the south, splashing through the jungle, a second road roughly paralleled the jam-packed trail below, then veered to the left and forded the San Juan River.

Derby leaned over the rim and yelled: "Is there a general officer down there?"

No answer issued from the wild confusion below.

"Is there a field or staff officer down there?"

Still no answer.

"Is there *any* officer?"

"Yes!" someone shouted. "Quite a few!"

"Tell 'em I see two roads in front!"

"Where do they lead to?"

"I can't tell exactly."

Derby scribbled a note telling about the second trail, wrapped a penny in the paper, and dropped it to an officer below.

Seconds later, sombreros popped up everywhere on the San Juan ridge. And now the Spaniards the balloonists hadn't spotted in the trenches were starting to shoot at the balloon, knowing it signaled the location of the Americans. Some bullets punctured the gas-bag. Many others struck the hapless Americans on the trail below.

Signal Corps balloon in Cuba, 1898

Soon Spanish cannon joined in, until every enemy weapon in range was blasting away at the balloon. Under the fearsome barrage, the foremost units of the American column reeled to a convulsive halt. But the inertia of the column of soldiers pressing on from behind was not so easily stopped. Now, throngs of soldiers milled about in the blizzard of slugs and shrapnel, cursing and shaking their fists at the same balloonists they had cheered the day before. In a frenzy of desperation, the ground crew tried to "walk" the balloon away from the clogged trail. But the jungle was too dense and the ropes snagged hopelessly in the trees. Maxfield and Derby, unable to ascend or descend while the ropes were fouled, were sitting ducks.

John Black Atkins of the Manchester *Guardian* watched the balloon being "drilled with as many holes as a pepper-box." Huge wrinkles creased the gas-bag. As hydrogen escaped through hundreds of holes, the balloon slumped into the jungle – and the Americans below cheered with wild relief. Correspondent Stephen Crane also saw it happen: "The balloon was dying., dying a gigantic and public death before the eyes of two armies. It quivered, sank, faded into the trees amid the flurry of a battle that was suddenly and tremendously like a storm."

The time was about 11:15 a.m.

From somewhere in the jungle, publisher W.R. Hearst also witnessed the balloon's expiration. A buzzing piece of shrapnel chopped into a tin of beef on his pack mule.

Miraculously, Derby and Maxfield escaped with only scratches from their plunge into the trees. But for all those soldiers near the balloon's finale, the aftermath was a maelstrom of death and tribulation.

Derby leaped from the basket and raced to tell General Kent where he had seen the second trail cutting through the jungle. Seeing Captain Howse of General Sumner's staff plodding on horseback down the jammed trail, the overwrought Derby yelled: "Tell the general I saw men up there on those hills! They're firing at our troops!"

Petty overheard this remark. With a sour laugh, he said to Ball: "By God, that Colonel Derby doesn't miss a thing!"

Derby realized, however that he had vital, if less obvious, information for Kent – about the existence of the auxiliary road that ran from the main road to the left, fording the San Juan River several hundred yards farther downstream. This was an opportune discovery, as the main road was frightfully clogged with soldiers almost totally demoralized by the intense concentration of enemy fire they had no way of returning. As soon as Kent could get the attention of his aids, he gave orders that hurled his first division, including the 13th Infantry, into the second road.

Sergeant O'Neill's roaring command galvanized Company H: "Double time...HARCH!"

No more the crowded trail: they had a clear road in front of them.

Everyone would agree that the balloonists erred badly in ascending directly over the large force of Americans crammed together – only to discover what scouting parties on the ground should have discovered a week earlier.

More than 400 Americans were cut down by death or wounds in that mad jungle corridor where the balloon's telltale presence pinpointed the American column and turned the advance into a shambles.

Not many minutes after the balloon fiasco, Grimes' field guns on El Pozo opened fire again in a desperate bid to draw some of the rage of Spanish fire from the agonized American column.

"Pour it on, buckos!" Grimes shouted, flinging sweat from his brow. "Take some of the heat off our boys on the trail. Fire at will!"

But Grimes' battery was only a pitiful token force, and no match for the monstrous Krupp cannon whose barrels bristled on San Juan ridge.

Chapter 13:
Hell in Panorama

Gazing up at the terrible crest of San Juan, flaming with Krupp cannon and Mauser rifles, correspondent Atkins of the *Guardian* wrote: "But this hill – the look of it was enough to stagger any man. Was this to be taken practically without the aid of artillery? Artillery should have battered, and battered, and battered the position, and then the infantry might have swept up on the run. But this had not been done. The infantry stood before the thing alone."

Shafter's biggest artillery still lay aboard the transports off Siboney, and he had failed to ask Sampson to lend a hand with his navy guns in the San Juan Hill sector – a criminal negligence, some would later call it.

The Spanish also had the alternate trail zeroed in, and scythes of lead lacerated the American advance. As Petty's outfit loped down the trail, a bullet struck brigade commander Col. C.A. Wykoff, mortally wounding him. Lieutenant-Colonel Worth took his place. Almost at once, he also fell, gravely wounded. Command then succeeded to Lieutenant-Colonel Liscum of the 24th Infantry. Five minutes later he also was wounded. Command then devolved upon Lieutenant-Colonel E.P Ewers of the 9th Infantry.

Suddenly an astonishing thing happened: as Company H

lurched through the hurricane of shot and shell, the body of a men fell through the air and crashed to the ground beside the trail. In the next instant, a Mauser rifle caromed downward through tree branches and landed beside the body.

"Son of a horsethief was in the *tree!*" Petty exclaimed in disbelief.

They could stop only for a stunned moment to look: the Spaniard's head, caught by a fury of shrapnel, was a bloody pulp. Palm fronds tied around his body camouflaged his uniform.

This was one of hundreds of snipers roosting in treetops, pumping slugs at the Americans. As protection from shrapnel, some wore double canvas jackets filled with sand and quilted. These daredevils not only fought in the very target zone where their own weapons were concentrating their fire, but doubled their hazard because discovery by the Americans meant certain death. No mercy would be shown to snipers – "back-shooters" who fired even at wounded soldiers borne on litters. Later it was learned that many had been prisoners in Cuban dungeons – life-term desperadoes who had been promised freedom if they survived.

Now Company H splashed across the shallow San Juan River at what would be aptly christened "Bloody Ford." As the men scrambled up the opposite bank, Petty saw a dozen officers huddled under a thicket of trees, but didn't recognize any. Running by, Petty passed close enough to hear the cacophony of voices, but not close enough so he could catch the drift of their words. It was only a moment's glimpse that he got as he charged by, but it was a moment etched in acid: they all seemed to be shouting, cursing and arm-waving at the same time. Faces were wretched with anxiety. *Look out, boys,* Petty thought, *don't lose your heads at a time like this.*

Some yards farther, they charged toward a scraggly opening in the jungle, and swung to the right to pass through. O'Neill's iron command shot from behind: *"Deploy!"*

As they burst through the jungle gateway, a volcanic scene engulfed them. To Petty it seemed like hell in panorama.

In a paralyzed couple of seconds, he took it in: in front loomed a ridge of hills running parallel to the jungle fringe they had just erupted from. Left and right, the ridge tapered off in a series of knolls, merging with the green jungle. In the center, the ridge humped abruptly to its highest point, which was crowned by a blockhouse roofed with red tile. Its sides of field stone and logs were loopholed for rifle fire.

On both sides of the blockhouse, the ridge boiled with flame and smoke. Torches of red fire blazed from Krupp muzzles, sending shells whistling over the savanna. Some exploded in the jungle while others burst on the savanna, scattering a devil's brew of shrapnel. In trenches and rifle pits along the ridge, countless sombreros bobbed as puffs of light blue smoke jetted from a thousand Mausers. Tornadoes of slugs cut grass around the Americans, while a din like hell's anvils hammered their eardrums.

Petty being six feet tall, was number two man in the first set of four in Company H. Number one dived into the waist-high guinea-grass. Then Petty hit the grass, taking his proper interval. But number three brushed Petty as he dropped.

"Move away!" Petty roared. "You're too damned close!"

The man didn't budge.

"Move it!"

Pale as candle-wax, the soldier didn't stir. Petty jabbed him with his rifle butt. He only squirmed closer, so close he impeded Petty's arm movements. The soldier stared pop-eyed as if hypnotized, oblivious of everything but the terrible ridge.

Any second, Petty figured, some officer or noncom would jump on number three because he hadn't deployed properly. But now those charging in from behind were also failing to deploy properly, piling into the grass and huddling together like terrified chickens. The Spanish could hardly miss. Green grass was turning red with American blood.

Petty raised his head and squinted at the blockhouse. Near the left corner he spied a long, narrow slot just wide enough for rifle barrels. In fact, puffs of light blue smoke were spitting from it. High on the corner above the loophole, a blood-and-gold flag shifted in a gentle breeze. No breeze cooled the flaming hell where Americans lay in the grass.

Petty's eyes darted about, scanning the terrain. From the jungle, the savanna by degrees rose for several hundred yards toward the base of the hill. The hill then lifted to a height of perhaps 150 feet at the blockhouse. A scatter of small trees and scrubs bristled on the hillside below it. Petty focused his eyes back on the flag.

All at once he found himself yelling: "They don't have to put that flag there to tell us where they are! *We know where they are!*"

To Petty, the flag posed an irritating challenge; *Here I am*, it seemed to boast. *What are you going to do about it?*

Batteries on the ridge continued to loose salvos. Black smoke and red fire blazed from Krupp muzzles and Spanish cannon. Shrieking shells burst among the Americans on the savanna and back in the jungle. Mauser bullets hummed past like mad hornets, many chugging into flesh and bone.

Petty, growing more incensed at the sight of the enemy banner, trained his rifle on the loophole below it and squeezed the trigger. Because of the din, he knew his rifle had fired only when the butt kicked his shoulder.

It was the first time he had ever fired his Krag. That first shot gave him a jolt of confidence. Wire-taut nerves seemed to loosen a notch.

He hadn't heard any command to fire or advance. But within only seconds after they had dropped into the guinea-grass, he and the others in his company were squinting along their sights and firing off their five-round clips. Trembling fingers snatched fresh cartridges from ammunition belts. Loaded clips. Snapped clips into rifles. Sighted. Squeezed triggers. Then automatically, the result of their long training, the regulars in Company H crawled forward a few feet through the grass and fired again. Petty and other rookies followed their cue. Sometimes he noticed that one or two soldiers close to him failed to move forward when the others did. Some writhed in pain. Others would never stir again.

They had wriggled forward some thirty or forty yards when suddenly a bugle sounded. To Petty, the signal seemed to waft from back where those jittery officers had been huddled under the trees.

"Cease fire?" roared a sunburned old private. *"Cease fire my ass!"*

At this moment, it seemed to Petty, there were only fifty to seventy-five men out in the grass mostly from his own company, with a scatter from other companies in his regiment.

Again the bugle sounded, louder and more insistently, its clarion notes stitching the rage of combat. Petty glanced at the regulars around him, ready to follow whatever example they would set. Roaring curses, they grudgingly began to slacken fire. Finally all stopped, flattening themselves on the ground, hugging the sweet earth, covering the best they could in the knee-high grass. The Spanish, apparently sensing the American confusion, redoubled their fire. Mauser bullets seemed to drive in sheets into the grass and jungle.

Thundering shells kept pounding across the savanna. Petty, sick with fear, pressed his face to earth, the peaceful smell of grass in his nostrils, the savage din of war in his ears and the merciless steel flying above. What now? They couldn't stay put, because the Spanish were chopping them to pieces. They couldn't fall back; the narrow trail was the only way back through the jungle, and it was glutted with troops pressing forward.

Maybe it was only four or five minutes they lay there, but it seemed like hours.

Petty gnashed his teeth. *Hell of a place to get us into*, he fumed, *then order us to stop firing, and just leave us here while the enemy wipes us out.*

They listened, listened as hard as they could for some additional command, listened with great longing, but heard none. They cursed and sobbed and prayed. Someone was asking for more than flesh and blood could endure.

It took all of Petty's self-control to hold fire, but the others were obeying the maddening bugle, so he followed suit. He sensed that the regulars around him felt as he did – that slow, excruciating, hours-long advance along the bloody trail, scourged by Spanish fire they couldn't return, had wound up muscles and nerves to a pitch of tension that only violent action could release. But they weren't about to turn tail and run – not mere minutes after plunging into the crucible, and for the first time having targets to shoot at.

To ask soldiers to like naked to pitiless enemy fire for any length of time, and not return it, was asking more than they could bear. At last, some high-strung old soldier let the enemy have a shot. Some other regular did the same. Two or three more did likewise. Petty aimed his Krag at the slot below the flag and gave them a good one.

Then that crazy bugler cut loose again, louder and more imperiously. This time nobody paid him any mind. They only quickened their fire until the roar of their fusillade drowned out the plaintive brass horn. Before long, a couple of American field guns chimed in.

Gathering up their fragmented courage, the soldiers in the grass started creeping slowly forward again, and now more and more Americans were boiling out of the jungle behind.

The mystery of why a bugler sounded cease-fire at this crucial juncture has never been explained. One possibility: some general officer decided that things had gotten so fouled up that they had better pull back and get organized – and also wait until General Lawton's 6,500-man division could finish the job at El Caney and link up with the main force for the San

Juan assault.

Lawton's original estimate of only two hours to overwhelm little El Caney would become an actual nine hours of savage combat, even though the Americans outnumbered Spanish defenders by more than ten to one.

Meanwhile, half a mile north of San Juan Hill, Roosevelt and his Rough Riders and a regiment of veteran black soldiers, the 9th Cavalry – all dismounted except for Roosevelt – were pushing on in a rip-roaring charge up Kettle Hill, so named because on its summit stood an enormous sugar-cane kettle, off which bullets were clanging.

In front of San Juan, it seemed to Petty that the crowding and bewilderment grew worse than ever, if that were possible. As the soldiers moved forward – crawling or dashing a few yards, then dropping in the grass to aim and fire – some began crisscrossing in front of Petty. As he sighted on the loophole below the flag, Corporal Seufert shifted directly in front of him, the back of his head almost in Petty's line of fire. Seufert had given him a bad time every chance he got. Just by lowering his Krag a few inches, he could put an end to that kind of crap. In the chaos of battle, who would ever know?

With a twinge of shame, he rejected the idea. Anywhere else, the thought probably wouldn't have occurred. But the frenzy of combat had fomented a reckless passion to strike at the enemy with all one's might. With the killing lust aroused, a guy could get a little careless about who the enemy was. Petty knew that Seufert hated his guts, and there was no love lost on his own part.

They scrambled forward a few yards, and hit the ground. They scrambled forward again, and hit the ground once more. The battle-din rose as more and more Americans stormed from the jungle gateway and out onto the savanna, their rifles adding to the crescendo.

Suddenly a terrific hammering resounded above the din. Lieutenant Parker's Gatlings were lashing the trenches on the hill, each hosing a stream of steel slugs at the rate of 350 per minute. A scatter of Spaniards leaped from the trenches and sprinted for the rear. Some were cut down in mid-flight, as if struck by an invisible giant. Cheers broke from the anguished Americans.

"Bully for Parker!"

"Give 'em hell!"

"The sound of the Gatlings," one man later wrote, "was the best sound I ever heard on a battlefield."

Minutes after Parker's Gatlings fired the sustained burst, Petty's jaw dropped at the sight: a Gatling gun and crew were hurtling across the savanna toward himself and other Americans in the grass. The driver, whipping his horses to a lather, yelled a warning: *"Hee-yaw! Hee-yaw!"*

Leaping to their feet, the soldiers flung themselves clear of plunging hooves and juggernaut wheels. *Must be switching to a better position*, Petty thought.

Farther and farther out on the savanna, the Americans were advancing. Loading and firing, sometimes kneeling, sometimes crouched, they fired as fast as they could squeeze off each five-round clip and re-load. Petty, re-loading, accidentally grabbed his rifle barrel. It was so hot he yelped in pain.

By this time, thousands of Americans had surged out of the jungle and onto the savanna. Bullets sprayed into the Americans, shells split with thunderclaps, earth rocked underfoot – Spanish steel was harvesting American flesh. The more Americans that poured from the jungle, the faster rose the toll of killed and wounded. Many Americans on the savanna had fired off perhaps two-thirds of their ammunition. At that rate, it couldn't last much longer, yet they could hardly be frugal with ammunition while the enemy was throwing everything they had.

To try to replenish their supply via the troop-choked trail would have been calamitous. To fall back into the jungle would have been equally disastrous – it would give the Spanish time to rush in the 8,000 reinforcements who at this very moment were pushing forward on a forced march from Manzanillo.

It was a dire moment.

Chapter 14:
"Sound the Charge!"

Crouching low and firing at will, the bedeviled soldiers lurched farther onto the savanna. It was impossible to retreat and suicide to stay put.

No prudent commander would have deliberately ordered this crazy frontal advance in broad daylight against such heavily-fortified heights. Without even scouting the terrain properly? With only token artillery support against a thousand magazine rifles? Someone had blundered – badly.

Mausers flamed and crackled in terrifying crescendos. Slugs buzzed through the air like angry bees. Petty heard the gruesome chug as a whizzing bullet smote the soldier next to him. Shells detonated among the Americans with crack-of-doom explosions. Flying steel tore into flesh and blood. Americans were falling, falling. Some vented low groans, some hollered in confusion, some dropped soundlessly. *Lord, help me*, Petty prayed.

Suddenly he realized there was no one in front of him and no one very close on either side. *At last*, he thought, *maybe now we're gonna deploy properly as we should've done when we busted out of the jungle*. He jerked his head right and left. This forward line seemed reasonably straight as far as he could make out. He was slowly moving ahead with the tremulous first wave. It was a wholly instinctive advance, unordered and unprepared.

His thoughts flickered back to the jungle exit from which the troops had boiled in such wild confusion, swept without warning onto the lethal savanna, propelled by the momentum of the onrushing column. *Like cattle pouring from the chute into the slaughter-pen*, it seemed to Petty. There was no turning back. The trail behind was clogged with troops pressing forward, unaware of what lay in front. Without even sending out scouts, the Americans had blundered into the abattoir.

Somewhere behind, correspondent Stephen Crane overheard a British attaché say to another Britisher as they stared at the drama unfolding on the savanna: "Why, they're trying to take the position!"

"I think they are," Crane interrupted with a gasp.

"But they can't do it, you know – it's impossible!" the Britisher said, his voice breaking. "By God it's plucky, but they can't do it!"

"Never in the world," his companion agreed. "It's slaughter, absolute slaughter."

As Petty's thoughts rushed back to the thousands of troops behind, he wondered if they, too, had reeled and staggered in the same horrible confusion as his own outfit had when it bolted from the jungle and hit the savanna. Glancing over his shoulder, he was momentarily transfixed. From rising ground, he glimpsed the whole field behind, a never-to-be-forgotten spectacle.

Up the gentle slope, through veils of smoke drifting across the wide field of grass, his comrades were coming on, a blue-shirted horde of Americans scattered over the savanna back to the shaggy jungle, loading and firing, yelling and cursing, agonizing in the vortex of enemy fire. Rifles and regimental colors glittered in the midday sun. It was magnificent and terrible – magnificent with the rage of thousands of men in combat, terrible with the havoc of Spanish steel.

It happened in a flash. All fear was blown away from Petty's mind by some wild madness that shook him, he would always remember, as a cat shakes a mouse. It was a kind of electric tremor, an ungovernable excitement, a primal ecstasy he had never felt before and would never feel again.

He whirled back toward the enemy hill. Again he saw that tantalizing flag on the blockhouse. An utterly reckless idea struck him, flooding his brain. *Petty*, he said to himself, *you're going up that hill!*

Whipping off his slouch hat, he waved it high, erupted with a barbaric yell – surprising himself with its force and suddenness – and sprinted forward.

Off to the left, Lieutenant Anderson watched with mouth agape. "Crazy son-of-a-bitch!" A moment later, an impulse overcame him. "Let's go!" he yelled and dashed after Petty, with several enlisted men charging behind.

Capt. William Auman, regimental CO, witnessed this peculiar happening. "Jesus H. Christ!" After a thunderstruck moment, he roared at the bugler: "*Sound the charge!*"

The dumfounded bugler raised his instrument to his lips. As the high, thrilling, prestissimo notes from the brass horn trumpeted through the iron din, thousands of bewildered soldiers cut loose with exultant cheers and surged forward. Stephen Crane heard another newspaperman yell: "*By God – there go our boys up the hill!*"

Crane later wrote: "There is many a good American who would give an arm to get the thrill of patriotic insanity that coursed through us when we heard that yell. Yes, they were going up the hill, up the hill. It was the best moment of anybody's life."

Another eyewitness, H.J. Whigham of the Chicago *Tribune*, wrote: "The assault came with astonishing abruptness from our center and left."

That was about where Kent's division had boiled out of the jungle gateway. The Rough Riders, of course, were engaged about a half mile away on the *right*.

Vaguely, Petty wondered why the Spanish didn't gun him down as he raced toward them in plain view. By plunging recklessly into the forefront, he was making a conspicuous target of himself, hazarding the focus of concentrated fury from enemy weapons. Paradoxically, this rash act may have been saving him. Before long, few bullets were drilling the air around him – perhaps because the thousands of Americans in the blue horde behind him offered an irresistible target, impossible to miss.

And now the contour of the hill began to shelter him from enemy fire. The Spanish also had blundered badly. They had entrenched on the hill's actual crest, instead of the "military crest," which is the hip-roof angle of a hill, the rim from which the defender can fire down on the assailant as he reaches the foot. Unwittingly the Spanish had created a blind zone screened from their direct fire.

Now the Gatlings, which had been trundled to a new position, ended what had seemed like a too-long silence. Three of Parker's "coffee-grinders" opened fire simultaneously, scourging the summit and blockhouse with a devil's tattoo of flying steel. A scatter of Spanish defenders leaped from their trenches and vanished over the hill.

Feverishly, Petty kept waving his hat high as he ran. The slightly-uphill distance to the foot of the hill was a power of yards farther than it had seemed. Gasping for breath and half-blinded by sweat, he nearly crashed headlong into a barbed wire fence six or seven feet high, barring his way at the foot of the hill.

Frantically he hacked at it with his bayonet – it was no use. He grabbed a post and tried to jerk it over. That was no good either. On each side of the post, the wire was strongly lashed to small trees. For a panicky moment he felt sick with defeat.

Then he grabbed the post, stepped up on the wires and scrambled over, ripping his pants. Now he thrashed farther up the hill, which from the fence pitched up sharply at about a forty-five degree angle.

Thirty feet farther, he was barricaded by another barbed wire fence. Just as he clambered to the top, a sharp command startled him:

"*Stop!*"

Halfway over, he hesitated, glanced back, then grudgingly dropped back on the downhill side. Five men from his own company loped up to within a few yards of the first fence – Lieutenant Anderson, Corporal Seufert and three privates.

Baffled, Petty just stood there, staring at Anderson.

Meanwhile the swarming thousands of other Americans, savaged by shot and shell, were pounding forward, their cheers ringing out across the smoky savanna.

Without a word or gesture, Anderson lurched forward.

Petty took that as a signal to go again.

Whirling, he flung himself at the fence, thrashed over it and scrambled another thirty feet up the rough slope as fast as aching legs could propel him – to a third fence! Just as he started to climb:

"*Stop!*"

Grudgingly, Petty stepped back to the ground and looked back at Anderson.

"Come back here!" Anderson yelled. "We don't know what's up there yet!"

Sullenly, Petty shuffled back to the second fence and stopped, alert for any move that Anderson would make.

"Hey, Petty," Seufert jeered, "who the hell do you think you are – the whole damn show?"

Petty let a slow grin crease his face. It seemed a bizarre time and place for complaints of that sort. If he had gotten out of line in sparking the charge, it was more the officers' fault than his, because they had let things get out of hand back there in the jungle. Now all that mattered was that he felt on fire with a reckless urge. All instincts for caution were overwhelmed by a crazy impulse to fling himself alone at any challenge he might meet up on top.

If I can just get that flag, he thought, *I'll die happy*.

Maybe he *was* trying to steal the show.

Standing there, bushed to the socks and sucking wind, mind whirling, eyes roving frantically, he spotted a gash under the third fence – torrential rains had gouged away some soil. Maybe he could weasel through that tiny gully, a damn sight easier than floundering over the barbed wire while toting his Krag.

In the last few minutes, while Petty had been scrambling up the hill and Anderson and his men pursuing him to the base of the hill, the banging of American field guns and the chatter of Gatlings had subsided by degrees. As Petty scrambled up to the third fence, the firing stopped utterly.

All at once the artillery and Gatlings exploded into life again, punishing the hilltop. Petty, hugging the ground some fifty yards below the blockhouse, watched dust clouds mushroom as the American guns worked over the fort, showering splinters from the log walls and churning up the trenches round about. For five solid minutes the Gatlings poured it on. If Petty had kept going, he no doubt would have caught it from friendly fire.

Suddenly at the Gatling emplacement, Parker saw someone frantically wave a white handkerchief. At the same moment, Captain Landis shouted to Parker:

"Better stop! Our own men are climbing the ridge!"

"*Cease fire!*"

As abruptly as it has started, the furious raking stopped. The time by Parker's watch was 1:23 p.m. As the rattle of Gatlings and din of shellbursts faded away, leaving only a ringing in his ears, Petty now heard the continuous crackling of rifles and waves of jubilant cheers from the oncoming Americans.

Without a word or gesture, Anderson quickly stepped

toward the first fence at the base of the hill.

That was Petty's signal to go again: he hurled himself into the hole under the third fence, wriggled through, and dashed up the hill on legs that were growing leaden. Now the rounding-off crest of the hill cut him off from any view of Anderson and his men.

Correspondent Stephen Bonsal also was watching the assault: "You could count on the fingers of your hand the brave men who were leading it, and even as you counted they grew fewer, the arms of some going up wildly in the air as they fell."

Correspondent Davis, from his vantage point on Kettle Hill where he was covering the Rough Riders, also observed that the number of men in the forefront of the San Juan assault appeared woefully small: "It seemed as if someone had made an awful and terrible mistake. One's instinct was to call them to come back.

"The thing that impressed one the most was that they were so few…You felt that someone had blundered and that those few men were blindly following out some madman's mad order…

"There were a few men in advance, bunched together and creeping up a steep, sunny hill, the tops of which roared and flashed with flame."

The Rough Riders, with great valor and energy, were assaulting Spanish entrenchments on Kettle Hill half a mile to the northeast, and it would not be until some hours later that they would link up with the infantry on the San Juan ridge. Aiding the Rough Riders was a superb regiment of veteran black troopers, the 9th Calvary, the legendary "Buffalo Soldiers" of the American West.

One Rough Rider, Capt. Bucky O'Neill, a famous marshal from Arizona, didn't think an officer should ever take cover,

"I'm here to lead my men, not to protect myself," he told Roosevelt.

"Let's go get 'em boys!" O'Neill shouted, pointing at

Kettle Hill. "You'll find 'em up there!"

Spanish bullets were coming thick and fast. "Get down, captain!" a sergeant yelled. "You're in plain view!"

"The Spanish bullet isn't made that will kill me," O'Neill scoffed with a grin.

Seconds later, he dropped, a bullet in his head.

* * * * *

The gentle breeze that had been wafting over the San Jan summit an hour earlier, ruffling the Spanish flag on the blockhouse, had gone away. The air was stifling hot and motionless.

Petty rushed toward the blockhouse, scanning the building for the enemy flag. In vain. Corpses of several horses lay about. Bodies of Spanish dead and dying were strewn grotesquely on the torn ground. Fanning his Krag from side to side, Petty was ready to nail anything with a suspicious twitch. Gasping for breath, he coughed in air that was still choked with dust from the bombardment. He felt slightly ill from the reek of fresh blood in his nostrils.

Closing on the blockhouse, he heard a mad scurry of feet and dashed around the corner, rifle at the ready – four Spaniards dashed pell-mell from the far side. Quickly he squeezed off several shots as the soldiers raced down the far side of the hill and dove into brush. Just then, out of the corner of his eye, he caught a light-colored flash on the ground a score of yards to one side of the blockhouse. Two sombreros, seemingly on ground level, slowly bobbed up and down.

As he charged with Krag ready to fire, the sombreros slowly rose above what Petty now saw was a two-man rifle pit, many of which had been excavated around the summit of the hill; long trenches had been dug on each side of the blockhouse.

Two pairs of hands shot up. The sombreros rose higher,

shading the stricken faces of two trembling Spaniards, both stammering at a furious rate. Petty didn't understand Spanish, but their demeanor was eloquent: they begged him not to shoot. Petty felt no hate – they were beaten men.

Just then, rapid footsteps pounded behind and he spun with his Krag, confronting a black private, probably from the 24th Infantry. Petty let go a profound sigh of relief and lowered his Krag. The black soldier trained his rifle on the prisoners.

"What we gonna do with 'em?" he asked.

Petty leveled his Krag back on the Spaniards.

"Nothing!"

"Le's dust 'em off!"

"Naw! We're taking 'em prisoners!"

Petty kept one wary eye on the Spaniards and one on the black soldier. The latter shrugged, turned and trotted back down the hill.

Before long, Anderson and his party emerged on the crest, perhaps eight to ten minutes after Petty had reached the blockhouse. When Anderson had heard Petty's shots at the fleeing Spanish, but couldn't see what had actually transpired, he may have surmised that Petty had caught it from the enemy. But when the black soldier jogged back safely, he no doubt concluded that the hill had been neutralized.

The prisoners, hands reaching high, were still standing in the rifle pit. Anderson directed his Colt .45 at them with one hand, and with the other motioned them to climb out. They obeyed with fear and trembling. Without a word to Petty, Anderson started back down the hill, escorting the two prisoners. They were the only prisoners captured in the San Juan battle.

Petty, grimy with dirt and sweat and drunk with fatigue, staggered over to the blockhouse where the men who had come up with Anderson were clustered. With a big grin, Pvt. Arthur Agnew triumphantly held up the red-and-yellow Spanish flag – the flag that had floated over the blockhouse, arousing Petty's animus as he lay with his outfit in the deadly grass at the bottom of the hill.

"Where'd you find that damn thing?" Petty asked.

"Dangling right here at the corner," Agnew said. "Staff was practically shot in two."

"Gimme that thing," a soldier said, snatching the flag. He tore off a strip and stuffed it in his pocket. "I'm gonna keep that as a little souvenir."

"Lemme have a piece," Petty said, and ripped off another strip.

Pvt. Harley Pierce did the same and others followed suit. Just then a tall, slender, white-haired officer stalked up to the group.

"What's that, boys?"

"That damn flag, sir."

"Why the hell did you tear it? We should've kept it as a battle trophy!"

Scowling and shaking his head, he turned and marched off, mumbling something about knot-heads.

As the soldiers looked at each other sheepishly, one fixed his eyes on Petty's face.

"What's the matter with *you*?" he asked Petty.

"Nothing – why?"

"Your face is *green*! As green as grass!"

"Really?"

"How ya feel?"

"Okay, I guess. Just pooped out."

Another solder squinted at Petty's face and offered a diagnosis: "His gall-bladder overflowed. He got too hot."

In fact, Petty had gotten so heated up during his ordeal in the midday sun that he had nearly passed out a time or two. Only his reckless impulse had kept driving him on. The weird color in his face, whatever the cause, vanished before long.

During this few minutes' recess in the battle, the increasing number of Americans collecting on the summit had been swaggering around heedlessly as if there wasn't a Spaniard any closer than Santiago. Down the slope in the west, the enemy stronghold sprawled two miles away, its red-tile roofs glowing in the sun – behind a diabolic maze of barbed wire and forts.

Suddenly a volley of bullets ripped overhead with a fearful noise. A sergeant, his face dark with fury, glared down toward the jungle. Thousands of Americans were still thronging up the slopes of the ridge.

"Tell those damn fools down there to stop firing!" he roared. "They'll kill us all!"

Seconds later, another volley stormed upon the hill, this time raking the soldiers on the crest. As half-a-dozen men dropped, some mortally wounded, the rest flung themselves into rifle pits and trenches. One soldier, with blood spurting from his chest, collapsed against Petty.

They got the direction that time: the Spanish had regrouped and were trying to take the hill back.

Illustration of the capture of San Juan Hill.

Chapter 15: Agony on the Ridge

Hour after seemingly endless hour during all that pitiless afternoon, with the world seeming one great throb of pain, the Americans crouched behind the enemy dead, propping up their bodies as shields against enemy fire, blasting away at Spanish targets.

Losing their comrades one by one: suddenly one would suffer a terrible wrench or be spun by an unseen force, then collapse like a marionette. And then the echo of enemy musketry, a soul-sickening death rattle.

The Spanish, now entrenched in their second defense line, were confident that the guns of Cervera's fleet, bristling in Santiago bay, posed a murderous threat to the invaders.

"Remember that bunch of skittish officers back there?" Petty asked, drawing a bead on an enemy flag. "Under the trees? Acting crazy like they didn't know what they was doing?"

Ball wiped sweat from his dirt-streaked face. "Yeah, what about 'em?"

"I figure that's how everything got all fouled up." He squeezed the trigger. "If they didn't know what to do, how the hell was we sposed to know? Reckon they was just looking for some excuse to pull back – any excuse at all."

"Maybe they had the right idea after all. Maybe we shoulda never charged the hill."

"We just gotta hang on," Petty said. "Grit our teeth and hang on 'til we can't hang on no longer. Then hang on another little bit."

"Times it seems them damn Spanish are gonna grab the hill back, and all the ground we got hold of and all the blood we spilled for it will be gone down by the crick," Fay said.

"Just remember, Fay, this ain't no picnic for the Spanish, neither."

At last some reserves trickled up the hill and crawled into firing position near the men of Company H.

"Where the hell you guys *been*?" Petty hollered in exasperation. "Where ya been hiding?"

"Just following the crowd," said one. "Nobody told us there was any big hurry."

Sergeant O'Neill crawled forward. "Hey, boys, pass the word along the line – General Kent's orders: dig in and get ready for a possible counter-attack."

Lacking picks and shovels, they chipped and hacked into the obstinate ground with their bayonets, scooping out the loose dirt with bare hands and empty meat cans. Bit by bit, they struggled to reinforce their feeble clutch on the fire-swept ridge.

A corporal leading a mule train halted the animals just below the brow of the hill. Wooden boxes were lashed on the mules.

"Ammo over here!" Petty sang out.

"Come and get it, soldier," the corporal said, untying ropes lashing the boxes to the mules, letting the boxes drop to the ground. Greedily Petty seized a box and pried off the lid with his bayonet. Grabbing handfuls of cartridges, he stuffed some in his pockets and refilled his two ammunition belts.

"Take it easy, boys," he said, as the other soldiers piled in. "Plenty here for everybody."

Somewhere back down there in the high guinea-grass near the jungle where so many good soldiers had been killed and wounded, Petty had snatched up a second belt, which was nearly full of cartridges. Maybe he had seized it from some fallen soldier, or picked it up where some poor wounded man had flung it off so he could breathe easier. He couldn't remember exactly.

The ammunition hadn't come up any too soon. Like Petty, most of the others had just about used up their original supply.

Soldiers entrench themselves on San Juan Hill to guard against a Spanish counter-attack (courtesy National Archives)

Meanwhile, General Shafter rode up El Pozo Hill for a wide-ranging view of the terrain. As he sat on his horse on the hill about 2 o'clock in the afternoon, he felt nauseated as he began to realize the terrible mistake he made in engaging his whole army on a front nearly seven miles long. Later, as casualty reports dribbled in, he began to divine the full measure of his blunder.

Where were Pando and his 8,000? That was the question that fretted Shafter the most. The day before, he had learned that Pando and his legions had thrust to within thirty miles of Santiago. If he attacked the Americans' rear – say, the almost totally unguarded supply base at Siboney – disaster would be virtually guaranteed.

By mid-afternoon, the Americans on San Juan were half-mad with thirst, having drained the last drops in their canteens by mid-morning. Their furious expenditure of energy in the broiling sun had sucked up all the excess moisture in their bodies.

"Never been so thirsty in all me born days," one soldier croaked weakly.

"Throat's dry as a bone," another said in a hoarse whisper.

"Been spitting cotton all afternoon," Petty rasped.

"Sergeant," Lieutenant Anderson addressed O'Neill.

"Sir?"

"Form a water detail, and go find some. Take as many canteens as you can carry."

"Yes, sir...okay, boys, let's have some volunteers!" O'Neill shouted.

"For what?"

"Go for water!"

"Sign me up!"

Four privates volunteered. "You going?" Ball asked.

"Naw," Petty said. "Don't wanna leave the line. If them damn Spaniards decide to take the hill back, I wanna be here to help give 'em a little ol' reception party."

The soldiers collected all the canteens they figured they could carry when full of water, fastened them to cartridge belts, and trekked down the hill. In an hour and a half, they staggered back, belts laden with heavy canteens.

"Water!"

One soldier drank and wrinkled his nose. "Smells pretty awful."

Petty chugalugged half a canteen. "Yeah, but I never tasted water before that was so close to heaven."

Late in the afternoon, breathless runners handed General Kent two requests almost simultaneously. One came from Colonel Wood, commanding the Rough Riders, and one from General Sumner, asking for aid for his "hard-pressed" cavalry, which included the Rough Riders. Kent dispatched the 13th Infantry, which had already suffered heavy losses in killed and wounded.

Roosevelt and his men on a crest overlooking Santiago. Roosevelt called his men "children of the dragon's blood." (courtesy National Archives)

Far from having spearheaded the charge at San Juan, as legend has it, the Rough Riders were in fact calling for help from the brutally-mauled infantry that had in actuality stormed the hill.

In the lee of the ridge, sheltered from enemy fire, the men of the 13th tramped three-quarters of a mile along the right flank of the American positions. Now they approached a patch of jungle.

"Halt...Deploy!"

Fanning out, they thudded to the ground on a grassy knoll, taking their intervals. Three noncoms, crouching low, slunk forward into the jungle. In half an hour, they filtered back.

"Find 'em?"

"Naw! But they gotta be here someplace."

The distinctive crack of Krag rifles reverberated from seemingly two or three hundred yards ahead.

"What outfit is it?"

"Rough Riders."

"Them's who we're looking for."

A scatter of slugs smacked into the ground close by. Instantly the soldiers flattened in the grass.

Petty raised his head cautiously. "Judging by the kind of light way they hit the ground," he said, "I'd say them Spanish are firing from a powerful distance."

Slowly and silently, Ball turned his face toward Petty. Though Petty was preoccupied in trying to spot some sign of friend or foe in the distant heat-shimmer, there was something in Ball's peculiarly sluggish contortion that penetrated his awareness. He glanced at him: Ball's face was twisted with pain.

"You hit?"

"They got me that time," he gasped.

"Where?"

"Leg."

"Lemme see it."

Petty gently pulled up the trouser leg. From a clean hole in Ball's calf, a moderate trickle of blood was flowing.

"Think you can walk?"

"Damn if I know."

"Try."

Petty helped him to his feet. But when Ball shifted some of his weight onto the wounded leg, he clenched his teeth to stifle a cry, and his face went white.

"Maybe a bone's broken," Petty said. "Hey," he called to another soldier. "Give me a hand, will ya?"

The two picked Ball up and carried him downhill about thirty yards, then gently lowered him into the grass.

"I'm gonna fix you a tourniquet," Petty said, and removed Ball's belt. He wrapped it around the calf several times and buckled it tight. "Unloosen it about every half hour, and let it bleed a minute or two, then buckle it up again," he said.

"You jus' gonna leave me here?"

"Got no choice. We'll be moving back to the blockhouse any second. Hospital corpsmen'll be along pretty quick. They'll give you a nice ride in a wagon back to Siboney. Looks like you'll be living the life of Riley for a spell." Petty gripped Ball's hand firmly, then let go reluctantly. "See ya later, pardner."

Petty felt keen remorse over leaving Ball there alone on the grassy knoll, wounded and with scant protection from enemy snipers. But there was nothing more he could do. There was no way to carry him.

Ever since Petty had joined the company in Tampa, Ball had been his friend and advisor. It wasn't Ball's fault that Petty wasn't inclined to take much advice from anyone. Being number one and number two in the first set of four in their platoon, they were always side-by-side on the march. Petty admired Ball as a first-rate soldier.

Leaving Ball behind, the soldiers crept back to the top of the knoll and rejoined the others. Petty looked back and Ball waved to him.

"All right, boys," a sergeant hollered. "Column o' twos!"

Scrambling to their feet, the soldiers scurried downhill a short distance behind the knoll and formed into two columns.

In the lee of the ridge, they plodded back to their old position near the blockhouse, where they were ordered to dig trenches.

"Sarge," Petty said to O'Neill, "Ball caught one in the leg over at the end of the ridge, and we need some corpsmen to take him down to the field hospital." Petty described the exact location where Ball would be found, and O'Neill saw to it that medics were dispatched.

"Seems like the fighting is dying down," someone said after awhile.

"Yeah, but never can tell when it'll flare up again," Petty said. "This war ain't over by a damn sight."

In a little time, the sporadic firing also died away. Now that all the weapons on San Juan were silent, the Americans beleaguered in sore straits on the ridge could plainly hear the firing at El Caney, borne on the hot air from four miles away – the sputtering crackle of rifles, the slamming-door sound of field guns and the ugly *crumps* of shell-bursts.

Battle-devastated blockhouse on San Juan Hill (courtesy National Archives)

At El Caney, the Spanish kept on fighting long after their cause was hopeless. Having heard rumors that the Americans slaughtered prisoners, they chose to die fighting, since death seemed inevitable. A strongly-built blockhouse defended by thirty-five Spaniards was offering the fiercest resistance. The Spanish were shooting through loopholes, and American bullets couldn't penetrate the structure's heavy timbers, and found the loopholes too small as targets.

Nineteen Americans were ordered to climb to the roof. The first four jumped into the courtyard and were killed immediately. Then the rest dropped in, all at the same time. For twenty minutes there followed an extremely desperate close-quarter combat. It ended with all thirty-five Spaniards dead, and the fifteen Americans as survivors.

A Spanish officer who lived through the day-long El Caney battle said, "I have never seen anything to equal the courage and dash of those Americans, who, stripped to their waist, offering their naked breasts to our murderous fire, literally threw themselves on our trenches, on the very muzzles of our guns."

All told, 377 Americans were killed or wounded at El Caney. Spanish losses were about 320 killed or wounded. The remaining Spanish defenders, something over 100, somehow escaped to Santiago. Among the American wounded was the black-bearded correspondent James Creelman, struck down when a bullet shattered his left arm as he led a bayonet charge. Like Davis at Las Guasimas, Creelman in the heat of action forgot he was supposed to be a noncombatant. Creelman, in 1894, had won fame during the Japanese invasion of Manchuria with his unvarnished account of the massacre of Port Arthur's population. He spurned a bribe from the Japanese to soft-pedal the story.

At El Caney, someone knelt in the grass beside the wounded Creelman and put his hand on his fevered brow. Opening his eyes, he saw his publisher, W.R. Hearst, straw hat on his head, revolver at his belt, pencil and notebook in hand. Slowly, interrupted now and then by Mauser bullets zipping too close for comfort, Hearst took down Creelman's story of the battle.

"I'm sorry you're hurt," Hearst said with a compassionate look. Then his face brightened. "But wasn't it a splendid fight? We must beat every paper in the world!"

Creelman later wrote: "The man who had provoked the war had come to see the result with his own eyes, and, finding one of his correspondents prostrate, was doing the work himself."

Ambulance trundles along after the battle (courtesy National Archives)

As the last bloody embers of a spectacular sunset flickered out in the darkening skies, General Wheeler – who had recovered enough to resume his place as senior commander at the front – scrawled a note to General Shafter:

The positions which our men have carried were very strong, and the intrenchments [sic] were also very strong. A number of officers have appealed to me to have our line withdrawn, and to take up a strong position farther back, and I expect they will appeal to you. I have positively discountenanced this, as it would cost us much prestige. The lines are now very thin, as so many men have gone to the rear with the wounded and so many are exhausted. We ought to hold on to-morrow [sic], but I fear it will be a severe day.

Shafter read the note while racked with a bout of fever. Some of the words stuck in his fevered brain, and for hours he kept hearing them over and over like a broken record: *"The lines are now very thin...so many are exhausted...I fear it will be a severe day."*

Restlessly, Shafter turned over on his cot and groaned to his aide, Colonel McClernand: "I don't know whether we've gained a victory or brought on a disaster!"

In the warm darkness, the Americans on San Juan now watched pinpoints of light sparkle in the Spanish lines as their field guns broke the uneasy silence, re-opening fire on the San Juan ridge. As the Americans dived for cover, an angry accompaniment of Spanish musketry joined the iron chorus.

Spanish resistance was stiffening, apparently anticipating the imminent arrival of Pando and his men. And more signs of dreaded disease were cropping up among the Americans. Shafter's problems would have been formidable even for a commanding general in the best of health. Even for an army in the best of health.

Chapter 16:
Shafter Ponders Retreat

All night the Americans fought desperately to hold the ridge, and in exhaustion's slow motion they dug trenches and buried the dead – American and Spanish. They also buried the Spaniards' dead horses. They buried the men and horses in the trenches the Spanish had dug that were too far back to be of any other use to the Americans.

Avoiding the Spanish error, the Americans were entrenching on the military crest – on the side facing Santiago.

In the nerve-racking hours of darkness, jittery soldiers blasted away at strange noises and peculiar shadows, shadows their overwrought minds had hallucinated into menacing shapes.

Many bone-weary frontline soldiers had to be called on by corpsmen to help carry the wounded back to the field hospital at El Pozo. This sapped the thin line of many able-bodied defenders. All night, knowing how bereft they were of fighting men, officers dreaded a counter-attack against their weak line on the ridge.

Hundreds of other wounded were not so fortunate as to be taken to the field hospital right away. Through the long night they lay on the battlefield in untended agony, haunting the darkness with their moans of pain and piteous cries for water.

Petty saw one wounded soldier lying close to the route his regiment followed as it was shifted here and there from time to time to cope with changing enemy pressures. Having rolled downhill from where he had been hit, the wounded man was caked with blood and dirt. His clothing had tangled around his arms and head, hiding his face. To Petty there seemed little resemblance to a human being in the filthy, blood-encrusted, misshapen heap that vented such unearthly moans. It was a tug-of-war between body and soul, with the soul begging the body to let it go free. Sadly, he thought of Fay Ball, wounded and abandoned on the grassy knoll far on the right, and wondered if hospital corpsmen had found him and taken him to the field hospital.

Meanwhile, Roosevelt dashed off a sulfurous letter to his friend, Senator Henry Cabot Lodge:

Not since the campaign of Crassus against the Parthians has there been so criminally incompetent a General as Shafter; and not since the expedition against Walcheren has there been grosser mismanagement than this. The battle simply fought itself; three of the Brigade Commanders, most of the Colonels, and all the regiments could not be surpassed; but Shafter never came within three miles of the line, and never has come; the confusion is incredible...

At last the supply wagons arrived at the front, and all night they creaked and rattled along the ridge, so that before dawn every soldier on the line had been doled out some hardtack, which they consumed with gusto only famished bellies know.

Back at El Pozo, Shafter was staggered by the incoming casualty reports. Much later, the final reckoning would disclose that 1,475 Americans had been killed or wounded between sunrise and sunset on July 1. To a foreign attaché, Shafter desolately unburdened himself: "I am prostrate in body and mind."

"He could confess this to a stranger," correspondent Davis scribbled wrathfully, "and yet, so great was the obstinacy, so great the vanity and self-confidence of the man, that, although he held the lives and health of 13,000 soldiers in his care, he did not ask to be relieved of his command."

Shafter not only was almost incapacitated from the infernal heat, his ponderous bulk, and the weight of his 63 years, but now he had been crippled by a "beastly attack of gout." Two privates were assigned to build a platform with steps, to enable Shafter to mount his horse. Thus he rode about, with his sore foot wrapped in a gunnysack and his head reeling with vertigo. Very likely his suffering affected his presence of mind and accounted for some of the blunders he would be blamed for.

Meanwhile, since afternoon, the wounded had been coming down from the front. Many, borne rear-ward in army wagons, suffered intensely as the jolting wagons plunged down, then were jerked up, the steep banks of the many streams that had to be forded on the way back. Some wounded walked the distance, if able. At the field hospital near El Pozo, surgeons were inundated by the tide of wounded streaming back from the front. Many of the wounded hadn't had water or food for twelve hours or more, and had been exposed all day to the merciless sun.

Late that night, surgeons worked partly by moonlight and partly under flickering candles held by attendants. Sometimes Spanish snipers roosting in treetops started trading shots with American sentinels. Medics had to blow out the candles so they wouldn't draw enemy fire.

Yet before dawn on Saturday, July 2, the surgeons performed over 300 operations. Most of the soldiers operated on had to then spend the rest of the night lying in the wet grass and drenching dew, without covering, without food or water. There was moaning everywhere. All night, two men called for someone to come and kill them.

At first light Saturday morning, all along the front line Spanish artillery opened fire, lobbing shells at American positions. A sudden assault by Spanish infantry ground forward to within 600 yards of the Americans before being stopped in its tracks.

At El Pozo, the agony of the wounded increased as the rising sun brought burning heat and aggravated their thirst. More creaking wagons loaded with wounded started surging down from the front, and the entire hospital corps turned out to take care of them. This left the suffering men on the ground in the care of camp cooks and lesser-wounded soldiers, who limped painfully about, fetching water and hardtack for their tormented comrades.

Back at Siboney, Dr. Lagarde, a bleary-eyed army surgeon, handed Red Cross nurse Janet Jennings an order from Shafter. It authorized Clara Barton to seize any army wagons she could find and use them to transport hospital supplies to the front.

"Where are the army's hospital supplies?" nurse Jennings asked the doctor.

"I don't know."

"Where's your service?"

"I don't know!"

"You don't know?" She threw up her hands, a look of sick dismay blemishing her young face. "You mean you brought 17,000 men to Cuba and rushed them up to the front without making any preparations for taking care of the wounded? How in heaven's name could you let that happen?"

"I don't know!" Dr. Lagarde moaned. Tears welled in his red-rimmed eyes. "God only knows what we could have done without the Red Cross. Our only hope is the help you can give us. If you can get supplies up to the front, you can do more than I can tell!"

On the *State of Texas*, a shocked Clara Barton heard the story, then gave crisp orders. That night, her aides ferreted supplies out of the ship's hold, landed them at daylight, and seized and loaded some army wagons. On one wagon, the plucky 77-year-old Barton bounced up to the front to see for herself what kind of medical folly this cockamamie army had brought on itself.

Some prisoners captured at El Caney were taken to headquarters on Saturday morning, dreading they would be shot. As a squad of rifle-carrying Americans approached to relieve the guard, the prisoners assumed it was a firing party: terror-stricken, they sank to their knees, awaiting their fate. It took an interpreter no little time to convince them they would be spared and would be well taken care of.

One Spanish lieutenant grumbled that the Americans hadn't fought fairly. "When they fire a volley only half fires," he said, "and the other half comes ahead, and then they fire and the rest come ahead, and they keep doing that."

Shafter's army now verged on utter exhaustion, teetering on the cliff-edge of disaster. Originally, he planned to capture the Santiago forts, snip the wires connecting them to harbor mines, and clear the way for Sampson to enter and loose his thunder on any remaining resistance. Now, knowing he could never overcome Santiago without help, he sent a message to Sampson:

I urge that you make every effort to force the entrance to avoid future losses among my men, which are already very heavy.

But Sampson refused to risk the loss of one or more of his warships on a job that the infantry could take care of. His ships, he explained, were irreplaceable. Soldiers, on the other hand, were expendable.

* * * * *

Early Saturday afternoon, Petty's outfit slogged back to its former place on the hill near the blockhouse, passing by the piteously-moaning soldier, who had been lying there now some thirty hours that Petty knew of. He began to think it would be a mercy to plunge his bayonet into the grotesque creature and put it out of its misery.

Later that afternoon, a tremendous storm buffeted the countryside, turning trails and roads into impassable bogs. Obviously, continued heavy rains would reduce transportation to utter chaos. Despite the storm, meager rations of bacon and coffee were carried up to the lines.

Skies cleared by evening. Sounds of rifle fire echoed sporadically and the great yellow moon glimmered on the rain-wet hills. General Shafer summoned his division commanders to El Pozo for a council of war. They found the commanding general lying supine on a door that had been taken from its hinges on the El Pozo farmhouse, and now rested on sawhorses. Shocked at the sight of their commander's obvious physical incapacitation, they gave him a rather strained greeting. Close by, Shafter's aides and his cavalry escort loitered by their horses, leaning on their saddles, gossiping and speculating on what would be the upshot of this powwow.

Now talking quietly, the generals huddled to study the problems: Santiago was surrounded by a diabolical maze of entrenchments and barbed wire tangles. On the east and southeast, ten blockhouses dominated the defense lines, each bristling with cannon. At Aguadores, a stone fort glowered, studded with cannon that threatened the coastal approach to Santiago. On the northern sector, no artillery had been placed: the Spanish were confident that Admiral Cervera's naval cannon would annihilate any American approach from that direction. And a Cuban scout had informed Shafter that 1,000 Spanish marines, with artillery, had been landed in Santiago from Cervera's fleet.

"I've called you here," Shafter said weakly, "to get your

opinions. I've been told by many people today that it's absolutely necessary for us to retreat to save ourselves."

"With all due respect, Bill," Lawton said, "Save ourselves from what?"

Shafter raised himself on an elbow and with his finger drew an imaginary arc on the map that Colonel McClernand had placed on his stomach. He ran the arc back to Siboney.

"Save ourselves from being enfiladed and cut off from our supplies. An attack by the Spanish with a few fresh troops could carry us down to utter defeat. We're totally unguarded at Siboney."

Some of the generals expressed dismay at the horrendous casualties, the enormous problems of transporting the wounded to the rear, the staggering difficulties of bringing up supplies – and their strong hunch that it would become nigh impossible if the rains increased. Some said they thought the imminent arrival of Pando and his formidable 8,000 would trigger General Linares into the offensive.

The talk was animated, but nobody committed himself one way or another except McClernand, who said, "General, I feel confident that with a little rest, nobody will want to fall back. All we have to do is hold on – and Santiago will fall into our hands like an overripe fruit."

"Well," Shafter said, "we'll just have to take a vote on it. Of course, I'll assume full responsibility for whatever movement we decide to make."

"I'm still kinda sick," Wheeler said. Then he added, with an impatient rasp in his voice: "But damn my eyes if I'm gonna vote to turn tail on them blankety-blank horse-thieving Spaniards!"

The results of the vote were supposed to be confidential, but someone leaked them to a correspondent: General Kent voted for retreat. Generals Lawton, Bates and Wheeler voted against it. Colonel McClernand, not a division commander, did not vote.

"Since we don't have a unanimous opinion here," Shafter said, "we'll stay where we are now while I study the problem for a while. I'll give all your opinions the most scrupulous consideration, gentlemen. But I have to make the decision myself, because I alone will be blamed for any failure. Even if I wanted to, I couldn't shuck off that responsibility. Thank you, gentlemen," he added, dismissing them with a feeble salute.

"Sir," Kent said, hanging back for a moment, embarrassed at discovering that he alone had voted for retreat. "Whatever you decide, Bill, you can count on all of us to back you up."

Early Sunday morning, Shafter sent for McClernand. "Take a telegram," he said.

"Yes, sir," McClernand said, with pencil poised.

Shafter now had a direct link with Washington: the Americans had raised a submerged costal cable running between Santiago and Guantanamo and cut it in two. Guantanamo was the terminus of the ocean cable. The severed end of the cable was dragged by a ship to Siboney, and signal corpsmen had strung a telephone line from Siboney to Shafter's field headquarters.

Shafter hawked to clear his throat, spat phlegm into a bucket, then dictated: "Secretary of War, Washington: Camp near Sevilla, Cuba, July 3." He paused for a long moment. At last, he haltingly dictated the rest:

```
WE HAVE THE TOWN WELL INVESTED ON THE NORTH
AND EAST, BUT WITH A VERY THIN LINE. UPON
APPROACHING IT WE FIND IT OF SUCH A
CHARACTER AND THE DEFENCES SO STRONG IT WILL
BE IMPOSSIBLE TO CARRY IT BY STORM WITH MY
PRESENT FORCE, AND I AM SERIOUSLY
CONSIDERING WITHDRAWING ABOUT FIVE MILES AND
TAKING UP A NEW POSITION ON THE HIGH GROUND
BETWEEN THE SAN JUAN RIVER AND
SIBONEY...GENERAL WHEELER IS SERIOUSLY ILL AND
WILL PROBABLY HAVE TO GO TO THE REAR TO-DAY
[sic]. GEN. YOUNG ALSO VERY ILL, CONFINED TO
```

HIS BED. GEN. HAWKINS SLIGHTLY WOUNDED IN
FOOT DURING SORTIE ENEMY MADE LAST NIGHT,
WHICH WAS HANDSOMELY REPULSED. THE BEHAVIOR
OF THE REGULAR TROOPS WAS MAGNIFICENT. I AM
URGING ADMIRAL SAMPSON TO ATTEMPT TO FORCE
THE ENTRANCE OF THE HARBOR, AND WILL HAVE A
CONSULTATION WITH HIM THIS MORNING. HE IS
COMING TO THE FRONT TO SEE ME. I HAVE BEEN
UNABLE TO BE OUT DURING THE HEAT OF THE DAY
FOR FOUR DAYS, BUT AM RETAINING THE COMMAND.

After sending the cable, McClernand rushed back to Shafter's tent with an audacious idea that had suddenly burst upon him, nearly bowling him over: "General, let's send 'em a demand to surrender!"

Shafter, lying on his cot, raised up on his elbows. "Surrender? Now?"

For a solid minute, he stared at McClernand, fixing him with the imperious gaze that had given the shakes to many a subordinate. McClernand fidgeted with his pencil and notepad, bracing himself for some caustic remark that would insult his intelligence. But Shafter sagged back with a profound sigh.

"Well, try it," he wheezed.

Under the tent fly that served as his office, McClernand carefully worded a terse message to General José Toral, the Spanish commander in Santiago. Shafter scrutinized it, then signed it, and said: "Give it to Colonel Dorst and tell him to deliver it immediately."

Dorst, the adjutant of Wheeler's cavalry division, carried the letter to the Spanish commander under a flag of truce:

Headquarters U.S. Forces
Near San Juan River, Cuba
July 3, 1898, 8:30 A.M.

Commanding General Spanish Forces, Santiago de Cuba.
 Sir: I have the honor to inform you that unless you

surrender I shall be obliged to shell Santiago de Cuba. Please instruct the citizens of all foreign countries and all women and children that they should leave the city before 10 A.M. tomorrow [sic].

Wm. R. Shafter
Major-General U.S. Vol.

Shafter's disturbing cable to Washington – in which he said he was seriously considering retreating five miles – arrived at 11:44 p.m. Saturday. Secretary of War Alger replied at 12:10 p.m. the same day:

YOUR FIRST DESPATCH [sic] RECEIVED. OF COURSE YOU CAN JUDGE THE SITUATION BETTER THAN WE CAN AT THIS END OF THE LINE. IF, HOWEVER, YOU COULD HOLD YOUR PRESENT POSITION, ESPECIALLY SAN JUAN HEIGHTS, THE EFFECT UPON THE COUNTRY WOULD BE MUCH BETTER THAN FALLING BACK. HOWEVER, WE LEAVE ALL THAT MATTER TO YOU. THIS IS ONLY A SUGGESTION. WE SHALL SEND YOU REINFORCEMENTS AT ONCE.

Shafter replied:

I SHALL HOLD MY PRESENT POSITION.

About 6:30 p.m. Sunday, Colonel Dorst brought back a note from General Toral indicating he was willing to have a talk with Shafter. Dorst returned to the American lines with British, Portuguese, Norwegian and Chinese consuls in tow.

"General," one consul asked, "will you permit the people to move out of the city and move into El Caney? They will be much better there. There is no food in the city."

Shafter pondered a moment. "I don't see why that

wouldn't be acceptable," he said.

"Honorable general," another consul said, "would you be good enough to delay the bombardment until 10 o'clock on the morning of July 5th, Tuesday, to give all the people time to move out of the city?"

"I will see that it is arranged, and that General Toral is informed of the revised deadline."

"General, I'm sure all the people will be very grateful."

Shafter was flabbergasted by the success thus far of his demand for surrender. But as word leaked out that he had been thinking of giving back the ground his soldiers had taken at such bloody cost, their morale plummeted to rock bottom.

So far the expedition had spent its strength in a phenomenal blaze of energy. But with the ever-mounting difficulties of bringing up food and ammunition, the extreme exhaustion of the soldiers, and more signs of dreaded fevers coming to light, the chance loomed big on the horizon that the whole expeditionary force could suddenly burn itself out like a Roman candle.

Chapter 17:
Desperation and Disaster

Abruptly the moon rolled through a slot in the clouds and lit up the dark slopes like an arc light. What the spectacle revealed swept chills through the watching sentinels, who shouted the alarm:

"Judas Priest – enemy in front!"

The sudden moon shone on slopes boiling with an oncoming wave of infantry. Mausers began raging as the Spanish threatened to overrun the American trenches.

"Fix bayonets – pass the word!"

Hands snatched bayonets from scabbards and clapped them onto rifles. Crouching in the trenches, Petty's outfit waited, sick with dread of meeting the enemy in the ferocity of hand-to-hand combat. Just then, hammering over the crackling lash of enemy Mausers and American Krags, a Gatling began spraying the moonlit enemy with a torrent of steel. In anguished convulsion, the infantry wave broke like a comber against a rocky shore, then began to ebb in roiling confusion. In the tense hours that dragged by, the Spanish discharged sporadic fire from field guns and volleys of rifle fire at the American trenches.

For three days and two nights, Petty and his comrades hadn't had an hour's sleep. At last, as the blackness of the sky paled a trifle in the east, a contingent of fresh replacements moved up, threading through the darkness and relieving Petty's outfit on the firing line.

"Boy, are we glad to see you guys!" Petty said, flinging down the shovel with which he had been enlarging a trench. "Where the hell ya been hiding?"

"Shaggin' ass all night to get here. Can't do more'n that. Now where's all this fighting s'posed to be?"

Just then a volley of slugs spanged around then, gouging the earth, klonking through somebody's canteen, and thudding into one of the replacements, killing hem before he even knew he was under fire. The other replacements hit the ground fast.

Petty picked out a spot in the lee of an earthwork, lay down, and fell asleep. It seemed to him he had hardly shut his eyes when he was jolted awake by a chain of explosions so powerful they shook the earth under him. Raising his head, he opened bleary eyes.

"Jumpin' Jehoseaphat! What in the holy hell?"

"Probably *Vesuvius* – chucking shells into the forts around Santiago again," somebody said.

"Dad-blame bilge rats! Can't even let a guy sleep!"

Petty rolled over in the mud and tried to find oblivion again, despite the blasts that continued to rock the earth.

The cruiser *Vesuvius* was equipped with dynamite-guns 15-inches in diameter and 55-feet long. Instant release of highly-compressed air expelled its huge projectiles freighted with dynamite and explosive gelatin, which its gunners at appropriate times aimed at likely targets.

But it was not *Vesuvius* this time.

That same clear sunny morning, a rumor of unknown source ricocheted through the trenches: Cervera's fleet had escaped from Santiago Bay.

With a loud groan, General Chaffee flung down his hat. "Gentlemen," he said to two officers of the 17th Infantry, "we've lost all we came for. The Spanish fleet is forty miles away on the high seas!"

"Rotten luck."

"Disgusting! Where the hell was our navy?"

It was a false rumor, but it cast the exhausted Americans into a deeper gloom.

One of the few soldiers who kept his equanimity and remained undiscouraged was Sergeant O'Neill of Company H.

"We got only 17,000 men here in Cuba, but most of 'em are regulars," he said, working on a quid. "When I think of all the damn fine soldiers we got here, I betcha my boots we're gonna come out on top."

Petty cast a critical look at O'Neill's boots, which had begun to split at the seams from long exposure to mud and water.

"If that's all you're willing to bet, we're in trouble."

* * * * *

U.S.S. Brooklyn

Earlier that same morning, at sea off Santiago Bay, not the slightest breath of air was stirring. The air was amazingly pellucid. Not the smallest cloud marred its pristine azure. Aboard the grim gray warships of the blockading fleet, it was Sunday and time for "quarters for inspection." On the bridge of the *Brooklyn*, Commodore Winfield Schley chatted with *Associated Press* correspondent George E. Graham.

Suddenly the lookout bawled: "Enemy ships coming out!"

Seizing his binoculars, Schley focused on an astounding sight: the entire Spanish fleet in column, led by Cervera's flagship *Maria Teresa*, was charging out of the narrow channel from Santiago Bay. *Maria Teresa* charged out under full steam, glinting in the sun, "a bone in her teeth," black smoke ripping from her stacks. She was headed straight for the Americans and the open sea.

"Come on, my boy!" Schley yelled to Graham. "We'll give it to 'em now!" To the officer of the deck, he shouted, "Call all hands to general quarters!"

"Aye-aye, sir...General quarters! General quarters! All hands man your battle stations! Look alive!"

There was no need to add that last, for these sailors were suddenly galvanized after chafing in endless boredom for months on this blockade duty.

Behind *Maria Teresa*, in the narrow strait between the headlands, with the Socapa artillery battery on one side and the cruel El Morro fortress looming on the other, emerged in single file the *Vizcaya*, *Cristobal Colon* and *Almirante Oquendo*, followed by the torpedo-boat destroyers *Furor* and *Pluton*. Red and yellow battleflags floated from their peaks. Golden figureheads glittered against the dark hulls of forty thousand tons of death and destruction.

But they had to come out of the narrow slot between the headlands like ducks in a shooting gallery.

All along the American line, emergency flags fluttered up signal halyards and sailors cheered as they dashed to their stations. Every ship immediately obeyed Admiral Sampson's standing order to close in and engage, if Cervera should try to escape. Gone were all the long days of endless waiting. Suddenly arrived – the rapture of action. And the terrible guns of the American warships unleashed a cyclone of death and ruin.

At one point, Schley feared the Spanish warships were making their escape. "Get the range on that one," he told Chief Yeoman George H. Ellis, indicating the *Vizcaya*.

"Yes, sir," Ellis said.

Stepping out from shelter, he raised a stadimeter to his eye and took his readings. "2,200 yards to the *Vizcaya*," he said.

A Spanish shell whistled across the ship. Ellis' body shuddered and slumped to the deck, headless. Other sailors, nauseated by the sight, wiped from their faces and uniforms fragments of the brain that had just given them vital information. Two officers lifted the decapitated body and prepared to throw it overboard.

"No!" Schley commanded, raising his hand in protest. "Any man who falls so gallantly deserves to be buried like a Christian. Take him below and cover him with a flag."

In a few short hours every Spanish warship was transformed into flaming wreckage. Some 400 Spanish sailors died in the holocaust. Ellis was the only American killed.

As the *Maria Teresa* struck the shore, American sailors vented lusty cheers. "Don't cheer, boys," cried Capt. Jack Philip. "The poor devils are dying."

While 400 of her crew were clinging to the wreck of the *Maria Teresa*, one of the American transport captains, according to correspondent Davis, refused to lower his boats and go to their rescue, despite the fact that all firing had ceased. All 400 probably would have drowned if the *Gloucester* and her two small shore-boats hadn't gone to their rescue.

In his yacht *Sylvia*, publisher Hearst approached the wreck of the *Almirante Oquendo* a few minutes after it was beached and lowered a boat to visit it. As Hearst's party moved alongside, a shocking spectacle greeted their eyes. All around, dead Spaniards were floating in the water, naked to the waist, as they had been while manning their guns. "We steered nervously among the bodies," Hearst recalled, "feeling much pity – and some satisfaction, too, that the *Maine* had been so well remembered."

Hearst and his associates spied a group of Spaniards on a distant shore, and cruised toward them, to capture twenty-nine terror-stricken prisoners on this beach. Most were wounded. The prisoners related that, as American gunnery became more and more destructive, Spanish gunners deserted their posts and were shot down by their own officers. As the battle raged even more desperate, bottles of liquor from the officers' mess were handed to the sailors so they could fight on with alcoholic bravery to the inevitable end.

Capt. Charles Edgar Clark, commander of the battleship *Oregon*, wrote about the *Vizcaya*:

As this last battle-torn wreck of what had once been a proud and splendid ship fled to the shore like some sick and wounded thing, seeking a place to die, I could feel none of that exultation that is supposed to come with victory. If I had seen my own decks covered with blood, and my officers and men dying around me, perhaps resentment would have supplied the necessary ingredient, but as it was, the faces of the women and children in far-away Spain, the widows and orphans of this July third, rose before me so vividly that I had to draw comfort from the thought that a decisive victory is after all more merciful than a prolonged struggle, and that every life lost today [sic] in breaking down the bridge to Spain might mean a hundred saved hereafter.

The news that Cervera's fleet had been destroyed was cabled around the globe and people were celebrating it with abandon all over the United States before the worn-out soldier on the Santiago hills even learned of it.

The erroneous report received in the morning that Cervera's fleet had escaped to freedom had been a grievous blow to the haggard Americans in the muddy trenches. One in six of their comrades had been killed or wounded. Many others were now dying of fever. It seemed as if all their sacrifices had been in vain. Utter desperation waxed imminent. For three days and two nights, since early July 1, the soldiers had gone without sleep, had precious little to eat, and for most of that time had been exposed to harassing fire as they clung to the embattled ridge.

A brigade commander snorted his exasperation: "By God, Shafter oughta show himself at the front and take charge, or resign!"

"Goddamn right," snarled another general. "It don't matter much who's in command, just so long as *someone* is. We just can't go on this way, with no one in charge!"

The army seemed to be coming unglued: correspondent Stephen Bonsal wrote that one could smell disaster in the air.

* * * * *

As the morning heat enveloped the hills, a squad from Petty's company started out with a load of canteens, to fetch water. Petty volunteered to go, too.

"Hold it, boys!" Petty said, after they had gone some distance.

Several dead Americans lay on the ground, still unburied and starting to putrefy in the blistering sun. The smell was sickening. Others had been buried, but none too well. From one low mound of earth, an arm protruded in a forlorn adieu. Petty found one unburied soldier whose shoes appeared about the same size as his own. His own civilian shoes, not in too great condition when he enlisted, were coming apart at the seams from many days in many weathers. Unlacing the dead man's boots, he laced them on his own feet.

"Hate to do this," he said, stamping on the ground to test the fit, "but this poor guy won't be needing 'em no more."

"Sumbitching Petty's got more gall than brains," a soldier said. "Catch *me* messing around with stiffs!"

"You guys got government shoes to begin with," Petty protested. "They ran out of my size. What's a guy to do? I can't go plumb barefoot forever."

They halted again at a stagnant pond ringed with marsh grass and cattails, its water festooned with ribbons of pea-green scum.

"This it?" Petty asked the soldiers who had gone on the previous water details.

"You got it."

"We been drinking' *that*?"

"That there's the only water we could find anywhere around here."

"How 'bout the river?"

"With all these canteens full of water? Too damn far to carry 'em. Besides, some dead horses are lying in the river."

"Farther upstream?"

"Yeah. Much too far to walk."

Petty, arms akimbo, spat in disgust.

"Well, don't *spit* in it, will ya? That's our *drinking* water!"

"We oughta haul ass back to the line, so let's get it done."

This foul pond may well have been one source of some of the diseases that later would devour such a ghastly number of Americans.

Meanwhile, Roosevelt ripped off another vitriolic letter to Senator Lodge:

Tell the president for Heaven's sake to send us every regiment and above all every battery possible. We have won so far at a heavy cost; but the Spanish fight very hard and charging these entrenchments against modern rifles is terrible. We are within measurable distance of a terrible military disaster; we must have help – thousands of men, batteries, and food and ammunition... Our General is poor; he is too unwieldy to get to the front.

Also in this one day, General Shafter sent three confusing cables to Washington about the whereabouts of Pando. In the first, he said Pando had arrived at Palma, a village about 25 miles northwest of Santiago. In the second, he said Pando was six miles north of Santiago. The third cable read: PANDO, I FIND TO-NIGHT, IS SOME DISTANCE AWAY AND WILL NOT GET INTO SANTIAGO.

But that very evening, the dreaded relief column entered Santiago.

The real story of what happened to Cervera's fleet when it fled from Santiago Bay crackled along the lines the next day like a string of Chinese firecrackers: every ship flying Spanish colors had been destroyed. On the Santiago hills, the tired men in the trenches celebrated their July 4th holiday with the reading of a congratulatory telegram from President McKinley, followed by wild jubilation. Soldiers danced jigs on earthworks, flung hats in the air, hugged one another and cheered deliriously.

"Bully for the navy!"
"They're dynamite!"
Shafter cabled Washington:

THE GOOD NEWS HAS INSPIRED EVERYBODY. WHEN THE NEWS OF THE DISASTER OF THE SPANISH FLEET REACHED THE FRONT, WHICH WAS DURING THE PERIOD OF TRUCE, A REGIMENTAL BAND THAT HAD MANAGED TO KEEP ITS INSTRUMNTS ON THE LINE PLAYED THE "STAR-SPANGLED BANNER" AND "THERE WILL BE A HOT TIME IN THE OLD TOWN TONIGHT," MEN CHEERING FROM ONE END OF THE

LINE TO THE OTHER. OFFICERS AND ME, WITHOUT
EVEN SHELTER-TENTS, HAVE BEEN SOAKING FOR
FIVE DAYS IN THE AFTERNOON RAINS, BUT ALL
ARE HAPPY.

Then a thunderclap: Cuban scouts reported to the Americans that Pando had entered Santiago. Garcia and his rebels had been unable to hold them back, much to the vexation of Shafter, who suspected them of gold-bricking. Shafter fired off a worried cable to Washington:

CAMP NEAR SANTIAGO, CUBA, JULY 4
WHEM AM I TO EXPECT TROOPS FROM TAMPA?
REPORT JUST RECEIVED, PANDO ENTERED CITY
LAST NIGHT BY COBRE ROAD WITH 5000 FROM
HOLGUIN. GARCIA WAS ESPECIALLY CHARGED WITH
BLOCKADING THAT ROAD.

This was the force that Cuban scouts had referred to as "Pando with 8,000 men." Actually, 3.654 reinforcements under Col. Federico Escario, not General Pando, had entered Santiago, and they had come from Manzanillo, not Holguin. Escario's army, leaving Manzanillo on June 23, had marched 150 miles over narrow trails, moving in single file much of the way as they hacked their way through the jungle with machetes, constantly harassed by Cuban rebels, who killed or wounded 98 Spanish soldiers along the route.

Nevertheless, the arrival of the relief column added a whopping increment to the number of Spanish defenders in Santiago. To capture the city, the Americans would have to advance through satanic tangles of barbed wire, while scourged by every rifle and cannon the Spanish could muster.

Chapter 18:
Surrender Talks

The citizens of Santiago were dreading that at any moment Sampson's squadron would force an entrance into the bay. All noncombatants were ready to light out for the boondocks at the first sign of it, as Shafter had agreed to allow them to pass through American lines.

On the night of July 4, the Spanish sank the Reina Mercedes in the channel to foil any attempt by Sampson to enter, but it failed to block the channel. American warships, although top brass weren't sure exactly what was happening, decided to play it safe by promptly bombarding this scene of suspicious nocturnal activity. The thundering cannonade threw the citizens of Santiago into a panic. Believing it could only mean the Americans were forcing an entrance to the harbor, they stampeded out of the city, glutting the road to El Caney.

For the next two days, the tragic procession dragged out of Santiago, congesting the road with thousands of sick and starving refugees. Old men and women barely able to totter, young mothers with babes in arms and crying toddlers lagging behind – all staggered along under whatever belongings they could carry. Ancient groaning carts transported the sick and frail and their baggage. Here and there, sleek horses pulled shiny black carriages crammed with foreign consular officials and their disarray of clothing and luggage.

Even before the exodus began, El Caney's 200-odd houses were crowded. Now a formidable multitude of more than 20,000 people was struggling toward the village's hopelessly inadequate lodgings. Nor would they find any food in El Caney, except some rations doled out by the Americans at the rate of 2,000 per day, a pitiful fraction of the amount so desperately needed. One trouble seemed to flow hard upon the heels of another: as a two-day downpour transformed the road into a chain of sloughs, the Americans found it impossible to bring up as many rations as before. Most of the refugees had to sleep in the jungle and eat mangoes and other wild fruit. Soon fever and dysentery broke out on a frightening scale, compounding the misery of famine.

Meanwhile, Spanish and American general officers had worked out a plan to exchange prisoners: on July 6, the Spanish prisoners – three lieutenants and eight privates – trudged up the trail from El Pozo, led by four mounted American officers and guarded by a cavalry detachment.

As the procession shuffled up to the American lines on San Juan heights, an officer ordered a halt.

"Blindfold the prisoners," he said.

This was to prevent the prisoners from learning vital facts about the American positions and the lamentable condition of the soldiers. That done, the party resumed its march, now in full view of the Spanish in Santiago. Riding ahead on horseback, an orderly held aloft a pole to which was tied a white tablecloth doubling as a flag of truce. Before long, a column of Spaniards wended its way out of the city, led by its own truce flag. The trail wound between high banks as huge trees arched overhead. The two processions continued to approach each other, until they met in a grassy field in the shade of a majestic ceiba, or silk-cotton tree, with a trunk nearly fifty feet in circumference. Blindfolds were snatched off.

Trenches near the trail were packed with American soldiers. Petty, seeing two familiar faces, nudged a comrade. "Them two guys on the end – them's the ones I captured on the hill. I'll never forget their faces."

Behind the trenches a thousand more soldiers stood four deep, all waiting impatiently for Lt. Richmond Hobson and the other heroes of the *Merrimac*. As their wait lengthened into hours, they sprawled in the grass, enjoying the respite from the rains, soaking up the blissful sunshine into the marrow of their bones.

"They're coming up the road!"

All scrambled to their feet, staring with profound curiosity at the approach of Hobson and his band of daredevils. A regimental band struck up *The Star-Spangled Banner*, and all doffed their hats.

When the anthem ended, a red-faced trooper cupped his hands to his mouth and shouted, "Three cheers for Hobson!" Frenzied huzzahs soared from thousands of throats.

Hobson, mounted on a horse, appeared a bit thinner. He looked natty enough, wearing his uniform cap and undress blouse, and somehow he had come by a pair of immaculate white duck trousers. Behind him followed six mules hauling an ambulance carrying half a dozen bluejackets, laughing and yelling. The sailors, with their faces white with prison pallor from long confinement in the stony walls of El Morro, rode through the contrasting sea of cheering bronze faces.

"Well, Jackie, how does it feel?"

"Great! Much obliged to you fellas for coming here."

"Hey, Jackie, what did they arrest you for – stealing a dog?"

"Naw! We stole this ambulance from the army!"

Hobson's spirited horse, prancing at the edge of the road, kicked up the duff and exposed the limb of a dead soldier buried in shallow earth. Cheered by soldiers all the way, Hobson and his men passed through the American trenches, then down the long crowded road on the lee side of San Juan Hill, while guns of American warships off Santiago Bay thundered, firing blank salutes to the repatriated prisoners.

A few hours later, long after dark, the sailors received another ebullient reception from their shipmates aboard the flagship *New York* where Hobson, in high spirits, regaled newspaper correspondents with his adventures.

General Shafter, after pondering the matter for a while, ordered that the remaining 140 Spanish prisoners, the rest of those captured at El Caney, be returned to General Toral. When the prisoners realized they wouldn't be slaughtered after all, their happiness knew no bounds, and they left the American lines only reluctantly. Shafter felt that returning them to their lines was the best way to scotch evil rumors fomented by Spanish officers that Americans massacred prisoners.

Now the trail between American and Spanish lines bristled every day with truce flags passing back and forth. To the rank-and-file Americans, the white flags were anathema. They had raised their own American flags, even though offering the Spanish perfect targets, along the entire line of trenches that formed a horseshoe-shaped curve five miles long. In the wind and sun, the waving flags created a stirring spectacle. But when the soldiers saw the big white truce flag slithering across the valley below, it seemed to them that somehow their hardships were being disparaged and denigrated. So they heaped scorn on the white flag, an emblem of appeasement.

Truce flags went by so often that the soldiers likened them to the different editions of a daily newspaper.

"Has the 10 o'clock edition come out yet?"

"Is this an extra coming out, or the baseball edition?"

Ugly churning clouds moving in on July 8 ushered in a week-long ordeal of tropic storms.

"Never seen it come down like this before," O'Neill said, gazing dismally out of his dog-tent as Petty splashed by.

"Worse'n a cow pissing on a flat rock," Petty said.

Surrender Talks

In Washington on the night of July 9, President McKinley was taken aback at learning that the War Department had received a defeatist message from Cuba. Shafter had cabled that he and his generals had agreed to accept Toral's request to withdraw his army intact into the hills, to avoid destruction of Santiago and its inhabitants by the naval bombardment. McKinley at once dispatched a brief wire with a strict order to accept only unconditional surrender. Later, he sent another wire to Shafter, elaborating:

```
WHAT YOU WENT TO SANTIAGO FOR WAS THE
SPANISH ARMY. IF YOU ALLOW IT TO EVACUATE
WITH ITS ARMS YOU MUST MEET IT SOMEWHERE
ELSE. THIS IS NOT WAR. IF THE SPANISH
COMMANDER DESIRES TO LEAVE THE CITY AND ITS
PEOPLE, LET HIM SURRENDER AND WE WILL THEN
DISCUSS THE QUESTION AS TO WHAT SHALL BE
DONE WITH THEM.
```

Shafter had to inform Toral that his request to evacuate Santiago was unacceptable, and he repeated his demand for Toral's unconditional surrender. Unless he received a favorable reply by 3 p.m. July 10, Shafter said, the Americans would resume firing.

Toral refused to surrender, and firing on both sides resumed about 4 p.m. July 10.

Struggling through the rainy morning of the following day, General Lawton's wet and bedraggled right brigade, commanded by General Ludlow, planted its guidon on the far shore of Santiago Bay.

"We have completed the investment of Santiago," Ludlow said in a written note to Lawton and Shafter.

The storms continued. The night of July 11 was the time of the largest one – nobody got any sleep that night. Furious torrents swirled around the soldiers' feet as the downpour intensified. Lightning zigzagged across the black heavens and dazzled along the mountain ridges. Paralyzing claps of thunder sent horses bolting with screams of terror. Wild gusts blew tents down and soldiers suddenly found themselves exposed to the pounding cloudburst.

Petty groped blindly for his clothing that the howling wind had scattered far and wide in the ooze and darkness. "Man," he groaned, "I thought we had gulley-washers back home, but *this*!"

The week-long onslaught of storms made it extremely difficult and dangerous to unload supplies from the transports, pitching and rolling off Siboney. On land, movement of supplies had bogged down to a virtual standstill.

Although the Americans now enveloped all landward approaches to Santiago, all their lines were perilously thin. And the many days of huddling, virtually paralyzed, in the muddy, rain-lashed trenches were wearing heavily on the miserable troops.

The same day that Ludlow completed the encirclement of Santiago, General Garcia took an interpreter along on a visit to Shafter.

"Buenas dias, general," Garcia said, then continued, pausing at the end of each sentence to give the interpreter time to translate: "My scouts report that a column of 6,000 Spanish soldiers will soon leave Holguin for Santiago…This column will join up with another column from Manzanillo…That is from where Escario marched…It is clear the combined column will march toward Santiago and make big trouble for the Americanos."

Shafter directed Garcia to post some of his soldiers several miles to the northwest of the city, to guard the passes.

Also that day, Major General Miles arrived at the front from Washington. Miles, 59 years old, one of the Civil War's "boy generals," was a handsome man with a silver mustache and chest covered with medals. "A brave peacock," Roosevelt called him.

During a slight break in the weather the following day, Miles and Shafter, together with their aides, and Robert Mason, British vice consul in Santiago acting as an interpreter, met under the giant ceiba with General Toral, a 60-year-old man with salt-and-pepper hair and mustache. The generals saluted each other respectfully.

"General Toral," Shafter said, "please excuse me for not getting off my horse. I'm not well."

Toral was not feeling very well either. His craggy face was drawn with deep lines of fatigue. "Comprendo," he said with a nod.

"General, you are completely surrounded," Shafter said. "We've cut off the water lines to Santiago, so that now you only have cistern water."

Toral shrugged, and a smile of amusement lit up his face. "Water lines, general? That is a very small thing. With all this rain, there is no shortage of water."

"Our reinforcements are moving up," Shafter said. "New batteries of artillery are being emplaced."

"I'm only a subordinate," Toral said, in a flat tone that suggested he was resigned to whatever fate held in store. "I obey my government. If necessary, we die at our posts."

Miles interrupted with impatience. "Sir, your situation is hopeless! Why not avoid sacrificing any more lives on both sides?"

"That I would like to do."

"Can you telegraph your government in Madrid?"

"It will take much time to get an answer."

"What do you think the answer will be?"

Toral shrugged and shook his head doubtfully.

"Will you telegraph?" Miles insisted.

"I will try," Toral said.

When Toral returned to the city, he conferred with the gallant General Linares, who was suffering from a serious wound received in the battle of San Juan Hill. That evening,

Give Me 10,000 Men!

Linares sent a poignant cable to Spain:

> TO THE COMMANDER IN CHIEF AND THE MINISTER OF WAR
> THOUGH CONFINED TO MY BED BY GREAT WEAKNESS AND SHARP PAINS, I AM SO MUCH WORRIED OVER THE SITUATION OF THESE LONG-SUFFERING TROOPS THAT I DEEM IT MY DUTY TO ADDRESS YOUR EXCELLENCY AND THE MINISTER OF WAR FOR THE PURPOSE OF SETTING FORTH THE TRUE STATE OF AFFAIRS.
> HOSTILE POSITIONS VERY CLOSE TO PRECINCT OF CITY, FAVORED BY NATURE OF GROUND; OURS SPREAD OUT OVER 14 KILOMETRES; TROOPS ATTENUATED; LARGE NUMBER SICK; NOT SENT TO HOSPITALS BECAUSE NECESSARY TO RETAIN THEM IN TRENCHES. HORSES AND MULES WITHOUT FOOD AND SHELTER; RAIN HAS BEEN POURING INTO THE TRENCHES INCESSANTLY FOR TWENTY HOURS. SOLDIERS WITHOUT PERMANENT SHELTER; RICE THE ONLY FOOD; CAN NOT CHANGE OR WASH CLOTHES. MANY CASUALTIES; CHIEFS AND OFFICERS KILLED; FORCES WITHOUT PROPER COMMAND IN CRITICAL MOMENTS...THE SITUATION IS FATAL; SURRENDER INEVITABLE; WE ARE ONLY PROLONGING THE AGONY; THE SACRIFICE IS USELESS; THE ENEMY KNOWS IT, FULLY REALIZING OUR SITUATION. THEIR CIRCLE BEING WELL ESTABLISHED, THEY WILL EXHAUST OUR FORCES WITHOUT EXPOSING THEIRS AS THEY DID YESTERDAY, BOMBARDING ON LAND BY ELEVATION WITHOUT OUR BEING ABLE TO SEE THEIR BATTERIES, AND FROM THE SEA BY THE FLEET, WHICH HAS FULL ADVICES, AND IS BOMBARDING THE CITY IN SECTIONS WITH MATHEMATICAL ACCURACY...
> IF IT SHOULD BE NECESSARY TO CONSUMMATE THE SACRIFICE FOR REASONS WHICH I AM IGNORANT OF, OR IF THERE IS NEED OF SOMEONE TO ASSUME THE RESPONSIBILITY OF THE DENOUEMENT ANTICIPATED AND ANNOUNCED BY ME IN SEVERAL CABLEGRAMS, I OFFER MYSELF LOYALLY ON THE ALTER OF MY COUNTRY FOR THE ONE PURPOSE OR

Surrender Talks

THE OTHER, AND I WILL TAKE IT UPON MYSELF TO PERFORM THE ACT OF SIGNING THE SURRENDER, FOR MY HUMBLE REPUTATION IS WORTH VERY LITTLE WHEN IT COMES TO A QUESTION OF NATIONAL INTERESTS.

* * * * *

A war of another sort – the circulation war between the two New York newspapers, the *Journal* and the *World* – heated up one day after the *Journal* published a story supposedly relating events in the siege of Santiago. It read in part:

"Colonel Reflipe W. Thenuz, an Austrian artillerists of European renown, who, with Colonel Ordonez, was defending the land batteries of Aguadores and the land batteries on the road from the latter place to Santiago, was so badly wounded that he has since died...Colonel Thenuz was foremost in the attempt to repulse the American advance and performed many acts of valor which excited the admiration of even the Americans."

Next day the *World* printed a long story speculating on how soon Santiago might fall. It continued with a nearly word-for-word report of the valor of Colonel Reflipe W. Thenus, as recounted by the *Journal*. Next day on Page 3 the *Journal* splashed a bold headline: "The *World* Confesses to Stealing the News!" The subhead declared: "Tired of Its Dispatches Being Stolen, the *Journal* Sets a Trap Which Catches the Thief and Makes Him Own Up."

"Reflipe W. Thenuz," the *Journal* went on, was an anagram of "We pilfer the news." Revealing passages from the two newspapers were published side-by-side, to the great amusement of all except the hapless World editors.

* * * * *

Along the muddy road toward the west side of Santiago, hundreds of soldiers were hauling and pushing field guns and caissons, helping horses and mules drag them through the mire. Correspondents interpreted this mass movement as indicating any assault on Santiago would strike from this sector.

But there was another reason. Shafter was bolstering the right side of the U-shaped line around the city. Each day, he received reports from breathless Cuban scouts that Spanish reinforcements were marching toward Santiago, variously from Holguin, Manzanillo, or San Luis.

If Spanish reinforcements tried to force their way into Santiago, or if Spanish forces inside the city tried to break out, Shafter believed they would make their bids on that vulnerable western sector, now guarded by Garcia's tatterdemalion rebels, weary from many years of war.

The arrival of the stubby field mortars had beefed up the American artillery at the front. But efforts to drag forward the ponderous five-inch siege guns, each weighing four tons, had failed utterly. After excruciating labors, two siege guns were unloaded from a transport at Daiquiri. But the soggy roads proved utterly impassable for such elephantine burdens. Each siege gun would have required twenty-four horses to lug it over the *best* stretch of the road from Daiquiri to the front. Whether it could have been dragged at all over the really abominable sections was doubtful. Some days later, the two siege guns, which never moved much beyond Daiquiri, were re-loaded aboard ship. Eventually, never having fired a shot, they went back to the United States.

Every evening at sunset, the tired and famished Americans hunched by their campfires, perhaps frying a bit of hardtack in sowbelly grease. Beyond the mighty blue of the Sierra Maestra, the setting sun kindled the storm-cloud remnants with flame. As some regimental band struck up the first chords of *The Star-Spangled Banner*, a hush descended on the miles of trenches. Soldiers rose on stiff legs, clambered up on the muddy earthworks, doffed hats and formed long rows of figures standing at attention. All eyes focused on the band of flags waving on the hills. When the last bars of the anthem died away, the soldiers clapped on their hats and went back to tending their skimpy suppers.

Illness was taking a heavy toll. As the buglers became ill, too, the daily calls that governed military life became weaker and more tremulous and disorderly. To one soldier, they sounded like "the ghastly echo of a thinning and dying army corps."

The Fifth Army Corps was, in fact, dying. Whether it could accomplish its mission before its portending demise was moot.

But events seemed to be sliding toward some kind of a climax. From time to time Generals Toral, Shafter and Miles met under the ceiba, conversing with the help of Robert Mason as interpreter.

One night in Santiago, the sorely beset Spanish commanders met in conference, the upshot of which was they drafted a gloomy assessment of their condition, which all signed. It read in part:

Considering further the great superiority of the enemy, who, besides a contingent of men said to exceed 40,000, possesses 70 pieces of modern artillery and a powerful fleet;

Considering further that no supplies can reach the city except by sea, and that there is no prospect of receiving any as long as a powerful hostile fleet completely closes the entrance of the harbor;

Considering further that, under these circumstances, to continue so unequal a fight would lead to nothing except the sacrifice of a large number of lives;

And considering, finally, that the honor of our arms has been completely vindicated by these troops who have fought so nobly and whose behavior has been lauded by our own and other nations, and that by an immediate capitulation terms could be obtained which it would not be possible to obtain

after hostilities have again broken out:
The junta is of unanimous opinion that the necessity for capitulation has arrived.

That night for the last time, American field guns fulminated against Santiago, but now it was only in mock wrath. Capt. Allyn Capron's battery was picked for the job, and he made sure the barrage had all the earmarks of the real McCoy. After several rounds had crashed off into the distance, Capron railed at the gunners for their execrable marksmanship:

"You punkinheads couldn't hit a barn if you was standing inside!"

In pretended anger, Capron rolled up his sleeves and then sighted the next gun himself. And likewise missed the mark.

"Devil take it! Send this crummy smoke-wagon back to the arsenal – it's got a crooked barrel!"

It was a lark for the soldiers, did no harm to the Spaniards, and satisfied General Toral, because now he and his men could truly be said to have laid down their arms under fire. Thus their honor remained unblemished.

At the next conference under the ceiba, Toral said he wanted one more item clarified.

"Does my capitulation embrace all my command?" he asked.

Shafter wheeled his horse while his mind worked on that. "What does your command consist of?" he asked.

"The Fourth Army Corps."

"Where is it located?"

Toral ticked off some numbers on his fingers: "I have 11,500 men here in Santiago, 3,500 at San Luis, 7,000 at Guantanamo, and 1,500 more scattered within twenty-five miles."

Shafter nearly fell off his horse. Toral seemed to be thinking of surrendering this tremendous force of 23,500 soldiers, without a fight, even though many of them were wholly outside the grasp of the Americans!

Shafter's jaw jutted grimly. "Your entire command is included," he said, and held his breath.

Chapter 19:
Last Days of an Empire

General Toral rubbed his chin, pondering a moment: the Santiago garrison was in desperate straits, hopelessly cut off from reinforcements and supplies by either land or sea.

At last he spoke, with an air of infinite sadness. "Que sera sera." What will be, will be. "I would not want my worst enemy to be in my place," he added sorrowfully. "My generals and colonels are all killed or wounded."

Generals of booth armies executed the final papers at 2:30 o'clock in the afternoon of July 15. By the surrender terms, the United States agreed to transport Toral's entire command back to Spain.

In the middle of the following morning, Petty's regiment and thousands of other Americans flanked the road to Santiago. All that Petty and the soldiers around him knew was that something was about to happen; something important, apparently. But an hour passed, and nothing happened. They lay down in the grass, soaking up the sunshine. Just then, General Shafter and his staff came riding down the road.

"Here comes the commanding general!" somebody yelled.

Petty had never seen Shafter before, but recognized him at once because of an indelicate comment he had heard about the general's dimensions: "He has a butt-end two ax-handles wide." Shafter reined in his nickering horse almost opposite Petty and for a moment fixed baleful eyes on him. Petty thought the general was about to speak to him. But Shafter shifted his glare to another rookie near Petty. The rookie scrambled to his feet and stood rigidly at attention, leaving his rifle in the grass.

"Have you boys got a good supply of water?" Shafter asked.

"Yes, sir," the soldier said.

"What outfit do you belong to?"

"Thirteenth Infantry, sir."

"Where's your rifle?"

Realizing he had blundered, the soldier snatched up his rifle and red-facedly resumed attention. "Right here, sir."

Shafter snorted, pulled out a red bandana and honked mightily. "You act like a 71st man," he said with a sneer. Turning in his saddle, he struck his horse with his crop, and centered down the road toward the city with his aides following.

"Well, I'll be shot for a jackrabbit!" the rookie spluttered, flinging down his rifle. "Plague take it!"

"Don't fret your guts," Petty said. "Anybody could've pulled the same boner."

"Biggest boner," said another soldier, lolling on his back and chewing pensively on a blade of grass, "was putting a blubber-belly like Shafter in charge of the whole shebang. Even if he's got the savvy, he's too old and too fat to cut the mustard."

"I hear the officers are saddling him with the blame for the big foul-up at San Juan Hill," another put in. "He was so far behind the lines he didn't know where we was at or what we was up against."

In the shade of the towering ceiba, where scattered shafts of sunlight lanced through the dust-laden air, General Toral and a score of his officers, having dismounted, waited for the

American commander. As Shafter came onto the scene, Toral stepped briskly forward, raised his hat, and saluted. Shafter returned the salute and remained on his horse. An hour later, General Miles and his staff, all mounted, trotted down the road to the ceiba.

The giant ceiba where the surrender occurred, which later became know as the "Surrender Tree." (courtesy the American Battle Monuments Commission)

"General Miles?" Toral asked. Tears sprang to his eyes as he advanced and handed Miles his unsheathed sword, butt-end first, in token of surrender. Toral pivoted, stepped back into the row of his fellow officers, and pivoted again. Wiping his eyes with a handkerchief, he spoke curtly to a lieutenant, who then shouted rapid commands.

From behind shrubbery bordering the road, fortissimo notes from a Spanish bugle sounded, marking cadence. In column of twos, a "king's guard" of 100 Spanish soldiers emerged through a gap in the bushes. As the Spaniards paraded past, they glanced with surreptitious curiosity at the Americans they had been shooting at only days before. Smartly they countermarched and halted, facing the Americans with stolid countenances that betrayed none of the bewildering emotions they must have felt in the humiliation of defeat. The Spanish lieutenant shouted another command: the soldiers presented arms. Captain Brett's command, "Present sabers," rang out. American sabers flashed in unison. The Spanish lieutenant gave more commands and his soldiers again trooped past the Americans, who remained at "present arms."

A few hundred feet beyond, the Spanish formation halted. Glumly the soldiers fell out and stacked their Mausers in neat rows of pyramids.

With the formalities ended for the moment, officers of both armies shook hands, exchanged cigarettes, and complimented each other on the courage with which they had fought.

General Toral sent an aide back to the city with a written order. In thirty minutes, thousands of Spanish soldiers began to march out of Santiago, to stack their rifles in pyramids in the open field. Since early morning, other regiments had been turning in their arms and ammunition at the government arsenal, a huge, lichen-dappled stone structure that rambled over several acres in Santiago. All told, the Spanish surrendered some 24,000 troops, together with their rifles, pistols and swords; they also gave up over 100 cannon, 18 Maxim rapid-fire machine guns deemed superior to the American Gatlings, and over 5 million rounds of mostly small-arms ammunition.

"Remember when I wrote you about Gen. Garcia and said he is fat and looks like he ate too much of your good cooking?" Petty said in a letter to his mother. "Well, we saw our Gen. Shafter this morning, and he looks like he gobbled up everything in sight."

In a letter to Dorothy, he wrote: "Looks like the Spaniards are calling it quits. Hope this means it won't be long before I can see you again, Sweetheart."

Shortly before noon on Sunday, July 17, American infantry and cavalry units massed in formation in the Plaza de la Reina. Thousands of Santiago's citizens, mainly women and other non-combatants, filled windows and doors and lined veranda rails and rooftops, watching the show. Shafter and all the other general officers had moved into positions facing the government palace, a grim, Moorish-style building fronting on the plaza. Opposite soared the bell towers of the Catholic cathedral. The flag of Spain had already been taken down from the government palace, after having fluttered over Santiago for four centuries, since conquistador Hernando Cortez became its first mayor. Lt. J.D. Miley, Shafter's aide, and a special detail mounted a stairway to the red-tiled roof, preparing to raise the Stars and Stripes on the staff from which the Spanish colors had so lately flown.

Sylvester Scovel of the New York *World* noticed photographers aiming cameras at the rooftop activity. Scovel was a brash newsman: Long before the American invasion, he had made several daring trips into Cuban jungles, once with a party that carried arms and ammunition to rebels, and skirmished with Spanish soldiers. Scovel's pro-Cuban reports had caused Spain to put a price on his head.

Now, realizing the scoop the World would have if photos showed him conspicuously in the flag-raising scene, Scovel dashed up the stairs to the roof. But Miley divined his motive.

"Get back down there!" Miley ordered.

"Just give me a few minutes, and it's all yours," Scovel said.

Shafter spotted Scovel on the roof and shouted, "Miley, tell that damn fool to get off there!"

"Sir," Miley said, saluting, "I *have* told him – but he won't go!"

"Well, goddamn it, throw him off!" Shafter yelled.

As the general's face took on a choleric red, he barked an order: two soldiers took off on the double, heading for the roof to help Miley carry out the commander's order. But Scovel saw them coming and wasn't about to wait for them. Incensed at being called a damn fool before the whole American army in the most dramatic ceremony of the war, he rushed down the stairs, three steps at a time, almost knocking down the two soldiers on the way up, and strode up to Shafter.

"Sir," Scovel said, "you have overstepped the bounds of decency! I demand an apology!"

"Apology be damned!" Shafter said. "I'd sooner apologize to a long-eared jackass!"

Scovel's eyes blazed with fury. Suddenly he let fly with a roundhouse right at Shafter's chops – but missed.

Shafter turned purple. "Arrest that man!"

Military police swooped in, grabbed Scovel and pinioned his arms. The soldiers with fixed bayonets made sure Scovel stayed in place against a wall while the ceremony resumed.

As the great bell of the cathedral bonged the first stroke of noon, Lt.-Col. Chambers McKibben pivoted around to face the formation and commanded: "Present...HARMS!"

Hands slapped rifle butts, sabers swished in the air, and Old Glory fluttered up the staff on the roof of the palace. Wind seized its folds, unfurling the banner above the vanquished city. As the soldiers saluted, the Sixth Cavalry band sounded the opening bars of *The Star-Spangled Banner*. When the band finished, McKibben gave the order-arms command. Then came the far-off booming of Capron's battery, firing a twenty-one gun salute, thus announcing to the navy at the harbor entrance that the American flag was flying over the Santiago palace, putting the crowning touch on the victory.

As the flag snapped in the breeze, the band played *Stars and Stripes Forever*. Strains of regimental bands echoed in the distance. A throaty cheering rose from the soldiers in the plaza. Like the waves of the sea, it spread: the cheering and oscillating arms and tossed hats undulated for miles along the trenches on the Santiago hills.

"Makes ya feel right proud, don't it?" said Pvt. Harley Pierce.

"Betcha they'll do some celebrating in St. Loocy," Petty said. "Some celebrating," he echoed longingly.

American Flag rises over the Governor's Palace in Santiago following the surrender by the Spanish. (courtesy National Archives)

When all the soldiers had marched out of the plaza, the MPs hustled the sheepish Scovel off to an old moss-tufted calabozo.

A day later, Shafter ordered Lt. Charles Dudley Rhodes to send Scovel under guard to Siboney, to be held there until he could be packed aboard the first ship leaving Cuba.

Rhodes, after many turnings of rusty keys in locks of the dungeon, finally found Scovel – looking as if he'd had a bad night. "General Shafter is sending you to Siboney," Rhodes said.

Scovel threw his arms around Rhodes. "My boy, am I glad to see you! If you'll only send me to Siboney, I'll walk every step of the way! Never again do I want to pass a night in this hellhole with these creeping things!"

Scovel didn't have to walk; the army provided a tug to transport him to Siboney.

Shafter, who had refused to let Cubans take part in surrender conferences and ceremonies, now issued strict orders: no Cuban soldiers were to be allowed to enter Santiago for any reason.

"General," Miley said, "the Cubans are demanding to know why."

"If we let 'em in now, they'd massacre the Spaniards. Tell 'em the Spanish civil authorities will remain in charge of all municipal offices until it's convenient for us to replace them with Cubans. That means when they've had a chance to cool off. God only knows how long that will take. Just keep stalling 'em."

Miley tried the best diplomacy he knew, but returned wearing a frown, saying: "General Garcia's really hopping mad. He says the right to operate their own civil offices was one of the main things they've been fighting for all these years."

But Shafter remained adamant. "I won't have a blood-bath on my conscience," he said.

* * * * *

Santiago, as seen from the trenches on the hills, seemed a drab jumble of hospitals, barracks and shed-like structures emblazoned with Red Cross flags, a checkerwork of white walls and red roofs. Thousands of green mango trees studded the cityscape.

"What say we take a closer gander at this city we conquered?" Petty said to Harley Pierce.

They followed the narrow streets down, past endless one-story houses and shops. Windows were unglazed, but covered with iron gratings.

Santiago had always been notorious as the dirtiest city in Cuba. Even in normal times, ship captains used to say they could smell Santiago ten miles at sea. At the time of the surrender, it had reached its nadir. Heaps of ashes, filthy rags, dung and garbage, the detritus of a stricken city, lay scattered on the broken pacements, picked over by dogs and flies. Gutters ran like open sewers, filled with garbage and stinking discharges from kitchens and cesspools. The air was laced with a horrible foulness.

"How can people live like this?" Pierce asked.

"Musta had years of practice," Petty said. "Naw. Just kidding. It's the war."

Emaciated figures reached arms from doorways, begging for food. Homeless children roamed like naked and haunted-eyed animals, picking through the garbage in a desperate hope of finding something to nourish them. Thousands of buzzards circled over the city. Some flapped down into the streets, like vengeful furies, stabbing their bloodstained beaks again and again into the bodies of dead dogs, horses, and even humans. Hundreds of corpses lay unburied.

At the governor's palace in Plaza de la Reina, they talked to a tall, skinny infantry private standing guard.

"Crikey," he said, "they carried out 300 loads of rubbish from this here place. By gosh, in one room where the Spanish was dumping garbage, the air was so bad a candle wouldn't even burn. Dozen dead dogs and cats was found, killed by the poisonous air."

Since early on July 17, the navy had been clearing mines from the entrance to Santiago Bay. Now, two days later, the entrance was deemed safe, and the Red Cross ship *State of Texas* began cruising in. Santiago's inhabitants had had literally nothing to eat, and the docks were crammed with starving people waiting for the ship's arrival.

Petty and Pierce watched as stevedores, under direction of Clara Barton and her aides, started unloading the ship's 1,400 tons of provisions. Each citizen was to be allowed a pound and a half of rations. But as the unloading began, mobs of half-starved people poured onto the wharf, fighting, trampling one another, smashing open cases and grabbing food.

* * * * *

Under American guards, the many thousands of Spanish prisoners of war were bivouacked two miles outside the city to await embarkation for Spain. Shafter wrote that the prisoners were "perfectly delighted" at the thought of going home, adding: "I believe this knowledge of the disposition made of them, as soon as it reaches other troops in Cuba, will utterly demoralize the whole island." This prediction was borne out by later incidents and by comments from many Spanish officers. It wasn't long before all Spanish resistance in Cuba faded away.

One day, Petty's regiment was ordered to pull up stakes and move back to a less crowded area, near the jungle. Top brass felt that dispersing the units would diminish the inroads of disease. But dysentery and fever ran rampant anyhow. Petty, clouded by gloom, watched many of his comrades waste away and die.

Each day as the sun dropped behind the mountains, three ceremonial volleys of rifle fire crashed over each new grave, and the haunting notes of *Taps* wafted over the hills. As burials multiplied, the growing number of rifle volleys and mournful buglings echoing among the hills began to jar morale badly. Finally these rites were suspended and the dead were quietly buried, with no more of that distressing fanfare.

For the last few days Pierce had been feeling badly out of sorts. Petty took his own canteen and Pierce's to the San Juan River to refill them. When he returned, Pierce, gaunt and long unshaven, rolled over and looked up at him with sunken eyes.

"Sure appreciate that, pardner," he sighed.

Petty's eyes widened at the sight. "Your skin's powerful yellow," he said.

"Reckon it's something I ate?"

If Pierce could still crack a joke, sick as he appeared to be, and when they were all literally starving for some half-decent meals, there must be a little bit of hope left somewhere.

Petty, his face a mask of worry, went to see Sergeant O'Neill. "I need some corpsmen for Harley," he said. "I think he's got the yellow jack."

The medics carried Pierce to the quarantine camp set up for yellow fever patients. Thousands of other soldiers were sick with dysentery, malaria, typhoid and smallpox. Some lay in Santiago hospitals and some in tents on the hills.

Petty also fell victim to disease – the ague and sweats of yellow fever and the horrors of bloody dysentery. The mere thought of food made him gag, yet he forced himself to eat. He stuffed himself with the monotonous army grub, sluicing it down with coffee. For a time he sensed the approach of the legendary pale horse – death. But he must have been doing something right. Because one day, after many very bad days, he felt a trifle better. Slowly he began to recover some of his old strength. As soon as he could put pencil to paper without shaking too much, he scrawled short letters to his mother and Dorothy, saying he had been sick, but was now coming out of it.

The day came when he felt well enough to pack his meager belongings and rejoin his regiment. And it was just in time to catch them as they started to march to the dock to board *Saratoga* for home.

Home!

Of all the men in Petty's regiment who had landed so arrogantly at Siboney in the springtime of their years, less than half remained on active duty. So many good men had been killed or wounded. So many had died of yellow fever. And many still lay in the yellow fever quarantine camp, never to leave except in death. Most of the actives were in deplorable condition, gaunt of face and weak from exhaustion and sickness of one kind or another. But the burgeoning awareness that soon they would be heading home was the best tonic they could have been administered.

"Where ya been goofing off?" Sergeant O'Neill demanded of Petty in mock gruffness.

"Sick as a dying dog. One foot in the grave and the other on a banana peel. If I had my druthers, I'd dodge more bullets, 'stead of taking any more of that cussed yellow jack." Puzzlement crossed his face. "What in tarnation causes it?"

O'Neill shrugged. "Lord only knows. Some say it's a 'miasma' or something that creeps into the air. God only knows where it comes from."

"Man, was I *sick!*" Petty said, shuddering at the memory. "I thought they was gonna put me to bed with a shovel."

On their final afternoon in Cuba, Petty's platoon labored on the docks, helping to load supplies and hardware onto a barge, to be trans-shipped out to where *Saratoga* rode at anchor. "You just take it easy," O'Neill said to Petty. "You don't look none too chipper yet." When they had dumped the last load onto the barge, O'Neill said they could take ten before getting ready to board the transport.

Petty, idly sauntering along the waterfront, came upon a wizened Cuban who was setting up a display of confections and other preserved edibles on a large wooden crate.

"Hey, Joe, you like cake?" the old man asked, whisking some flies off a large chocolate layer cake. "Caramba, he taste good!"

The sight of food intensified Petty's craving for something tasty to eat. He was sick to death of army chow. "How much?" he asked.

"Feefty cent."

Petty explored his pockets. A dime and a nickel were all he could dig up. He tapped a jar of preserved peaches.

"How much?"

"Thirty-five cent."

Petty picked up a jar of olives. "And this?"

"Forty cent."

Reluctantly Petty set it down. Pricing everything on the crate, he found that his meager fifteen cents would buy precious little of anything he really had a yen for. Glumly he stared with red-rimmed eyes at the unattainable luxuries. Suddenly he slapped his fifteen cents on the crate, snatched up the chocolate cake with both hands, and dashed off, beating a hasty retreat from the Cuban's rising outrage.

"Hey, Joe, no *feefteen* – is *feefty* cent! Hey, come back, Joe, you dirty son-om-beesh!"

Aboard the *Saratoga*, Petty shared the cake with some comrades.

"I feel a little guilty," he said, licking his fingers, "giving him only fifteen cents."

"Don't sweat it – he didn't lose much," Pierce said, wiping the crumbs off his face. "Besides, we stomped the shit out of the Spanish. He oughta be grateful for that."

As the sun began to slip behind the western horizon, *Saratoga's* skipper emerged on the bridge, made a quick survey of the harbor, and snapped out an order: "Make all preparations for getting under way!"

"Aye-aye, sir!"

"Stand by to get under way! Weigh anchor!"

The snorting steam winch tractioned the clanking chain, reeling it up on the steel drum until the anchor banged into the hawse-hole with a clangor that reverberated throughout the ship. Weak cheers wafted from the soldiers lining the railings, and even echoed throughout the dim, odorous holds, where many soldiers drooped in their bunks in the stupor of exhaustion.

"One-third speed ahead."

"Aye-aye, sir."

With engines throbbing with a beat that excited the pulses of everyone on board, *Saratoga* began to maneuver out of the darkening bay.

Chapter 20:
Comic-Opera Invasion of Puerto Rico

The red light of waning day glimmered on the wine-dark water, and the smell of salt laced the air with the heady promise of a voyage over the open sea. Aboard a small craft riding at anchor a hundred yards off Saratoga's starboard, some regimental band struck up *When Johnny Comes Marching Home Again*:

> *The old church bell will peal with joy,*
> *Hurrah! Hurrah!*
> *To welcome home our darling boy...*

The *hurrah-hurrahs* echoed through the dusk and swelled with a chorus from the soldiers on the transport. Tears brimmed in Petty's eyes; it seemed to him he had never heard sweeter music. As *Saratoga* maneuvered through the narrow harbor entrance, now shaded from the sun's dying rays, it carefully skirted past the sunken hulk of the *Merrimac*. Just about all of the collier still protruding above water was the smokestack, riddled by Spanish bullets and trailing an oil slick. Lining *Saratoga's* railing, the soldiers fell silent, staring at the riddled stack, thinking with pain of the deadly storm that had lashed the brave ship. Now they caught faint strains from the

Comic-Opera Invasion of Puerto Rico

distant band's wildly exultant *Get Ready for the Jubilee*...

* * * * *

A surprise landing in force began the American invasion of Puerto Rico at Guanica on July 25, General Miles commanding. The landing quickly turned into a triumphal procession as the invaders met, not force, but a joyous welcome by the natives, and a conspicuous absence of Spaniards in the opening stages. Three days after the Guanica landing, American transports cruised into Ponce's harbor with similar results. Hundreds of small boats jammed with near-delirious Puerto Ricans taxied out to offer their greetings to the invaders. When the cutter carrying General Miles started for shore, the cortege of Puerto Rican boats charged after it in a seemingly endless procession, firing volleys of cheers: *"Vivan los Americanos!"* The Americans had barely landed when Miles and his staff received dinner invitations from local VIPs.

Flags of a dozen nations waving over the consulates dressed up the waterfront like some mad carnival. Streamers of red, white and blue fluttered from every roof and balcony. Musicians twanged strings in the streets and plazas, which shimmered with crowds in fiesta costume. Puerto Rican soldiers and firemen paraded in uniform, then petitioned General Miles to enlist them in the U.S. Army.

One night in a plaza, the 3rd Wisconsin Infantry band gave a concert of American patriotic airs. As the Americans belted out a chorus of *Hurrah for the Red, White and Blue*, 5,000 Puerto Ricans surged to their feet and cheered with a frenzy that was almost volcanic.

Prospects for an effervescent social season seemed more likely than chances of bloodshed. Almost every day, the Americans occupied another town on the island. Citizens welcomed them with flowers and bottles of wine and spirits, and fell over one another in their eagerness to surrender.

The Puerto Rican campaign may be unique in warfare in that news correspondents captured towns all by themselves. The City of Ponce surrendered officially and unofficially four separate times, according to correspondent Davis, who personally accepted one surrender. "It was possessed of the surrender habit in a most aggravating form," he reported. "Indeed, for anyone in uniform it was most unsafe to enter the town at any time unless he came prepared to accept its unconditional surrender." On a number of occasions, American officers were miffed to learn that a town, whose surrender they had accepted in good faith, later had the gall to surrender again to someone else. It was damned inconsiderate. Had they no respect for protocol?

Davis racked up another surrender when he and three other reporters, all riding on ponies, managed to reach the town of Coamo ahead of American army scouts. The fact that they were all mounted, and the proud display of campaign ribbons on Davis' chest, convinced the citizens they were dealing with no small potatoes. Davis accepted the surrender with the proper ceremonial flourishes. Just as he and the mayor were working out the capitulation terms, American troops came marching in.

Stephen Crane also had his immortal hour at Juana Diaz, as the citizens surrendered the village to him. Next morning, a colonel and 800 American soldiers crept up, planning to take Juana Diaz by surprise, not knowing Crane had the village in his hip pocket.

As the Americans burst onto the scene with shooting irons at the ready, they found Crane calmly drinking coffee in a sidewalk café with some of the locals. Recognizing Crane, the colonel beamed with delight at the thought of having his triumph recorded by the illustrious author of *The Red Badge of Courage*.

"Glad to see you!" he said, approaching Crane with a broad smile and an outstretched hand. "Have you been marching with my men?"

Crane grasped the hand. "Haven't had the pleasure, colonel."

"I'm sorry. I would've like you to see us take this town."

"This town? I'm really very sorry, colonel, but I took this town myself before breakfast yesterday."

Hostilities in Puerto Rico, such as they were, ended on August 12 with the arrival of the news that a peace agreement had been signed, ending the war with Spain. The two-week campaign in Puerto Rico comprised six skirmishes with the Spanish, in which four Americans were killed.

The signing of the peace treaty with Spain on August 12, 1898, presided over by William McKinley, ending the Spanish-American War.
(courtesy the National Archives)

Despite everything, despite the battle casualties of the Santiago campaign, despite the several-fold greater casualties from the illness and disease that followed, despite the charges of bungling in high places, there were some who said Americans should focus their eyes on the larger picture. One of these was Secretary of War Alger, who wrote to a friend:

When we think of calling for an army from civil life, gathering it together, arming and equipping it, when there was no equipment for it, fighting battles all the way from Manila to Porto [sic] Rico, and closing the whole matter in three months, we realize it is something that has never before been equaled, and I doubt if it ever will be.

To the thousands of individual soldiers, however, homeward bound from Cuba, the big picture was irrelevant to their wounds, disease, and the exhaustion and inanition that wore them down, wore them so far down as to break many of them. Among all the veterans of that campaign against Santiago, many and many a soldier would never be the same, never anywhere near the same as when he enlisted at the high tide of his young energy.

One afternoon late in August, a flurry of excitement swept the decks of the *Saratoga* as all eyes strained to see the tiny white tower gleaming on the distant horizon.

Chapter 21:
Home From the Hill

As *Saratoga* cleaved the blue Atlantic toward the eastern end of Long Island, the gleaming white lighthouse, beacon of Montauk Point, bulked larger and larger. Soldiers lined the ship's rails, eyes puckering as they squinted at the sandy shores of the big, low-lying island. The shores of America. The shores of home.

Cocking a weather eye at the cloud-dappled sky, one soldier shoved his hands in his pockets and hunched his shoulders against the breeze.

"Seems a might chilly for August," he said.

"When you come out of a furnace," Petty said, "anything else seems nice and cool."

The transport threaded its way into the haven, and the disembarking began. As the troops stepped onto American soil for the first time in over two long months, some were so grateful to be back they got down on their knees, bent over and kissed the earth.

"How far we gotta walk?" Petty asked a hospital corpsman.

"Four miles."

"Hell's peckerneck!"

"'Spect 'em to send you a taxicab?"

Wearily, the veterans of Santiago slung on their blanket-rolls and haversacks and staggered onward – a long column of gaunt and hollow-eyed ghosts shambling along in slow motion. It was a long four miles. Many collapsed and lay helpless by the road for hours. It was impossible to give immediate care to all the invalids and exhausted men arriving from Cuba so suddenly in such overwhelming numbers. Doctors and nurses slaved long hours, but the medical people were too few and far between.

Yellow fever had taken such a fearful toll of the Americans in Cuba that the returning soldiers were being quarantined at Long Island's new Camp Wykoff, named after the colonel of the 3rd Brigade who had been killed July 1 at San Juan. The slap-dash camp, with its rough-plank sheds and hitching rails, had sprung into life almost overnight on the Montauk sands like some western boomtown. Ten thousand white tents lined the breezy streets.

* * * * *

Petty thought he was seeing a ghost when Fay Ball walked into his tent. He stretched out his hand.

"Thought you was *dead*, pardner!"

"Naw! Take more'n a little nick like that to kill an old war horse like me."

"But we never *saw* you again! Nobody knew what happened to you! Where'd you disappear to?"

"Corpsmen patched my leg up and hustled me back to Siboney, then put me on the first boat heading for home. Been here ever since."

* * * * *

General Shafter, arriving at the end of August, hobbled on a cane down one of the tent-lined streets, casting appraising glances right and left. "Best camp I ever saw," he said, nodding approval.

But there were others who didn't think it was all that great. Day after day, returning transports loomed relentlessly on the horizon, with their holds crammed with diseased and exhausted soldiers. The medical people threw up their hands in horror. This was too much. For a time, disembarking of troops from each transport had to be postponed while emergency care was given the droves of invalids preceding them. And the death rate continued to spiral upward.

Except perhaps in the first days, the camp wasn't so badly organized and equipped. But there were problems. Commissaries bulged with supplies, but were unevenly distributed: only two wagons were allocated for distribution. Adding to the confusion, a certain element of roistering troublemakers had acquired the annoying habit of descending on the food-laden wagons in surprise raids, whooping and ki-yi-ing like bands of feathered Comanches.

Another problem was that soldiers assigned to guard the storehouse – not yet equipped with doors – apparently felt they had earned the right to help themselves to its larder, and they did so with commendable energy, not stinting themselves in the slightest.

So Camp Wykoff was something less than perfect. But the sensational newspapers, deprived of the Spanish as a target for invective, now began to horsewhip McKinley's administration even more lustily than they had the Spanish. They depicted conditions at Wykoff with such uninhibited exaggeration that a thunder of outrage rumbled across the nation like a sizzling train of gunpowder. One father, writing to protest the "cruel and horrible treatment" inflicted on the soldiers, said he wouldn't be surprised "if the feeling should lead to a revolution of some kind."

At the same time, a wave of sentiment in favor of the Spanish, spawned by a natural tendency to accentuate the strength of a conquered enemy, washed the land. So recently the butt of curses and insults, the Spanish now found themselves becoming heroes. Admiral Cervera and 78 of his officers were being accommodated at the Naval Academy in Annapolis, with all the courtesies the Americans felt were due their rank. When Cervera was escorted to Portsmouth, New Hampshire, to visit twenty Spanish officers and 1,661 men interned on nearby Seavey's Island, the locals gave him the red-carpet treatment. In fact, he became such a popular personality that a fund-raising campaign was launched to buy him a house in Florida.

Meanwhile, visitors descended on Wykoff in multitudinous numbers, carting in plain and fancy luxuries for the allegedly suffering soldiers. Vessel after vessel arrived at Montauk, unloading bountiful contributions of fresh fruit, milk and many delectables. The upshot was that many soldiers learned to sneer at such plebeian fare as beef and bread, opting for fine delicacies drowning in rich sauces. They stuffed themselves on pheasant and squab, sluicing it all down with slugs of bourbon and brandy. Some paid the piper for their indiscretions. But not since the triumphal returns of Roman legionnaires had homecoming soldiers partied so unrestrainedly.

Payday for Petty and the other recruits came at long last on the final day of August. It was the rookies' first payday since they enlisted. There was little gambling and larking, as there had been at Tampa in those long-ago days when they impatiently waited to sail on the great adventure. Most of the soldiers now were subdued by illness or wounds that still needed a good deal of time to mend properly, and their constitutions were still recuperating from the hardships and deprivations of the tropic ordeal.

Petty received more than four months' pay. He flicked his thumbnails over the end of his small packet of new one-dollar greenbacks. "Over fifty bucks," he said.

"That's a lot of money," Ball said. "Whatcha gonna blow it on?"

"Gonna keep four bucks for myself and send the rest home to Ma. Whatcha gonna shoot yours on?"

A frown wrinkled Ball's forehead. "I only got a lousy month's pay. I'm not rich like you rookies. Hell, I'm already in hock to the boys in the poker games for thirty bucks. Might as well fling my dough into the pot and try to get my bundle back."

* * * * *

Sergeant O'Neill's wide grin revealed tobacco-stained teeth as he made the announcement at reveille on September 3: "President McKinley's coming today!"

Anticipating the President's arrival, the troops were organized into a U-shaped formation, the better to hear the speech he would give. Officers on horseback galloped about in all directions. They seemed to enjoy charging perilously close to standing troops, letting their horses kick up dust and dirt in the soldiers' faces. O'Neill wasn't about to put up with antics of that sort without a squawk.

"Where in the hell were all these officers at San Juan Hill?" he roared.

The soldiers thought that was hilarious.

Touring Wykoff, McKinley had ridden in an open carriage over miles of sand with Secretary of War Alger at his side and Roosevelt riding at the head of his cavalry escort. The sun was hot but a fresh breeze wafted in from the Atlantic, blowing little clouds of dust along the tent city's sandy streets.

McKinley doffed his straw hat. "Glad to meet you," he said, sweating in his dusty frock coat, a flush of sunburn on his face. "You've come home after two months of severe campaigning, which has embraced assault and siege and battle..." He paused to mop his brow with his handkerchief.

"So brilliant in achievement, so far-reaching in results as to command the unstinted praise of all your countrymen."

To Petty, the president seemed a kind and gentle man who talked to the soldiers not unlike the way a father might talk to his children. Several news media photographers captured the scene, including a man in a brown derby, teeth clenched on a cigar butt, aiming a new-fangled Vita-graph motion picture machine at the President.

* * * * *

Corporal Seufert walked into Petty's tent and curtly told him to get off his can and report to Lieutenant Anderson. Anderson had given him the silent treatment for months. What in the world would he want to talk to him about now?

* * * * *

Anderson, sitting at a small table in his tent, looked up, his steel-gray eyes focusing on Petty's face.

Petty saluted. "Corporal Seufert told me to report to you, sir."

Anderson returned the salute in a perfunctory manner. After what seemed to Petty a long moment, Anderson asked, "You boys getting enough to eat?"

"Sir, when we come into this camp, we was hungry enough to eat the south end of a northbound polecat. Never saw so much food in my life since we been here."

Anderson fiddled with his pencil and looked down at his papers. "Your beds comfortable?"

"Yes, sir. When you sleep on the ground for weeks, an army cot seems as comfy as a feather-tick."

"How about the boys who've been sick – are they doing any better?"

"Most of them are feeling much better now, sir. They're so

glad to be going home they're batting their eyes like a toad in an ash-pile."

"All you men get your issues of the lightweight uniforms?"

"The tropical uniforms we should've had in Cuba, sir? With half the men still sick, I kinda think flannel shirts and pants would've been better in these damn sea breezes."

Anderson looked up, his eyes seeming to bore into Petty, his face taking on a faint flush. *Dammit,* Petty thought, *there I go again, shooting my mouth off when I shoulda been using my noggin a little.*

An uneasy pause followed as Anderson regarded Petty without expression. It was a disconcerting stare that Petty didn't know how to interpret or deal with, so he merely remained at attention, looking directly at Anderson. "Sir?" he finally asked.

Anderson spoke only one crisp word: "Dismissed!"

Stumping back to his tent, Petty found himself puzzling over the reason for the interview. Couldn't Anderson have gotten better answers to those questions from Sergeant O'Neill? Why had he asked *him* those questions? He racked his brain to think of some good reason. He could come up with only one: perhaps Anderson was just beating around the bush because he couldn't bring himself to ask the questions he really intended to.

Petty believed it was Anderson who wrote – for the company commander's signature – some of the reports of Company H's participation in the campaign. Ordinarily the company commander would have done the report on the San Juan assault. But Lieutenant Hughes had been elsewhere and hadn't witnessed it. Could Anderson have intended to write an amended report to include something about Petty's action? Or recommend him for some decoration? The original report, written six days after the battle, mentioned Petty only as being one of several men in Company H who were the first

Americans to reach the top of San Juan.

Petty speculated that, when he entered Anderson's tent, Anderson was confronted again with what he must have regarded as the stubborn and willful face of the rookie with the wiseacre answers. And the rankling memory of how Petty had twice deliberately disobeyed his orders to retreat came back with such overmastering impact that the questions he really wanted to ask got stuck in his throat.

Neither Anderson, nor anyone else, ever asked him for details of his lone action on the summit, unseen by Anderson and the others just below the brow of the hill. Maybe Anderson merely wanted to satisfy his curiosity about that. Maybe Anderson feared that if he *had* asked, Petty would have stung his pride with some sardonic remark such as, "Why didn't you follow me fast enough to see what happened?" But that was all supposition on Petty's part, and he never found out for sure the reason for the bizarre interview. Yet it never ceased to puzzle him whenever he thought of it.

* * * * *

Celebrating the soldiers' return in Watertown, New York, 1902.
(courtesy The National Archives)

Home From the Hill

The whole country was still in a dither over the soldiers who had fought in Cuba when the 13the Infantry boarded a train one day in late September, bound for the regiment's home post near Plattsburg, New York. Citizens of Albany, learning the troop train would stop in their city, prepared a gala. As the train steamed into the depot about 11 o'clock at night, hundreds of people milled about the platform, cheering and waving hats, welcoming the soldiers to tables groaning with refreshments.

A repeat of the same hoopla was in store the next day. As the train, whistle shrieking without letup, ground into Plattsburg, the soldiers were greeted by more tables overloaded with good things to eat and drink, and a crowd that surpassed the first in numbers, noise and exuberance.

* * * * *

Unknown to most of the Santiago veterans in the 13th Infantry, some of the officers at Plattsburg, mostly those who had never left the States, were cooking up something special to satisfy what they felt was a public demand: they were drawing up plans for a sham battle on the parade grounds, in which the troops would re-enact the assault on San Juan Hill.

When the public announcement of it came to the rank and file via Sergeant O'Neill, Petty heard the news with mixed emotions. This could be his chance to show what he had done at San Juan Hill to an appreciative audience, an audience harboring no feelings of hate or envy. At the crucial moment, he could spring from the line, wave his hat high, cut loose with a rebel yell, and charge toward the audience, toward some pretty girl in a fancy sunbonnet – the bonnet symbolizing the Spanish flag on the blockhouse. He could go through the motions of climbing two barbed wire fences, and crawling under a third. Just before reaching the lass in the bonnet, he could veer off to one side, train his rifle on two spectators, and hold them "prisoners" until Anderson arrived.

He could be what Seufert had accused him of trying to be – the whole damn show.

That's what he *might* have done. But something nettled him.

"Whatcha think about this ol' sham battle garbage?" he asked some comrades.

"Buncha crap," Ball said, scowling. "Turning it into a circus. Too many guys *died* there!"

Another soldier dropped a cigarette butt on the barracks floor and ground his heel on it. "Just one more boner by someone with the typical mind of a brass-hat dust-inspector," he said.

"Dingleberries either don't know how the boys in the ranks feel," said a third, "or just don't give a shit."

Petty's sentiments exactly. To avoid taking part in something cheap and disgusting, a travesty designed only to titillate the public, he decided to feign illness. Many good soldiers had died on that blood-soaked Cuban ridge. It was wrong, Petty felt, to profane their memory with a burlesque of their heroism.

Only wild horses could have dragooned him onto the parade grounds on that farcical morning.

On the day scheduled for the sham battle, Petty went on a sick call. "Got the mulligrubs something fierce, Doc," Petty said, and complained of so many miseries the doctor must have wondered how he had ever managed to stagger into his office.

"Stay in your barracks and rest until you feel better," he said kindly. He gave Petty some pills and scribbled a note excusing him from duty for a week.

* * * * *

Petty received his honorable discharge on October 1. He collected another month's pay, shook hands warmly and said goodbye to Ball, O'Neill and some others, and entrained for St. Louis.

* * * * *

Ma was speechless with joy. When she found her voice, she stammered, "Why, Alfred, oh, thank goodness you're all in one piece!"

She dabbed at her eyes with a handkerchief.

"Course I am, Ma. Didn't I tell you in a letter that I'd come out of it okay?"

"Son, I was just so worried. Just *worried sick!* Thought maybe you left part of yourself over there and didn't wanna tell me the awful news in a letter."

"Naw!"

"Woman down the street, her boy came home and she didn't know 'til he hobbled in the door on crutches that he left a leg in Cuba. The gangrene got to him. Didn't say nothing about it in none of his letters, the rascal."

"Ma, even some guys lost an arm or leg could be worse off. There's a lot of poor boys who ain't never gonna come back at all." He strode to the door. "Be back in a scratch."

"You just *got home!* Where ya off to now?"

"I gotta see somebody – you know."

* * * * *

Dorothy, rocking in the squeaky porch swing, sprang to her feet and waved when she saw the young man in army uniform cycling down the rutted dirt road.

As she ran to meet him, Petty propped his wheel against a pyracantha bush, grabbed her hands, cocked his head, and shot a quizzical look at her pale green dress.

"How come you ain't wearing that pretty pink dress with the white collar?" he asked. "I always did like that one."

She laughed and broke away from him, then dashed back up the porch steps, offering Petty an enchanting glimpse of lissome calves. Plumping herself in the swing, she motioned him to sit beside her.

"Lordamercy, Al, you said you liked it, so I decided I liked it, too, and I wore it all the time, and just plumb wore it out. Guess I should've saved it to wear for you. Or bought another. You forgot how long you been gone?"

"Hey, I just decided – green suits you fine. No, I ain't forgot how long I been gone. Didja get my letters?"

"Sure did. They were sweet. I keep 'em in my hope chest, tied together with a pink ribbon." She laughed and pushed her feet hard on the floor, to set the swing in motion.

"Didja miss me?"

"Reckon I did. You know that."

"I don't know it unless you tell me."

"Course I missed you. I hardly ever stopped thinking about you, and wondering how you were."

"Really?" His voice grated with emotion. He cleared his throat and, with a comical sidelong look, asked, "Sure you ain't been making eyes at some of them lolligaggers around these parts?"

"Al, you know better than that."

He put his arm around her and pulled her close. "Dorothy!" She turned her face up to his and their lips met hungrily.

After a long moment, he said, "I sure missed you, too. Kept thinking about my sweetie in St. Louie." With a little laugh, he added, "Hey, I could write a song – *My St. Louie Sweetie!*"

"Silly!" She snuggled closer and breathed into his ear, "I thought about you all the time you were away. I thought about that time down by the creek, where we went on a picnic... Now stop it! *Stop!* You got grabbier hands than an octopus! Ma and Pa'll be coming back *any minute!*"

Home From the Hill

* * * * *

Some days later, as Petty and his friend Zachary Clayton bicycled near the baseball park, huge posters tacked onto the board fence brought them to a halt. The posters advertised a coming attraction: some entrepreneur had recruited five dozen cowboys to do some wild riding in a spectacular billed as *The Rough Riders Capture San Juan Hill By Assault.*

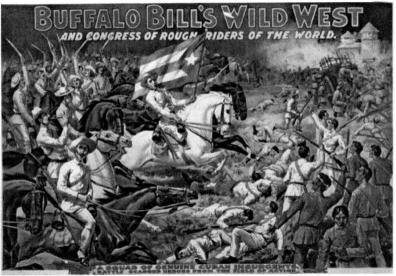

A typical exploitation poster of the day, with Teddy Roosevelt leading the charge up San Juan Hill with all the Rough Riders on horseback.

Petty's lips curled in a sneer. "Zack, look at them stupid pictures!"

The gaudy scenes depicted the troopers charging up the hill on horseback.

"What's stupid about 'em?"

"Whoever the highbinder is who's promoting this farce either don't know or don't give a rat's ass that the Rough

Riders had to leave their horses behind in Florida. And it was the *infantry* that took San Juan, goddamn it!"

Petty was carried away by emotion as the searing memory of the San Juan cataclysm welled up in his mind – churning, churning. Tears sprang to his eyes.

"Aw, let's take a gander," Zack said. "Might be a good show anyway. We could take our gals."

"Naw!" Petty said with a sour laugh. "I ain't got the stomach for it."

"How come you know so much about it?"

Petty could only shrug, too full of emotion for more words. He had never told Zack he had fought in the war.

* * * * *

He and Dorothy were married the following June. Petty took a week leave from the railroad so they could go on a short honeymoon. From St. Louis, they traveled down the Mississippi to Memphis and back aboard a great sternwheeler, the *Natchez Belle*.

It was a floating palace, plush with red velvet and a-glitter with crystal chandeliers. In the grand salon, a hard-eyed gambling man wearing a beaver hat and jeweled studs in a frilled shirt sat at a table covered with green felt, smoking a Panatela cigar and trying to lure the innocents into a game of three-card monte.

"Naw!" Petty said, beaming at Dorothy. "You know what they say – 'Lucky at cards, unlucky in love.' So I'll pass."

The years came and went, and there was no way to hold back the relentless onslaught of time. For years, Petty never told anyone, except Dorothy and a few relatives, about his exploit at San Juan Hill. And now he had stopped talking to them about it. If he did start to talk about it, the onrush of memories assaulted him with overpowering, almost unendurable, emotion and pain. He would seem almost to relive his ordeal on the Hill, and the baffling official defalcation that came after. This upset his composure and bothered him for hours. Even days. His job as a telegrapher, demanding a clear head and steady nerves, suffered because of it. The memory of what he had done and how he had been cheated out of recognition for it was so disturbing, each time it was called up, that he pushed it back from his consciousness as far as he could. He kept it, as he later said, as a secret locked in a mental drawer labeled: *San Juan Hill – Do Not Open.*

For forty years.

Only his wife and close family members knew his nearly incredible story.

And one can only wonder if, in the absence of official recognition, they really found it possible to believe. That perhaps it was just a bit too incredible.

But after forty long years had gone by, something happened that made Petty vow he was going to get what he had coming to him. The year was 1938.

Chapter 22:
Forty Years After

Year 1938's arrival found Petty an old man of nearly sixty-one years with iron-gray hair, crow's feet dancing around his eyes, and packing a tidy bit more poundage than he had during his hell-for-breakfast days in Cuba.

By this time, he had punched the time clock for twenty-seven years with Western Pacific in Stockton, California, and pounded the brass key all those years, his *dit-dah* helping speed the trains on their grinding way, trailing plumes of smoke.

One day in that year, thumbing through an issue of *Liberty* magazine, Petty was pulled up short by a reader's letter. His jaw dropped as he read. The correspondent presented the case that – contrary to the obstinate legend racketing around all these years – the infantry, not the Rough Riders, had done the job at San Juan. Petty read the letter over and over, while a windstorm of emotions blasted though his brain.

Lord, how the time did pass. Was that all of forty years ago? Time didn't simply march, it seemed to fairly sprint. Who was it that said of time: what arm can hold his swift foot back?

Swift is the word, he thought. By Godfrey, the lie often travels in seven-league boots, while the truth stumbles far behind on crutches, humping as best it can, hoping to catch up if and when the lie takes a little siesta. Remember the hare and the tortoise. Maybe now was the time, after four decades, when the truth about San Juan Hill at last would catch up, maybe even scamper out in front. Hallelujah. And how did that old proverb go? "Truth crushed to earth shall rise again."

After so many years, it was about time; he reckoned the hour had come to pluck his own story out of that locked mental drawer, brush off the cobwebs of forty long years, and set the record straight once and for all.

Flash back to turn-of-the-century Nebraska: Petty was working there as a railroad telegrapher, and his and Dorothy's union had produced three winsome daughters – Lucille, Lela and Erma – all born in the Cornhusker State.

But Petty was a restless man, and Nebraska wasn't his kind of state – it was too far east. California, on the other hand, lured him because he would be following Horace Greeley's advice to go as far as a man could go and stay on dry land. And if a man couldn't find an end to restlessness on Continent's End, where could he find it? So California echoed in his mind like a magic word, or a siren's song.

Petty kept his ears cocked so that any time opportunity rapped sharply on the door of the railroad shack he heard it – and promptly signed on for any new job that would transplant him and his family farther west.

As an agent for Denver & Rio Grande, he railroaded in Colorado, first at Pueblo, then at Larimer, where the family had to set up housekeeping in a boxcar – not a novel way of life for railroad families in that rough-and-ready era. Came time to move on again. Their new home was Wendover, Utah, hard by the Nevada border, where Petty "slung lightning" for Western Pacific Railroad and the family bedded down in a canvas tent like the other locals. Then only Nevada obstructed his path to El Dorado – the Land of Gold. In 1911, they did it – pulled up stakes, beat the dust of Utah out of their clothes, and made the final jump, leapfrogging over Nevada to Western Pacific's Stockton terminal.

Give Me 10,000 Men!

* * * * *

After studying that letter in Liberty, Petty started to set down his own story, pecking it out on an old grotesque Oliver typewriter that he had bought somewhere for five dollars.

Excerpt from his story:

When I first began to write this narrative, I was in doubt as to whether I could remember enough details to make it worthwhile... But as I wrote, events came back surprisingly vivid and clear. It was like dusting off an old phonograph record that has lain in the attic for forty years and again starting it revolving on the machine.

When I came to that part of the narrative describing the events of July first, second and third, 1898, I became abnormally alert mentally, my nerves and muscles became taut, and for three days and two nights I slept only fitfully. I was living over again the events of those three days and two nights.

Petty's slim little book was printed in 1939 by a subsidy publisher. If he expected any earthshaking reaction to his book, he was sorely disillusioned. The reaction was on a par with that cited by a poet, who said publishing a book of poems is like dropping a feather into the Grand Canyon and waiting for the echo.

In the years that followed, Petty pushed on in his fight for recognition as the first man up San Juan. As he persuaded local politicians and veterans' organizations to go to bat for him, these efforts were reported by his hometown newspaper, The Stockton *Record*, and on occasion carried far and wide by wire services. He first made his claim while thousands of San Juan Hill veterans were still alive. Any one could have challenged it. None ever did.

As a newly-hired reported for the *Record*, I first met Petty in the fall of 1961 when our receptionist at the front desk telephoned me in the city room. "There's a man here with a press release," she said.

He was a rather large old guy with large facial features and wearing a rumpled gray suit and tie. Although his thinning hair was gray, his bushy eyebrows were almost black. His press release announced plans for a barbecue by the Spanish War Veterans' Stockton Camp, for which he served as publicity chairman.

I was a mite surprised that there were enough ambulatory veterans of that ancient war still lingering in the local area to hold a clambake. I motioned him to a seat in a leather armchair. "Where'd you serve during the war?" I asked.

"Cuba," he said gruffly.

"Where in Cuba?"

"Ever hear of San Juan Hill?" he asked in a ringing voice.

Of course I had, but like almost everyone else I had to be disabused of the notion that Roosevelt and the Rough Riders captured it. Briefly he related his story in a bold voice.

As to his claim to have sparked the charge, I was automatically skeptical of that whopper. Sparked the charge? Sounded like a lot of malarkey.

Days passed and the thought kept nagging: what if? I started looking into it, tentatively at first. I read everything in the *Record's* "morgue" about Petty's long fight with Washington to gain recognition as the first American up San Juan. Now plunging into it, I read everything I could find about the Santiago campaign. Everything Petty told me that could be verified by research, I did verify. By slow degrees, doubt changed to a tentative belief. That belief strengthened when I found some evidence Petty didn't know about.

In 1899, Petty had received – via registered mail – a Certificate of Merit for being "a member of the first squad to reach the top" of San Juan. Petty's smile, as he studied it, gradually turned upside down. Hold your horses, he thought.

Just wait a minute. The document was unsigned, undated, and contained no other details of the action. These were flagrant omissions that at first puzzled Petty mightily, and later would irk him to no end.

In 1954, this award was superseded by the Distinguished Service Cross, also delivered by the postman, which Petty thought was a rather casual way of conferring such a military honor. (By this time, anyone who had received the Certificate of Merit was automatically eligible for the DSC.)

Of that first squad to the top, who was actually first? No record indicates. Nor does any record offer an explanation for this puzzling omission.

It is puzzling because, when First Lt. William N. Hughes, commander of Company H, on July 6 penned his first report of the July 1 battle, he felt *the first officer* on the Hill deserved special mention.

For some inexplicable reason, the entire last paragraph of Hughes' report was deleted when published with all the other battle reports in the *Annual Report of the Secretary of War for 1898*.

I discovered that strange circumstance when National Archives sent me copies of various documents, including the handwritten version of the July 6 report.

The deleted paragraph contains vital and interesting information disclosed nowhere else – the names of the first men up the Hill, including Petty's.

That paragraph reads:

Second Lieutenant Thomas M. Anderson, Jr., 13th Infantry, deserves special mention for his gallantry and for the capture of two Spanish prisoners near the blockhouse, he being the first officer on the Hill, with some men of the regiment with him. Sergeant Anton Weber, Sergeant Fred L. Smith, Corporal Ludwig Seufert, Privates Federick Binckli, Paul Klick and Recruit Alfred C. Petty and Private Arthur Agnew – all these men belong to Company H and were with Lieutenant Anderson when he reached the blockhouse.

National Archives could not explain why that last paragraph was omitted in the published report.

Could it have been omitted for brevity's sake? It seems unlikely. Many other published reports run twice as long. Besides, the contents are too important, one would think, to omit. They focus on the veritable climax of the campaign. One can only wonder.

Hughes' description of Anderson as *the first officer* on the Hill can only force the conclusion: some enlisted man or men got there ahead of him. Which coincides with Petty's account.

Petty believed it was actually Anderson who wrote that July 6 report – for Hughes' signature. At any rate, that Hughes himself did not write the report, though he apparently signed it, seems evident from two facts: one, *the slant of the writing* in the body of the report is noticeably more pronounced than the slant of the letters in Hughes' signature; two, the *H* in Hughes' signature is as radically different from the *H* in "Company H" in the report as day is from night.

I wrote again to National Archives, asking if any of the other Company H men who were first on the Hill were decorated. National Archives replied:

The War Department records in our custody show that Sgt. Fred L. Smith, Sgt. Anton Weber, Corp. Ludwig Seufert, Pvt. Arthur Agnew, Pvt. Frederic Binckli and Pvt. Paul Klick received Certificates of Merit. Lt. Thomas M. Anderson did not receive a Certificate of Merit because it was only awarded to privates and noncommissioned officers. However, Lieutenant Anderson was recommended for a Congressional Medal of Honor and a brevet rank, but we have been unable to locate any documents showing that he received either honor.

Petty's opinion of the conduct of company commander Lieutenant Hughes in the battle of San Juan Hill was something less that unconstrained admiration. On June 29, 1957, while Petty was visiting Washington in connection with H.R. 7201, a bill to award him the Medal of Honor – a bill introduced by Congressman John J. McFall of California – he wrote to Secretary of the Army Wilber M. Brucker, declaring that Hughes' July 6, 1898, report "is of little value because Hughes was one of the few officers who displayed a yellow streak in the battle. He did not take part in the assault and capture of Fort San Juan."

Petty continued:

"When our attacking forces came under the withering fire of the enemy at the edge of the jungle, Hughes, along with three or four privates, crawled back into the thick jungle and did not show up on the battle line until mid-afternoon – hours after the hill had been captured...

"I feel confident that my old comrade, Harley L. Pierce of Los Angeles, Calif., can verify the foregoing facts."

Regarding the capture of the two prisoners, Petty had this to say in the same letter:

"The manner in which various officers (three of them) reported the two prisoners that I captured is very significant. While they were able to give me the silent treatment they could not hide those prisoners. In their reports they all lied, and very significantly their lies were not in agreement. One officer said they were left in the trenches by the enemy..."

In his 1939 book, he had made this acid comment on the matter of the prisoners: "How thoughtful and big-hearted of the enemy to leave us a couple of prisoners in the trenches! Consider for a moment that absurd statement and then laugh as I have laughed...

"Someone should have smothered feelings of hate or envy and made a record of this incident for truth's sake."

Stephen Crane, having covered the Greco-Turkish War of

1896-97, perceived that there is more than a particle of fudging in battle reports. He also appreciated that the San Juan charge was an abortive assault:

> No doubt when history begins to grind out her story we will find that many a thundering, fine, grand order was given for that day's work; but after all there will be no harm in contending that the fighting line, the men and their regimental officers, took the hill chiefly because they knew they could take it, some having no orders and others disobeying whatever orders they had.

Any doubt I may have had about Petty's story vanished when I discovered that his old comrade-in-arms, Harley Pierce, was still alive, and corroborated Petty's account. Pierce, living in Los Angeles, was a former commander of Theodore Roosevelt Camp No. 9, Department of California, United Spanish War Veterans.

I outlined Petty's story on the telephone and asked Pierce for his reaction. I listened to the slightly quavering voice of an old man, but it carried a ring of sincerity: "Yes! That's just the way it happened!" he said. "Just the way it was!"

I mailed him an affidavit, which he signed and returned.

As a private, Pierce went through the thick of the San Juan inferno.

He was *there*. He saw it with his own eyes.

He was a living eyewitness to Petty's wild courage at San Juan Hill.

Since Petty was awarded a Certificate of Merit, and later the Distinguished Service Cross, for being "a member of the first squad to reach the top" of San Juan, what should he have rated as the first man in that squad?

Congressman John McFall of California thought it called for nothing less than the Medal of Honor. Three times he introduced bills in Congress, asking the Medal for Petty. The bills never got as much as a committee hearing.

Explained Secretary of the Army Brucker in a letter July 22, 1959, to Carl Vinson, chairman of the House Committee on Armed Services, regarding one of McFall's bills:

"Since 1918, various statutes have required that awards of the Medal of Honor be made within three years... because of the difficulty in securing reliable evidence and unbiased reports of witnesses more than three years after the event." Therefore, he said, the Department of the Army "strongly recommends" that H.R. 7668 not be enacted.

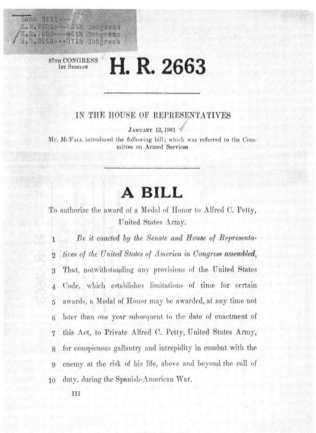

One of Congressman McFall's three attempts for Petty's Medal of Honor

Yet in 1933, Congress – apparently without any compunction about "various statutes" – got around to awarding the well-deserved Medal of Honor to Richmond Hobson of *Merrimac* renown for what he did thirty-five years before.

Teddy Roosevelt, largely on the myth that the Rough Riders captured San Juan Hill, rode the crest of popular adulation all the way to the White House. From all reports, Roosevelt was a soldier of extraordinary valor and energy. And his hell-for-leather hooligans, whom he extolled as "children of the dragon's blood," were the stuff of legend.

But one legend is merely a legend – a myth.

For the simple fact is that the infantry, not the celebrated Rough Riders, captured San Juan Hill.

A sad irony: while the mythical conqueror of the Hill rode on to political glory, the intrepid soldier who was really first on the Hill lived all his days in obscurity, euchred out of the honors he deserved as one of America's military immortals.

Another ironic note: "The immodest Roosevelt even put in for a Medal of Honor for himself, only to be rebuked by Secretary of War Russell Alger. Although it took until 2001, Roosevelt, through the lobbying of his family, eventually won the Medal of Honor posthumously for his bravery during the battle for San Juan Heights." – from *The Wilderness Warrior* by Douglas Brinkley, HarperCollins, 2009.

* * * * *

I never met Petty's wife Dorothy. She died in Stockton in 1957, a day after being admitted to a hospital with extreme fatigue. She had suffered a heart attack ten years before. She told the nurses that the medicine the doctor had given her didn't agree with her and was making her sick. The nurses pooh-poohed that notion. Dorothy had to die to prove it.

During the fall and early winter of 1961-62, I was in fairly constant communication with Petty by personal visit, telephone, and letter, because I was getting all the facts together for a magazine article.

From an undated note Petty sent me in the fall:

"I had been assigned to a regular Army outfit whose privates and officers were neatly dressed in regulation uniforms." (Petty, by contrast, was still wearing mostly his shabby civilian hand-me-downs.) "This fact made it most difficult for those West Point officers to consider my behavior in an impartial way."

Among many other letters he sent me was one on Jan. 11, 1962, that touched on a similar theme:

"Human nature being what it is, I am convinced that if the feeling is strong enough, under certain circumstances envy can cause proud and sensitive men to stoop to low and harmful discrimination. It is discrimination that I am asking Congress to remove in my case."

Nobody knew that Petty had less than a month to live.

Article describing Petty's fight for recognition of his part of the capture of San Juan Hill from the Washington Daily News, June 17, 1957.

Chapter 23:
Petty's Final Days

All the letters Petty had sent me thus far had been cranked through his ancient Oliver typewriter. Suddenly I got an awkwardly-penciled note dated Jan. 14, 1962. It was headed: Veterans Hospital, Livermore. The town of Livermore reposes in the rolling hills of the Diablo Range, east of San Francisco Bay and about forty miles southwest of Stockton.

Bill:

I got away from home yesterday (Saturday) in a hurry and didn't have time to answer your letter.

I developed a case of lumbago or something in my old back that really put me down for the count. However, I don't think it is anything very serious and hope to be back home within a short time – soon as I can get a correct diagnosis and proper treatment of my ailment.

The next time you come through Livermore – soon, I hope – please come by to see me.

When a five-day chain of rainstorms ended, leaving a blue sky festooned with snowy cumulus, I tooled my '55 Buick Roadmaster along Highway 50, over Altamont Pass amid the voluptuously-rounded, treeless hills that lifted and dropped in massive sweeps. It was the season when the hills were arrayed in the incredible luminous green of new grass. Grass was born and old soldiers were dying.

Cruising through the town, I followed signs and drove four miles through the Livermore Valley, then rattled across an old iron bridge that spanned a swift, dark creek. The hospital, a congeries of cream-colored buildings with red Spanish-tile roofs, rambled over a great hillside. The grounds were ornamented with palms, eucalyptus and evergreens and great expanses of lawn.

I found Petty in a large, sunny ward where other grizzled veterans were either abed, navigating shakily on crutches, or maneuvering about in wheelchairs. Petty was propped up on pillows in bed, his face puffy and his gray hair wildly askew. His sharp brown eyes had caught me the second I entered.

Alfred C. Petty in 1961, the year before he died. (Author's Photo)

"What's all this garbage about being sick?" I asked, grabbing his big, weathered hand. "Sure you ain't goldbricking?"

His lips curved in a wry smile. "Wish I was," he said with a sigh, then added, jabbing a finger toward the foot of the bed: "See that crank down there? How's about giving me a few spins?"

As I cranked, the hinged bed lifted his head up several inches.

"Few more," he said... "Fine!"

"They got your problem diagnosed yet?"

Petty braced his big hands on the sides of the bed, lurched to a sitting position, reached for a glass of orange juice on the bedside table, and took a long drink. He set the glass down and wiped his mouth with the back of his hand. "Naw!" he rasped. "Docs are still running tests."

As we talked, he seemed chipper enough. Certainly not like a man with mere days to live. But neither of us had any inkling of that.

Some days earlier, I had sent him a letter telling about my discovery of the missing paragraph in Lieutenant Hughes' July 6 report that mentioned Petty, along with Anderson and half a dozen others, as being in the first squad up San Juan.

"Got any idea why that last paragraph was deleted from the published report?" I asked.

His eyes focused on mine and widened in puzzlement. "Ain't got the foggiest," he said, shaking his head slowly. "Just wish I *knew*. Kinda suspect somebody did it deliberately to avoid raising any embarrassing questions about what really happened during the charge." He sighed loudly and sagged back against his pillows. "But I don't know how I'm ever gonna prove it. Not after all these years."

* * * * *

Two days after I visited Petty, the mailman brought me a short, penciled letter headed: "A few minutes after you left." The note asked me to mail copies of my letter to him about the missing paragraph to Congressman McFall and Francis W. Stover, Director of the Veterans of Foreign Wars' National Legislative Service, who was also interested in the case. I sent the copies as he requested.

The old soldier was still fighting – down to the wire.

By this time I was no longer working for the *Record*, having accepted a job in Sacramento as an information officer in state government. Coming home on February 6, I picked up the *Record* from my porch and was stunned to see a front-page story saying Petty had died unexpectedly the previous day in the Veterans Hospital – the day after he celebrated his 85th birthday.

Died? It was awfully hard to believe. What the hell was he trying to pull?

I was quite saddened by the old soldier's passing – dying without ever having won what he had been fighting for, for so many years.

Funeral services at the Victorian-type chapel of B.C. Wallace & Son in Stockton drew a sizeable contingent from the Stockton Camp of Spanish War Veterans – men with doddering figures, palsied limbs, ash-gray faces, heads fringed with snow. The Old Guard. Unbelievably, three still wore their uniforms of 1898, or a reasonable facsimile. Many others ex-soldiers on hand were wearing the insignia of Stockton's Luneta Post 52, VFW, of which Petty also was a member. After the funeral, Petty's body was entombed in Stockton's Rural Memorial Mausoleum.

Now it was all over. Finished. The big gruff, contentious voice was forever stilled.

Some months afterward, my article about his San Juan exploit came out in the pages of Impact magazine. I was only sorry he hadn't lived long enough to read it.

Petty's Final Days

* * * * *

After all is said and pondered, it doesn't seem too farfetched to regard Petty's wild charge at San Juan as a bright flash of courage – or madness – that defied the black clouds of onrushing disaster. Consider that, at the moment he took off hell-bent for the crest, the Americans on the savanna and in the jungle fringes were firing off their ammunition at a frenetic rate. Most probably had less than half the 105 rounds each began the day with. To re-supply them quickly, by driving wagons or pack mules along the clogged trail, would have been nigh impossible. Pulling back, while more ammunition was labored forward and jittery officers hassled-out a battle plan they could agree upon, would very likely have spawned all the horrors of a full-scale debacle.

As Petty assessed it, more delays, if only for minutes, would have practically forced issuance of orders to pull back. Was not that mysterious cease-fire bugle the first sign of demon panic ripping through command levels?

Falling back into the jungle, the regular outfits would have mingled with the volunteer regiment, whose totally demoralized condition would have infected the regulars with the deadly virus of disaster. The upshot of hasty conferences very likely would have been a cautious postponement of the assault until days later – if not longer - when reinforcements could arrive from Tampa. Prudence would govern the situation: better wait and assess the matter carefully. Meanwhile, the virus of disaster would have been breeding in the army corps at an exponential rate.

Procrastination would have given the Spanish precious time to double or triple their defenses on San Juan with the oncoming thousands under General Escario. Worst of all, fever and dysentery would have struck the troops in the jungle in front of San Juan Hill – *before the battle* – just as they did strike not long after the Hill had been captured, and the battle won. Petty's conclusion: "No one would have been able to see the end of the chain of events that could have followed."

But one might foresee, as General Shafter did in his study of the Caribbean campaigns of Napoleon and Lord Vernon, the all-too-likely possibility of disaster piled on disaster, and no end to horror.

It was at this momentous juncture, this crisis on the terrible savanna, that Petty's wild impulse galvanized him into reckless action – sparking the infantry charge. It was this abortive charge that won the battle – the battle that won the campaign – the campaign that won the war – and the war that dismantled the empire that had flown the blood-and-gold colors of Spain since Columbus.

Roosevelt called his Rough Riders "children of the dragon's blood." Petty, though not one of that legendary band, did a job the army in effect assigned him to do, and did the job with the audacity legends are made of. In battle, he proved himself a real berserker, a child of the dragon's blood.

Through bleak years after, he fought on. But victory in that baffling struggle forever eluded his grasp, and he had to bear up with stoic heart as visions of honors for what he had done vanished like smoke, and the chronicle of his futility unscrolled like an age without a name.

Yet surely one can assume with some degree of certainty that he must have drawn some sustenance, some comfort, from the fact that, if the world didn't know, he knew – *he knew* what temper of soldier and mettle of man he was; knew what he had done for America, and Cuba, on a little hill near Santiago. And wore that knowledge with the same invincible pride that Cyrano de Bergerac wore his plume.

Rest in peace, Alfred C. Petty, soldier of '98.
Never victorious – but never defeated.

Epilogue

To be sure I was describing the terrain with authenticity, I felt I had to see for myself the mountains and jungle the soldiers of '98 had to push through to get to their rendezvous with destiny at the gates of Santiago.

This I knew: Americans were allowed to visit Havana and its environs. But I wondered: would Cuban officials let me make a quick aerial jaunt down to Santiago on the southeast coast, over 400 miles from Havana? A San Francisco travel agent was offering seven-day flings in Havana, but couldn't give a yes or no to my question: could I sneak off to Santiago for, say, a couple of days? He suggested I get the answer by telephone from Señor Robles, sales manager for Cubana Airlines in Havana.

For two weeks, I tried to make phone connections with Señor Robles, to no avail. A couple of times I came tantalizingly close: "He just left the office," or "He should return in a few minutes." If he ever came back, he never found the time to return my call.

Back to square one: I sent Señor Robles a cable asking if I could fly from Havana to Santiago. The silence was almost deafening. I'd have been delighted to pay in advance for a cable from him, just to be sure of a response. But that would be asking too much. Sending money to Cuba – even a bagatelle such as payment for a return cable – is prohibited by United States authorities. Never mind that Uncle Sam allows Americans to personally take Yankee dollars to Cuba and toss them to the four winds.

If I took a chance on Havana, but then was forbidden to do the Santiago caper, my whole trip would be an exercise in futility.

As any rate, my wife Patricia finally learned that the Soviet cruise ship *Kazakhstan* would dock for the whole day on Dec. 31, 1979, in Santiago – one port-of-call in a Caribbean cruise departing from New Orleans. That would guarantee our reaching Santiago. And *Kazakhstan's* arrival made it the first cruise ship to sail into Santiago Bay since the 1959 Castro revolution. Cuba being a Communist country, Soviet cruise ships get parking privileges there that are off-limits to cruise ships of non-Communist nations.

Jose Alvarez of Santiago de Cuba guided author, right, and his wife Patricia around San Juan Hill, where Americans fought the battle that changed the world forever. (Photo by Patricia E. Holden)

Epilogue

From the Santiago waterfront, my wife and I headed out in a yellow subcompact taxi with Roberto Madrugo at the wheel and José Alvarez as our guide. Both were congenial Cubans, probably in their mid-twenties. Our taxi was a 1972 Dodge – made in Argentina, José said. The only American-made cars in Cuba are the antiquated, wheezing – but nicely simonized – survivors of the years before the 1959 revolution.

We scampered through narrow streets flanked by old buildings whose ground-floor windows were barred – our taxi lifting us bit by bit as we approached the low range of hills ringing Santiago.

José pulled up to the "Surrender Tree," the gigantic ceiba still standing in a groin of the hills. After all the years that had gone by, I was mildly surprised to find that it hadn't succumbed to storm, disease, or the works of man, although I understand that it has unfortunately since died. Encircled by a wrought-iron fence, the silk-cotton tree at that time was identified as the surrender landmark by bronze plaques in both Spanish and English.

Horse-drawn cart enters grounds at San Juan Hill. The Lome De (hill of) part of entrance sign is on a similar pillar to the left. (Author's Photo)

Farther on, we wheeled up onto a hill on the eastern rim of the low range confining the city. A sign identified the slight prominence as Loma (Hill) de San Juan. Surprisingly, only some one hundred feet high compared to the surrounding terrain, the green knoll scarcely seems grand enough for so epic a struggle – the crumbling empire of Spain versus the brash new imperialism of the United States.

Tall trees arched overhead. At the time of the battle, the hill was practically bare, except on the side facing the river, where the Spanish had lashed barbed wire to a scatter of stubby trees. They had chopped down most of the other trees to clear fields of fire for rifles and cannon. A pastoral hush wrapped the lovely knoll that once erupted with the terrible din of Krupp cannon and crashing volleys from Mauser rifles. Several ancient cannon hunkered mutely on cement pads. A few trenches are preserved with rock-and-mortar retaining walls, but no trace of the blockhouse remains.

Spanish cannon reposes mutely on San Juan Hill near Santiago de Cuba. Even in 1898, some of the cannons were ancient, having been manufactured in Spain during the mid-1770s. Krupp cannon also fired at the Americans during the battle. Our guide poses with the cannon. (Author's photo)

Epilogue

Monuments honor the American and Cuban soldiers who fought here. A bronze plaque on the Cuban monument cites "decisive support" by the Cubans, adding: "Therefore this must not be called the Spanish-American War, but the Spanish-Cuban-American War."

Now we swung off the paved highway and jolted several hundred yards over a bumpy dirt road that parallels the shallow, jungle-fringed San Juan River. We stopped and looked across the river, a stream ten or fifteen yards wide, eddying past its tangled banks. From far on the other side, the American invaders had pushed forward along the jungle corridor – and had run into a meat grinder as the observation balloon unwittingly pinpointed the column's location. At about this point, the stunned Americans had splashed across the rain-swollen river, boiled out of the jungle, and flung themselves into the guinea-grass.

Jose Alvarez of Santiago de Cuba, who guided two American visitors to San Juan Hill, shows a preserved trench. (Author's photo)

As we turned our gazes to the opposite direction, San Juan Hill loomed low in the middle distance, perhaps some 300 yards away. On this field rising gently toward the base of the hill, as the torrid sun hovered near its zenith, Petty had been thunderstruck in a mercurial moment. Suddenly his whole being had been given over to mad action – and the blue-shirted horde of Americans, without orders, had followed, charging toward the enemy guns on the hill.

Today, lettuce crops grow in the plow-scarred soil watered so long by the blood of the Fifth Army Corps. Birds chitter in the trees and wing through air that once warbled with flying steel.

Time to move along; on we zipped toward Siboney Beach, with the cab's tires swishing along a fine, paved road. For the men of the Fifth Army Corps, this route had been a horrible quagmire, despite its proud name of El Camino Real, the Royal Highway. Banana palms lift their canopy-like leaves besides solitary cottages taking a siesta in the emerald tangles. Lean cows amble on stiff legs by the road, foraging. A sign flagged the little hamlet of Sevilla – site of General Shafter's field headquarters for some days before the momentous events of July 1.

Royal palms soar above the green mat of jungle, which smolders here and there with the red embers of bougainvillea. To the north frowned the cloud-topped Sierra Maestra. Another sign told us we were a few miles from El Caney, off to the north, where the all-day battle by Spanish defenders against ten-to-one odds tossed the American timetable for the San Juan attack onto the trash-pile.

Time for lunch: José said he knew a good restaurant near Siboney, which was the way we were heading anyway. We caught a glimpse of its ground-floor cantina, in which locals wearing straw sombreros quaffed from foamy mugs of cerveza. José smiled. "Is to celebrate the anniversary of the revolution, which comes tomorrow," he said. "They start early." He was

Epilogue

talking about the 20th anniversary of Fidel Castro's revolution.

With a wave of his arm, he ushered us up an exterior flight of wooden stairs to the restaurant. Tables covered with clean white cloths ranged over a freshly-scrubbed wooden floor. A tiny lizard scooted off a chair to make room for a cash customer. The restaurant was wide open on two sides. There was no window glass. The openings offered views of steep, jungle-matted hills. We knocked back a couple of cervezas, although Patricia limited herself to one, then ordered pollo con arroz. Not bad.

Moving along again, we cruised down to Siboney Beach, where a grove of palms, their fronds rustling in the soft wind, crowds hard by the curving sandy shore. To the east, a steep cliff lifts its craggy, jungle-masked eminence from the gleaming blue sea. This bluff shelters the cover from the prevailing trades, and this made it an ideal invasion beach for the American expedition. Today the beach seems to be a popular playground for Cubans.

Siboney Beach, scene of the 1898 invasion, today is a popular swimming area for Cubans. (author's photo)

Give Me 10,000 Men!

Too soon came the time to rush back to Santiago, say "Gracias" and "Hasta la vista" to our new friends José and Roberto, and re-board *Kazakhstan*. And none too soon. In less than an hour, the great ship was working its way out of the twisting channel. Darkness was falling over the land and the scattered lights of the city were vanishing behind.

* * * * *

Perhaps one of the strangest monuments in the world, this memorial is dedicated "to the Spanish soldier, who knew how to die heroically in the performance of his duty." The monument was erected on San Juan Hill by the Republic of Cuba – after Cubans had suffered through eleven revolutions in 75 years, trying to eject the Spanish from the island. (Author's photo)

Of what we had seen at Santiago, the most boggling thing has got to be a certain monument – a kind of symbol of what one might loosely call "the greening of San Juan Hill." Remember that the Cubans had agonized through eleven

Epilogue

revolutions in seventy-five years as they struggled to cast off the iron yoke of Spanish despotism. Their hatred for their oppressors must have been rabid beyond measure.

Yet on San Juan Hill there stands a monument erected by the Republic of Cuba and dedicated "to the Spanish soldier, who knew how to die heroically in the performance of his duty."

Is this the ultimate meaning of San Juan Hill? Was the burning hatred of seven decades interred with the bones of the heroic soldiers on both sides who fought here? Did the Cubans somehow find it in their hearts to forgive the Spanish soldiers? Is forgiveness too strong a word? Yet surely this must be one of the world's most astonishing monuments. The amazing legend on the bronze plaque, one might say, spells out a kind of tangible paraphrase of Petty's musing as he trained his rifle on the two Spanish soldiers standing, hands in the air, in the rifle pit: *I felt no hate – they were beaten men.*

Mercy.

And perhaps the beginning of forgiveness, or something akin to it.

The world does turn, and sometimes it takes a turn for the better.

CPSIA information can be obtained at www.ICGtesting.com
262579BV00005B/5/P